W9-AKX-443

MUNICH

Edited by Susanne Rick
Photography by Gerd Pfeiffer, Günter Schneider,
Werner Lüring, Stefan Reuther and others
Directed and designed by Hans Johannes Hoefer
Translated by Marianne Rankin

APA PUBLICATIONS

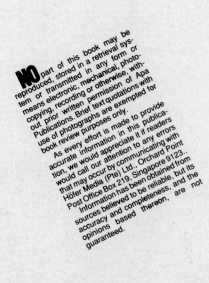

NO part of this book may be reproduced, stored in a retrieval system or transmitted in any form or means electronic, mechanical, photo-copying, recording or otherwise, with-out prior written permission of Apa Publications. Brief text quotations with use of photographs are exempted for book review purposes only.

As every effort is made to provide accurate information in this publica-tion, we would appreciate it if readers would call our attention to any errors that may occur by communicating with Höfer Media (Pte) Ltd., Orchard Point Post Office Box 219, Singapore 9123.. Information has been obtained from sources believed to be reliable, but its accuracy and completeness, and the opinions based thereon, are not guaranteed.

MUNICH

First Edition (Reprint)
© **1990 APA PUBLICATIONS (HK) LTD**
All Rights Reserved
Printed in Singapore by Höfer Press Pte. Ltd

ABOUT THIS BOOK

I t was pure chance that brought editor **Susanne Rick** from Paris to Munich in 1986. For a long time, the journalist was homesick for the city on the Seine. But everything changed after she had been offered to project edit the *City Guide to Munich*. So having arrived in Munich against her will, she now has no wish to leave, and that is in no small measure due to her work on this book.

With the writers and photographers of this volume, she worked out a concept to present Munich to the reader, "from the inside", from the point of view of people who live there. The result is a portrait of Munich, which, despite their love for the city, or perhaps just because of that, includes criticism too. They also tried to do justice to the typical Bavarian mentality, which gives the city its unique atmosphere.

One Entity

It would be difficult to imagine the writer **Bernhard Setzwein** and the city of Munich as two different entities. Sendling is at the centre of his novel *Wurzelwerk* (Root Work) of 1984, and *Hirnweltler's Rückkehr* (Hirnweltler's Return) of 1987. He has written a literary sight-seeing tour as only a true inhabitant of the city can. His contributions to this book are written in his natural Bavarian style.

Meinhard Prill, a historian with a doctorate in Germanics, took himself off to the fathomless depths of the many libraries of the city, and the results of his research are contained in the historical section of the book.

In her walk through the Lehel, **Christine Lubkoll** discovered a new world herself. Born in Bremen, she attained her doctorate in Berlin, and in 1986 came to Munich, where she works as a literary scholar at Ludwig-Maximilians-University.

Travel journalist and geography graduate **Armin Herb** shares his enthusiasm for the Westend with the reader. In his articles about the outskirts of the city, he takes the visitor to parts of Munich which are not often included in the tourist itinerary, but which are nonetheless fascinating.

In 1972, after the Olympic Games, Munich born **Peter Neugart** moved into the Olympic Village which had been taken over for student accommodation. There he makes films, and is active in "forum 2", the cultural centre of that part of the city, and is responsible for the film programme there.

Georg Weindl, who is a freelance writer on economics and travel, shuttles between Munich and Chiemgau, and has written articles on walks in Venice for the *City Guide to Venice*. For the Munich guide, he concentrated on the inner city.

Klaus Schmidt was inspired by the surrounding areas of Munch, near and far. As a T.V. writer for the news sketch *Show and Tell*, he was most interested in the unintentional humour to be found in some aspects of the life of Ludwig II, the Bavarian "Fairy-Tale King".

The art historian **Gerhard Ammelburger** followed the trail left by the artists of Munich, and for his contribution, rummaged in the immeasurable art treasures of Athens on the Isar.

Andreas Ammer has lived in Munich since he was born, and is of the opinion that life would be quite impossible elsewhere. In

Rick

Setzwein

Prill

Lubkoll

Neugart

seminars, studios, galleries, pubs and projects, he has devoted himself body and soul to the cultivation and evaluation of not only the higher, but also the more dubious side of Munich life. Thus he compiled his "archeological" articles on the "social scene" in the city and in the district of Au.

Klaus Hübner has a doctorate in Germanics, is editor of a professional journal and also works at the Munich Iudicum Publishing House, where he is responsible, among other things for the publication of the illustrated volume of *Bayerns Bier-Burgen* (Bavaria's Beer Castles). He intended to write about the literary side of Munich, but during the course of his research, he decided that Munich was more a city of beer than a city of literature. Incidentally, he is just as much an authority on the beer gardens of Munich, as he is on the writer Lion Feuchtwanger.

Born in Paris, **Etienne Bellay** grew up in Munich, and then studied in New York, Paris and Houston. He then returned to Munich where he rediscovered the city for himself and others. He used his knowledge of the film and literary scene in the *Münchner Stadtbuch 1984/85*. In *City Guide to Munich* he turned his attention to the Bavarian Hollywood and the comedian Karl Valentin.

For 13 years, **Peter M. Bode** worked as arts editor and architecture critic on the *Süddeutsche Zeitung* and the *Spiegel* newspapers, before becoming editor of the Munich's *Abendzeitung* (Evening Newspaper). He is the author of specialist books on architecture and town planning, as well as of various T.V. programmes, and his essay in this guide gives a critical evaluation of town planning in Munich.

Gerd Pfeiffer has been working as a photographer in Munich for over 15 years, and there is hardly a corner on which he has not focused his lens . His favourite place is the Viktualienmarkt (Victuals Market), and he has in fact published a beautiful book on it.

Fleeting glimpses of the city have been caught and preserved by **Werner Lüring** with love and patience for this guide.

Other photographs were contributed by **Günter Schneider, Werner Gebhardt, Rainer Hennings, Robert Srzentic, Heiko Schiemann and Tony Holliday.**

Particular thanks go to **Fritz Fenzl** of the Monacensia Library, who gave the editor access to important material in the archives.

—APA Publications

Schmidt

Ammer

Hübner

Bellay

Pfeiffer

CONTENTS

TRAVEL TIPS

MUNICH—A MYTH

Munich. The name alone has an exciting ring to it. It's a name which conjures up a city where you'll find the best of life in the post modern era. You're not far from the natural beauty of the Bavarian uplands, and yet you are able to notice the culture of a city which holds dear a love for the arts. The architecture ranges from Gothic to Functionalism and the place has a colourful local atmosphere of its own. There are business opportunities for the high-tech generation as well as for the bureaucrats, the service industries and the media. But that's not all. Munich has a glamourous image, a whiff of high society and show-biz too—it's got what it takes!

Munich. It's also, one has to admit, a new Bavarian city. Nowhere else in Bavaria is "the Bavarian" so stylised, embellished and marketed as in Munich. And it's not surprising. Two thirds of the inhabitants are newcomers, who have arrived from other parts of the country during the last ten years, and who, even if feeling slightly inhibited, are determined to do justice to the character of the city.

Munich has created its own self portrait, and keeps its own myth alive. The city seems to draw its energy from living in a state of tension between appearance and reality. Munich has always basked in the limelight. It's a cosmopolitan city and has never shrunk from illustrious comparisons: Athens on the Isar, Little Paris, the German Silicon Valley, world city with a heart, movie metropolis or the secret capital of Germany. Despite all this, Munich has always retained its friendly atmosphere of a village of a million, somehow idyllic and open. However, its cultural and political psychology is more petit bourgeois and provincial than rural. Munich has never been innovative, and has always been averse to new ideas—unless it was opportune to move with the times. But when times changed, so did attitudes, and that adaptability came to an end—as King Ludwig I had to learn, as well as the pacifist Eisner, not to mention anyone who has ever pitted himself against the Bavarian authorities.

Nevertheless, many come to Munich. The Oktoberfest (October Festival) alone attracts about 7 million visitors each year—in fourteen days. People want to live and work in Munich, and have high expectations of success and fulfillment. Even the weather is supposed to be better on average than elsewhere. Yet about 30,000 leave each year because good weather can be changeable, and there's many a provincial beauty who has waited in vain to be discovered on the Leopoldstraße.

"Munich sparkles", wrote Thomas Mann, attempting to explain the attraction which has drawn outsiders to the city for more than a century. A traveller once remarked, "Munich is anxious not to appear to be an international city, but tries to remain a provincial capital. Munich has the opposite of delusions of grandeur, a love for the small. But forces beyond its control make it a metropolis."

Preceding pages, FC-Bayern fans; a bird's-eye view of the Olympic Complex; all kinds of beer tankards; a performance on Marienplatz. Left, a young couple appreciating art.

Der Marc

24

München.

BEGINNINGS OF THE BAVARIAN METROPOLIS

The history of Munich begins with an act of violence. In 1156 Emperor Friederich Barbarossa bestowed the Duchy of Bavaria upon the Guelph Heinrich der Löwe (Henry the Lion). Shortly after taking power, Heinrich destroyed the bridge over the Isar at Oberföhring, which was owned by the bishop of Freising, and which brought revenue from tolls, as it laid on the salt trade route from Reichenhall and Hallein to Augsburg.

The Guelph Duke had a new bridge built a few kilometres further upstream, near a small settlement by the name of *Ze den Munichen*. This was no more than a group of farmhouses, partly run by monks (Munichen), with a small stone church.

Heinrich der Löwe, realising the importance of towns in the development of a province, and who, as Duke of Saxony, had founded Lübeck, Rostock and Schwerin, conferred upon the small settlement of *Munichen* those rights necessary for it to prosper: the right to hold markets and the right to mint coins.

Bishop Otto von Friesing was helpless in the face of this injustice, as Heinrich der Löwe was one of the most powerful Dukes of the Empire, and Emperor Barbarossa, a Hohenstaufen, had entrusted Bavaria to him, principally to end the rivalry between Guelphs and Hohenstaufens for dominion within the Empire. Thus on 14 June 1158, the Emperor legalised the step taken by the Duke, and since then that has been taken as the date of the foundation of Munich. However, the settlement had to pay a third of its annual coin and toll revenue to the bishopric of Freising as compensation. This agreement stood until 1803, when the bishopric fell to Bavaria. In 1852 the matter was finally settled as the city bought itself free of all obligations by paying 987 Guilders to the Bavarian State, as successor to the bishopric.

Preceding pages, the Marienplatz, copperplate engraving by Michael Wemig, 1701. Left, Emperor Ludwig and his wife Margarethe von Holland in a medieval display of power.

Thus Munich is a relatively young city, without the traditions of cities such as Augsburg or Regensburg, which were founded by the Romans. However, excavations under the Marienplatz and under the Alte Peter (St. Peter's Church), have unearthed remains of a settlement and of a stone church, which date from before 1158. So attempts are still being made to set the founding of Munich back to the time of the Romans or at least to A.D. 6th or 7th century.

A Roman Settlement

All that is certain, however, is that at the end of the era, the Munich area was a Roman settlement. In A.D. 17 a Roman military post was set up in Gauting (Lat: Bratanarium), and traces of Roman habitation have been found in Denning and Grünwald. In the 5th century, in the wake of the retreating Romans, Bavarians settled the land. Even today, no-one is entirely sure where they came from. The preponderance of place names ending in "-ing" found in this area date from this period. There are early records of Sendling (760), Pasing (763), Schwabing (782) and Giesing (790) and places such as Laim, Haidhausen, Ramersdorf and Bogenhausen have been established much earlier than the settlement of *Ze den Munichen*.

However, the name alone indicates that there is not much history of Munich before 1158. The annals of the monasteries of Schäftlarn and Tegernsee are unclear as to which of them originally had jurisdiction over Munich, and there's still many a lively argument around the beer table about the exact history.

No-one knows either, just why, in the 17th century, the monk, displayed on the settlement's coat of arms right from its earliest days, was changed into the now famous Münchner Kindl (Child of Munich). The Child of Munich was quickly adopted as a charming symbol of the city. The citizens became so attached to their child, that when, after World War II, the city fathers were on the look out for a new coat of arms, the old having become tainted by association with the swastica, they were only able to adopt the original monk with reservations insisted upon by the residents. The child of Munich is still on the coat of arms today, in a monk's cowl, holding a book in his left hand.

The First City Wall

After 1158, the small settlement grew rapidly, even though in comparison with today, its dimensions were very small indeed. The

named the Schöner Turm (Beautiful Tower); the inner Sendlinger Tor on the southern exit of the Rindermarkt or Cattle Market; and the two northern gates at the end of Wein and Diener streets. The city wall was defended by peel towers, none of which remains today, and although the tower at the Cattle Market is often referred to as dating from this period, it is merely an old water tower.

From the very beginning, the Marienplatz was the centre of the city, although until 1854 it was simply known as the Market Place or the Grain Market, because it was

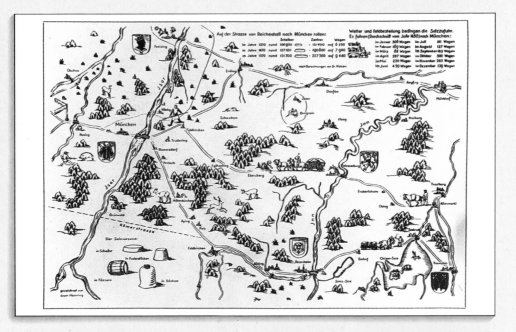

first encircling wall, recorded in 1173, enclosed 2500 inhabitants, and followed what is today the Augustinerstraße, over Löwengrube (Lion's Den), Schäfflerstraße, Hofgraben and Sparkaßenstraße to today's Viktualienmarkt (Victuals Market), to complete the circle over Rosental and Färbergraben. Long after the city had expanded, water flowed here in the inner city moat.

Entrance to the city was through five gates—the Talburgtor (Valley Fortress Gate) near today's Alte Rathaus (Old Town Hall) on Marienplatz; the Obere Tor (Upper Gate) at the end of Kaufinger Straße, later

here that from the 14th century onwards, the grain market was held. Here, the Salzstraße (Salt Route) from Salzburg to Augsburg crossed the road which connected Sendling with Schwabing. This crossroads can still be seen on a map of the city today.

As the centre of the city throughout the centuries, the Marienplatz has been the venue for joustings, tournaments and duels, festivals and uprisings, and also the site of executions. During the Thirty Years' War, the King of Sweden had the gallows set up in the square, after he had occupied the city, and the survivors of the Sendlinger Bauernschlacht (slaughter of the peasants) in 1705, known as the *Mordweihnacht* (night of murder), came to a ghastly end there.

The existence of the small settlement of Munich was seriously in jeopardy once more in 1180, when Heinrich der Löwe refused to support Emperor Friederich Barbarossa in his campaign against the cities of North Italy, for which he was outlawed by the Emperor. He lost the duchy of Bavaria, and the Bishop of Freising believed that he could put the clock back.

It was even recorded in the annals of the

monastery of Schäftlarn, that "Munich has been destroyed, Föhring rebuilt." But it seems that the place was now too well established for the bishop to be able to destroy it. So until 1240, the Bishop of Freising ruled over Munich, which was now referred to in the annals of the monastery of Scheyern in 1214 as *civitas* or a town.

During this period, Munich's revenue came above all from the lucrative salt trade, and its related bridge tolls. The town had

Left, the salt trade routes and Isar crossing at Munich. Above, city seal from the 14th century.

risen to be the trading centre of the Upper Bavarian region, which had already recognised the Munich *Pfennig* (penny) as valid currency, when the Wittelsbach family took power in 1240. The Wittelsbachs received the crown of Bavaria in 1180 and retained power over Munich and Bavaria until 1918. No other dynasty in Germany held onto power for so long, and even though the Wittelsbachs were autocratic—the early rulers in particular were very stern—the Bavarians have quite fond memories of "their" ruling dynasty with its dukes, electors and kings. "Benevolent despots", is how they are referred to by loyalists even today in Bavaria, and no-one seems to disagree. Every year, even today, there is a gathering of the Wittelsbach faithful in Gammelsdorf in Lower Bavaria, for as they say in Bavaria, "*Mir braucha koan Kini, aber scheena wars...*", or in ordinary German "*Wir brauchen keinen König, aber schöner wäre es...*" or in English "We don't need a king, but wouldn't it be nicer..."

The First City Fortress

Duke Ludwig II der Strenge (The Stern), is the first Wittelsbach to choose to live in Munich. He had to share dominion over Bavaria with his brother, who lived in Landshut, the capital of Lower Bavaria. This marks the beginning of the complicated land divisions of Bavaria, which hampered the development of the province and were only rectified in the early 16th century.

First, however, Ludwig der Strenge had the Alte Hof (Old Court) built on the northern outskirts of the city as the city fortress. There was apparently already an administration building on the site dating from the time of Heinrich der Löwe. Despite the sympathy with which time has endowed this ruling family, the relationship between citizens and rulers was not without conflict during the middle ages. The Wittelsbachs very wisely built their fortresses and residences on the outskirts of their cities, so that in times of rebellion, they would be able to make a quick getaway.

In the second half of the 13th century Munich grew to five times its former size. Franciscans, Augustinians and nuns of the Order of St. Clare set up their cloisters in the town, and although the church of St. Peter had been built in 1260 (it then had a double tower), another parish church soon became necessary, for, as the Bishop of Freising remarked, "The congregation of the church of St. Peter in Munich, has, by God's grace grown so immense, that a sole shepherd cannot look after the flock without danger to their immortal souls…" The Marienkirche (Church of Mary) was built, and made way for the Frauenkirche (Church of Our Lady) in the 15th century. The poor settled in the valley between the Marienplatz and the Isar. The growing suburbs were included within the encircling wall, the first city fortifications, and there too the monks of the Holy Ghost, receiving a portion of the bridge toll, set up their hospital for the treatment of the poor and sick.

Social Unrests

The expansion of the town was not accomplished without its share of social tension. The citizens' town council (Council of Twelve), first recorded in the late 13th century, was dominated by a small group of rich patrician families. They were supposed to represent the interests of the town against the town rulers and sovereigns and their representative, the town judge.

The majority of the inhabitants of the town were artisans, small traders, waggoners, workers and day labourers. In addition there was a small Jewish population, which suffered a terrible pogrom in 1285, when they were accused of the murder of a child. One-hundred-fifty Jewish citizens were burned alive in their synagogue, which, like the ghetto, was located in the area behind the Neuen Rathaus (New Town Hall). It wasn't until 1287 that Jews again took up residence in the city, and as punishment, all trades bar moneylending were forbidden them. They were again persecuted in 1348, and finally banned from the city in 1442.

In 1295, the citizens rebelled against the Duke, who had set up his own mint in the marketplace, where, to ease his financial difficulties, his coins were stretched with base metals. The artisans rose up and stormed and razed the house, and, it was said, killed the mint master. For this crime, the citizenry had to pay 500 pounds of Pfennigs to the Duke as punishment.

Due to the taxes it collected, Munich was the richest city under Wittelsbach dominion, and by the 14th century, the surrounding lands yielded enough revenue to maintain the inhabitants, who now numbered 10,000. Foodstuffs were sold in the grain market, and at the top of the Weinstraße, there was a wine market. During the middle ages, wine reigned as the preferred drink in Munich. Much of it was distilled from vineyards in southern Tyrol which were owned by the monasteries of the city.

But wherever possible, vineyards were cultivated in Bavaria itself, and even today, the slopes on the banks of the River Danube at Regensburg are known as "Winzerer Höhen" (Vintner Heights). In the late middle ages, traders who did not live in the city had the right to sell their wares, but only in the open air, so a wine shed was set up in the late middle ages (Burgstraße 5), where the casks could be stored overnight. In the early morning meat stalls were set up around the Peterskirche, which is why so many butcher shops are still found there today. Fish have been bred in the city moat since the 15th century. Most of the foodstuffs which were offered for sale in the town were liable for the bridge toll, as were all the items for sale in the Jakobsplatz or "Jakobidult" after the 14th century. A trader was not allowed to pass through the city or go round, without offering his wares at the market for at least one day. It was through such means that the medieval cities were assured of their standing as market towns.

For the development of Munich, it was of particular advantage that it was elevated to imperial and royal city early in the 14th century for in 1314, the German princes elected the Bavarian Duke Ludwig IV as the

German Kaiser (Emperor), to be known as Ludwig der Bayer (Ludwig the Bavarian). It was because Ludwig was not among the most powerful of all the German princes—a reason, in fact, for his being elected, that for the next few centuries Munich was to be at the centre of German and European politics.

Ludwig's rival for the Imperial throne, the Hapsburg Friedrich der Schöne (Frederick the Handsome), laid siege to the city in 1319, but Ludwig finally managed to defeat him in the battle of Mühldorf and took him as his prisoner.

politics of the German Kaisers was even then a thing of the past.

As a gift to Munich, the Kaiser brought a holy relic back from his journey to Italy, the upper arm of St. Anthony, which can still be seen in the church of St. Anna im Lehel.

But Munich gained in other ways from the feud between the Kaiser and the pope. The city became the centre of antipapal dissent and propaganda. Intellectuals and scholars, mostly Franciscan monks like Marsilius of Padua, who was also the Kaiser's personal physician; Bonagratia von Bergamo; Mi-

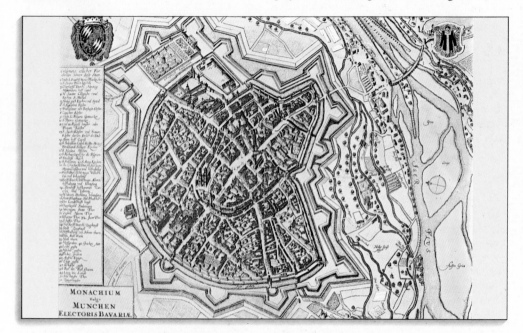

However, the pope, then resident in Avignon, declared himself in the Hapsburgs favour, and he excommunicated Ludwig. This was the last intervention by a pope in German affairs of royalty. On the other hand, Ludwig was the last German king to be crowned Kaiser in Rome (1328). It was more a nostalgic link with the claims of his predecessors, to stand as the Kaiser of the Holy Roman Empire of the German Nation, in the footsteps of Ancient Rome, for the Italian

Munich of the Prince Electors, copperplate engraving by Matthäus Merian, 1640.

chael von Cesena; Heinrich von Thalhelm, Ludwig's chancellor; and Heinrich der Preisinger all wrote polemical pamphlets and preached against the claim of the pope to bring the temporal ruler under his sway.

These men constituted the *Geistliche Hofakademie* (Spiritual Court Academy) of the Kaiser, and the most notable member was William of Occam. He studied in Oxford and Paris, until, pursued by the pope as a heretic, he fled to Munich. "Kaiser, defend me with the sword, and I will defend you with the word," was his offer to Ludwig. He was one of the first rationalists, and differentiated strongly between knowledge and belief and advocated church reform by means of a convened council, as well as the subordination of the church to the state. Through his efforts, the liberation of European philosophy from theology was begun, and his name and memory still live on in the Occamstraße in Munich.

But even then, the general public was less interested in the learned disputes between scholars and pope than in the measures taken by the Kaiser to augment the power and wealth of Munich. For Ludwig der Bayer had, as the chronicle tells, *"grosse lieb zu der Stadt gehabt"* (a great love for the city), and even today his imperial black and gold colours are on the coat of arms of Munich. In a golden bull of 1322, he ordered that salt mined in Reichenhall or Hallein could only cross the Isar in Munich. This monopoly ensured Munich's wealth in the years that followed, and has resulted in the blossoming of bourgeois art in the city during the 15th century.

At the same time, the city was expanding, even though the great fire of 1327 destroyed almost the whole of the eastern part. A new encircling wall became necessary, and as an indication of just how far the town had grown by the 14th century, the new limits of the city remained as such until the 18th century. The wall ran from today's Stachus, then the Neuhauser Tor, over what is now Sonnenstrasse to the Sendlinger Tor and followed today's Blumenstraße over the Angertor to the Isartor. Then, bypassing the area where the Residenz (palace) stands today, it continued to the Schwabinger Tor (Odeonsplatz) along what is now the Maximilianstraße and back to the Neuhauser Tor (Stachus).

People involved in trade and industry mainly lived in the valley, in the Anger quarter around the Cattle Market and in the Hacken quarter, while those of religious persuasion preferred the Kreuz quarter, northwest of the Marienplatz. The nobility resided in the Graggenauer quarter, near the Platzl today.

The city owed it to the Kaiser that the Marienplatz remained intact through the

centuries, as he forbade any alterations or additions, for all time, in order to preserve its unique character for gentry, citizens and guests to enjoy.

The increase in population led to a change in the city parliament. There was an "External Council" comprising 24 members, and the "Commons", a committee of citizens, which complemented the original Council of Twelve, now exclusively for the patricians. In the final analysis, however, power was in the hands of about 40 patrician families.

Munich's great period as an imperial city

ended with the death of Ludwig in 1347. He was killed on a bear hunt at Fürstenfeld (now Fürstenfeldbruck). However this had possibly spared the city further military conflict, as Ludwig had pursued a policy of unrestrained dynastic aggression, bringing Brandenburg, Kärnten, Tyrol and Flanders under Wittelsbach rule, thereby provoking resistance by other princes of the Reich. In 1346, they had elected Karl von Maehren as a rival king. After Ludwig's death, he took the Imperial crown jewels, which had been guarded day and night in the Alte Hof, by four Cistercian monks: the Imperial crown,

Imperial orb, sceptre, the holy lance, the royal mantle, the ceremonial sword and the Imperial and Mauritius swords.

Civic Rule

With the death of Ludwig, unquiet times came to Munich and the province. His descendents divided up the land, and made war on each other and then inherited from each other. Bavaria was no longer one of the princedoms of the Reich to elect the king. Brandenburg and Tyrol were lost and Land-

zenry, to award specific freedom in return for the payments, which would eventually develop into taxes. They were awarded more legal rights, but above all the right to resist princes who broke covenant. As early as 1302 even before Ludwig was regent, the Schnaitbacher Document had an agreement between the ruler and the Upper Bavarian estates, inclusive of Munich. It was the citizens of Munich who, in the 14th century, defended their rights most vehemently against the Wittelsbachs.

It was with some misgivings that the

shut, Straubing and Ingolstadt, where the first Bavarian university was founded in 1492, become the new centres of power in Bavaria, only to fade back into sleepy provincial towns after a few generations.

These towns were able to profit from the warring Wittelsbachs. The Dukes, seeking to shift their debts onto the province, were required by the representatives, the so-called three estates of church, nobility and citi-

people—the artisans and small tradesmen—viewed the close links which had developed between the rich patrician families, who held political power in Munich, and the Dukes. In 1385, Hans Impler, the patrician, was beheaded on the Marienplatz for being a favourite of the Dukes, and soon there was open conflict with the Wittelsbachs. In 1397 the patrician families fled the town, and did not return until 1403, after the Dukes Wilhelm and Ernst had subdued the citizens by laying siege to the town. In return, the citizens were granted a greater say in political matters.

Left, in the Old Court. Above left, coat of arms with the *Münchner Kindl* by Erasmus Grasser, 1477. Right, Morisk dancer by Grasser.

The Wittelsbachs rapidly drew their own conclusions from this uprising. Through the expansion of the city wall, they found themselves in the centre of the town, in the Alte Hof. So in 1400, a fortress, the Neuveste, was built outside the city, where the Residenz now stands. It was not until 1476 that this became part of the city fortifications. In the 17th century, the new palace then took its place.

It was during this time of civic power that the landmarks of the city today were constructed in quick succession. The year 1392

tious facades of the later princely edifices.

From Poland came Jan Pollack, who, as town painter, not only adorned the towers and walls of the town with coats of arms and religious scenes, but also the Dom (cathedral) and St. Peter's. Apart from Pollack, the most important artist of 15th-century Munich was the Upper Palatian, Erasmus von Grasser. He was responsible for the sculpture of St. Peter, and the famous Moriskentaenzer (Morisk Dancers), which were first placed in the Town Hall. Today, only the copies are there, while the originals are kept

saw the now superfluous Taltor, dating from the Guelph times, altered to become the Ratsturm. At its side, in 1470, one of the most beautiful examples of Gothic art in Germany was built. The Alte Rathaus (Old Town Hall) with its glorious state room, was designed by Joerg von Halsbach, known as Ganghofer. It was he who, at the request of the citizens, built the Frauenkirche (Church of Our Lady), between 1468 and 1488. This late Gothic construction, without ornamentation, without decorative additions and without marble adornments, stands out in its simplicity in contrast to the rather ostenta-

in the Stadtmuseum (Town Museum). Only 10 of the original 16 figures remain.

Thus the landmarks of Munich were, for the most part, created by artists from outside the city. Up to the 14th century there was no local artist of high calibre, nor, was Munich the intellectual centre of Bavaria. In 1482, the first printer in Munich, Hans Schauer, was still not using the latin printing letters which were used in learned documents elsewhere. His task was mainly to deal with prayer books and holy songs. However, the town could afford to bring artists in from outside. The city annals reveal that by 1400 over 25,000 carts from outlying districts, carrying foodstuffs, and more than 3,000 with other articles passed through the city gates. In addition there were many unregistered two wheeled vehicles, and, of course, there was the salt transportation. Paving of the main thoroughfares was begun in 1393, and soon, the first traffic rules were passed.

Outside the city gates, there was stabling for the horses, and the attendant craftsman's workshops. Near the bridge over the Isar, more than 3000 rafts landed each year, bringing building materials, coal and articles

cludes one of the first illustrations of Munich, depicts a wealthy and well-fortified city despite the many fires which destroyed various parts of the city, and despite the plague which recurred intermittently after 1349 (25 epidemics were recorded up to 1680). The city had acquired a second walled circle and many peel towers, for defence against the Hussites.

In the year 1500, a total of 13,447 inhabitants were counted, of which 700 were members of religious orders, 600 connected with the nobility and the court and 350 beg-

for trade from Wolfratshausen to Munich. In 1492 the pass over the Kesselberg at Walchensee was built, to improve communications with Venice, which had moved its northern trading centre from Bozen to Mittelwald. By now, Munich was not living by the salt trade alone, but more and more from long distance trading with Italy. From Venice came cloth, spices and precious metals.

The *Schedelsche Weltchronik* (World Chronicle of Schedel) of 1493, which in-

Historical city view of 1493, *Schedelsche Weltchronik* (World Chronicle of Schedel).

gars. One-hundred-twenty-four shoemakers and tailors were working in the city, 80 grocers, 69 butchers, 76 linen weavers, 38 brewers, 23 inn keepers, 2 book sellers and just 1 printer. The Law of Purity for Munich beer was passed in 1487, and from 1475 it was forbidden to keep pigs in the Innenstadt (inner city area), apart from the "Antonius pigs", complete with bell, who in their fashion performed the duty of keeping the streets clean. Munich still could not compare with cities such as Augsburg or Regensburg, but it was easily on par with those like Frankfurt or Basel.

SERENISS.º PRINCEPS. AC. DN. DN. FERDINANDVS. MARIA. VTRIVSQ. BAVARIÆ
AC. PALATINAT, SVPERIORIS. DVX, COMES. PALATIN. RHENI. S. R. I. ARCHIDAPIE
ET ELECTOR. LANDGRAVI, IN LEICHTENBERG.   Sᵃ Cels. Electorali   Abraham Aubry Calcographus et Cinis
                                          Francofurten humillime   D.D.D. 1658.

With the reunification of Upper and Lower Bavaria (1506) Munich became the residential city of the Wittelsbachs. Originally Duke Albrecht IV wanted Regensburg as the capital city of Bavaria, but the Kaiser was against this plan as the free Reichs city of Regensburg, like Augsburg and Nürnberg were under his suzerainty. Those cities were still richer and more powerful than Munich. However, by the end of the 18th century, Munich had surpassed them all. This progress was not without its setbacks, and has left little of the medieval city intact.

The Expansion of Princely Power

From Munich, the Wittelsbachs attempted to regain political importance for Bavaria within the Reich and to ensure for themselves the monopoly of power in the Land. As yet, Bavaria, like the other German princely states was not a cohesive national territory. The province was interspersed with numerous enclaves, which did not fall under the rule of the Bavarian Dukes, but which were independent. There were reichsfrei (free Reich) knight's castles, and cities, under the direct protection of the Kaiser. There were spiritual principalities, like the bishopric of Freising, in possession of their own lands, who lived in constant danger of having their rights curtailed by the Wittelsbachs. But even within their own areas, the Dukes did not wield absolute power, but were financially dependent upon the three estates of the province, as well as on the cities and the landed gentry. For it was they who collected taxes from the province, and in their Landtag (Diet) they granted the Duke a certain annual revenue.

In Bavaria, the Landtag sessions were held in Munich, in the Alte Rathaus (Old Town Hall). The absolutism which prevailed in Europe until the 18th century sought to rescind these ancient rights. The Dukes settled

Left, Prince Elector Ferdinand Maria of Bavaria, copperplate engraving of 1658.

upon the amount they were to receive from the Land and the cities, court expenses were to be written over to the estates, and in the towns, autonomy such as that granted to Munich by Ludwig der Bayer, became a thing of the past.

In the 16th century the Wittelsbachs began to fashion the city of Munich to their own design. Artisans and traders of the city were increasingly required to cater to the demands of the court for tapestries and decorative work, high quality cloth and intricate carpentry. The town council records of the time proclaim displeasure at the extravagance and surfeit of workers on the palace, as well as express disapproval of the excess entertaining which was taking place.

For the Wittelsbachs were not only great builders, they also loved celebrations, festivals and sumptuous feasts, such as were held for the visit of Kaiser Karl V in 1530. For the nuptials of Wilhelm V and Renate von Lothringen (Lorraine) in 1568, the celebrations lasted three weeks, and the Glockenspiel (carillon) in Marienplatz is an ever present reminder of the jousting which took place then.

It was Wilhelm V who, in 1587, considerably weakened the city. He ran up large debts through the construction of a Renaissance palace, the Maxburg (destroyed in the war), between the cathedral and today's Lenbachplatz. He removed the salt trade privileges from the city in order to set up a state salt trade monopoly. Such was the power of the Dukes over the town, that the citizens were unable to rebel against this violation of their ancient rights. During the Thirty Years' War, the Wittelsbachs had consolidated their power, and from 1643 onwards it was they who elected the mayor of Munich.

The New Belief

By this time the people had long lost the battle, fought behind the scenes of courtly festivals and bourgeois life, over the protestant teachings of Luther. In the beginning, the Bavarian Duke Wilhelm IV was, like the majority of believers, a follower of the Reformation. The Catholic Church had lost credibility with the people, through its ruthless power politics, prebendal profits and the general conduct of its clergy.

The Duke, however, was quick to see that criticism of the authority of the church could well lead to an attack on his own position. He began to fear "revolt, rumour and assault" and so banned the writings of Luther.

In 1522 he ordered a journeyman, who had professed himself a protestant, to be beheaded on the Marienplatz. It was a fate which also befell some itinerant preachers, such as the Minorite monk, Hans Roth, who had called for revolt against "heathen temporal authorities". The peasants' wars of 1525 in Schwaben (Swabia) and Thüringen (Thuringia) exacerbated the situation. A Baptist community with about 40 members was apprehended in Munich in 1527, and nine of them were burned or drowned. Even the great Bavarian historian of the 16th century, Aventin, could only save himself from the consequences of the charge of heresy, by fleeing. Like him, many patrician families of

the protestant persuasion left the city, and as many people from Munich made their way to Lutheran Augsburg for Sunday worship, the Duke had the roads watched.

"German Rome"

For in 1583 Wilhelm V had decreed that in Bavaria, only the Catholic faith was permitted. So Munich became the centre of the Counter Reformation in Germany, "German Rome" as contemporaries called it. As a reward for their papal and imperial loyalty,

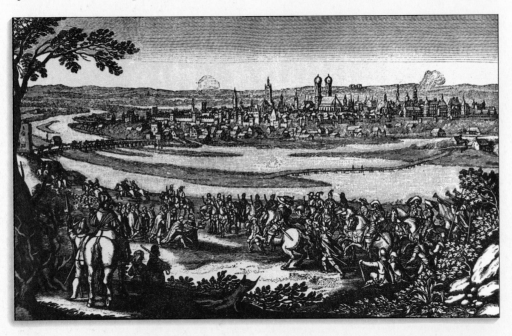

the Wittelsbachs were given the seat of the Archbishop of Cologne, a right they kept until 1806. As early as 1559 Albrecht V had called the Jesuits to Munich, and under his successor, Wilhelm V, they set up a college, the Alte Academie (the Old Academy) in the Neuhauserstrasse. Wilhelm also had the Michaelskirche (St. Michael's Church) built for them in 1583. It was the largest Renaissance church north of the Alps and the immense building costs almost caused a national bankruptcy.

With the Counter Reformation, the Renaissance came to Munich. Apart from the

Michaelskirche and the simple, but rather dark Münzhof (1563-1567), the Residenz also reflects this style in Munich especially the parts which were built earlier. Albrecht V had a chamber of art built, one of the first museums north of the Alps, and the Antiquarium, considered the finest secular building of the German Renaissance. He thus laid the foundation for one of the most glorious princely edifices of Europe, and when King Gustav Adolf of Sweden occupied Munich in 1632 during the Thirty Years' War, he forbade his troops to touch

the buildings, saying that to harm them would be a crime, not merely against an individual, but against the whole world.

These buildings mark the beginning of the history of art in Munich. Wilhelm IV had created the first Hofgarten with an art gallery on the site of the present-day Marstallplatz, and had invited artists such as Hans Burgkmaier and Albrecht Altdorfer, who had painted the *Alexanderschlacht* (Battle of

Left, handing over the keys of the city to Gustav Adolf in the Thirty Years' War. Above, Prince Elector Maximilian I in 1635.

Alexander), to work for him. His son Albrecht V, whose other love was architecture, was also a bibliophile. He bought literary treasures from the Augsburg entrepreneur Jakob Fugger and acquired the collection of books of the orientalist Johann Albert Widmannstetter. Thus he laid the foundations for the Bayerischen Staatsbibliothek (Bavarian State Library), now one of the largest libraries in the world.

Under Albrecht V and his successors, Duke Wilhelm V and Maximilian I, later elevated to Prince Elector, the Munich court gained fame within Europe. Peter Candid was the court painter, and Orlando di Lasso, the most important composer of his time, spent almost half a century (1556-1594) as leader of the court orchestra in Munich. In the field of plastic arts, Munich mannerism of the late Renaissance developed into an individual, early Baroque style. Hubert Gernhard created the figure of St. Michael for the facade of the Michaelskirche, and possibly the figure of the Madonna in Marienplatz. And finally, Hans Krumpper was responsible for the *Patrona Bavariae*, the patroness of Bavaria, just on the west side of the Residenz.

Eve of the Thirty Years' War

The Munich court glittered, and of course, to later generations, the collections and patronage of the arts of the Bavarian Dukes of the Renaissance seem most laudable. Particularly admirable, perhaps, was the founding of the Rubens collection in the Alte Pinakothek with Maximilian I's purchase of the *Lion Hunt* and his acquisition of Dürer's *Four Apostles* by means of gentle force from Nürnberg. For the city of Munich and its folks, however, this Wittelsbach style was a great economic burden, and the chronicles complain of "heavy taxation". Prices of foodstuffs rose, and craftsmen became poorer as the Dukes utilised any surplus from the city coffers for their own ends. Everyday life in the city had its darker side, and the religious fanaticism of the Counter Reformation reigned.

The Women's House was closed, and the first witch hunts took place in 1578. Processions of flagellants wound through the streets on Good Friday, and from 1608 onwards, only plays with religious subjects were permitted. The guilds mounted biblical dramas, and everywhere audiences were captivated by powerful Jesuit productions. The performance of *Esther* on Marienplatz lasted three whole days, with over 2000 in the cast, and after a production of *Cenodoxus* by Jakob Bidermann, who lived in Munich, 14 courtiers sought to enter monasteries. It was a time of excessive cruelty and collective penitence, a time of ecstatic preaching and dark warnings of destruction, which were ultimately fulfilled in the apocalypse of the Thirty Years' War (1618-1648).

The year 1619 saw the beginnning of a strengthening of Munich's defences. Yet in 1632, the city surrendered without a fight to the Swedish King Gustav Adolf, leader of the protestants, who protected the city from destruction in return for a payment of 450,000 Guilders. The citizens were unable to find the money immediately, and so had to give 10 hostages, who were only allowed to return home after three years. In gratitude for the preservation of Munich as well as Landshut, Maximilian I had the Mariensaule (Maria Tower) built in 1638.

Baroque and Rococo Dreams

The war left a ruined city, and financially too, the state of Bavaria, elevated to an electorate in 1628 and expanded to include Upper Palatine, was not to recover until 1806, the end of the Old Reich. The fault laid at court. Court life under Prince Elector Ferdinand Maria and his wife Adelheid von Savoyen modelled itself on the fantastic goings-on at the French court. There were pastoral plays and knights' tournaments. There were gondolas on the Nymphenburg Canal and festivals on the state ship *Bucentaurus*, built on Venetian lines for the Starnberger See (Starnberg Lake). Operas and ballets were performed. The first opera to be performed in Munich was *L'arpa Fes-*

tante by G.B.Maccioni, which was held in the Residenz in 1653.

The settings for courtly festivities included the Theatinerkirche (Theatiner Church) and the Nymphenburg Palace. The Theatinerkirche was built as the fulfillment of a vow, made by the royal couple on the birth of their son and heir Max Emanuel. Its design, by the architects Barelli and Zuccalli, brought the Italian Baroque style to Munich, a style which was to be reflected in monasteries and village churches all over Bavaria. The Bavarian historian Karl Bosl summed it up, "The ordinary man believes with his eyes through looking at architecture and artistic images, and with his ears by listening to preaching and music. So Bavaria, which remained Catholic, became a land of glorious Baroque, even in the smallest villages."

It was Barelli who conceived the central part of the Nymphenburg Palace, around which the most extensive palace grounds of Europe were created, modelled on Versailles, of course. In the 18th century, master builders and artists such as Joseph Effner, the Asam Brothers, Francois Cuvilliés, Johann Michael Fischer, Johann Baptist Gunezrainer and sculptors Johann Baptist Straub and Ignaz Günther, extended these buildings in the late baroque and rococo style. New buildings were constructed, such as the Amalienburg and the Pagodenburg in the Nymphenburg Park, the cloister church of St. Anna im Lehel, the Kirche St. Michael (Church of St. Michael) in Berg am Laim and the Asamkirche (Asam Church) in Sendlingerstrasse. Francois Cuvilliés the Elder was still practising in Munich, and he created the glorious Gruenen Galerie (Green Gallery) in the Residenz and above all the theatre bearing his name, the best example of rococo art in the world, according to Jakob Burckhardt.

The money to build these wonderful edifices came, for the most part, from taxes paid by the citizens, whose efforts were hardly adequate to meet such demands. The town was forced to supplement its income by selling land to the nobility. This is how the Promenadeplatz of today came into being, with the palaces of the Preysing, Lerchen-feld, Holnstein and Törring families. Obviously the lifestyle of the rulers did not find favour with the people, and when in 1674, the Residenz went up in flames, because a lady-in-waiting had forgotten to extinguish a candle, it took well over an hour to rouse the people to help.

Bavarian Power Politics

It was not only the costs of holding court baroque style and the resulting imperial

Belgrade. Thirty thousand Bavarian soldiers lost their lives in this campaign, which cost the Land 20 million Guilders and brought nothing in return apart from some Turkish prisoners-of-war, who were brought to Munich by the Prince Electors, and who added colour to the city by becoming sedan bearers. Max Emanuel almost lost his lands through this engagement, but was rewarded by the Kaiser with the hand of his daughter.

A son was born of this union, who was chosen by the European powers as heir to the Spanish throne. When the child died in

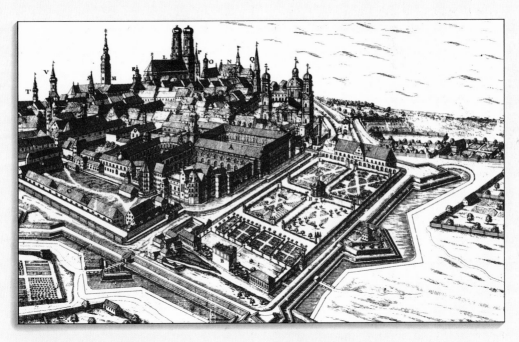

demands which sapped Bavaria's strength, but also the ambitions of Max Emanuel, who sought by all means within his power to attain a higher standing. The palace he built in Schleissheim was decidedly kingly in its attributes. He took part in the Hapsburg uprisings against the Turks, who laid siege to Vienna in 1683 and in 1688 conquered

Copperplate engraving of 1701 on aerial view of Munich. In the foreground are Hofgarten and Residenz; in the background stands the Church of Our Lady; on the left lies St. Peter and to the right, Theatiner Church.

Nymphenburg at the age of six, in 1699, the War of the Spanish Succession (1701-1714) broke out. The Prince Elector took the side of the French in this conflict, against his father-in-law, who was residing in Vienna. Max Emanuel moved his residence to Brussels, and planned to exchange Bavaria for a larger territory. But in the final analysis, he remained a pawn in the hands of greater powers, and for ten years (1705-1715), Austrian troops occupied Bavaria. In 1705 the peasants of the Bavarian uplands rebelled against the cruel regime. Armed with scythes, they marched towards the headquarters of the

Austrians in Munich, their battle cry was that they would rather die Bavarian than be corrupted by the Kaiser. But the peasants were betrayed, and in Sendling, outside the city gates, the rebels were massacred by the Kaiser's troops. This slaughter, known as the Sendlinger "Mordweihnacht" (Night of Murder), is commemorated by the memorial to the blacksmith of Kochel, one of the leaders of the insurrection, on the Sendlinger Berg (Sendlinger Hill).

When Max Emanuel finally retook Bavaria, with the help of the French, the popu-

land was occupied." His death in 1745 brought this episode of Bavarian history to an end.

Signs of New Times

Under Prince Elector Max III Joseph, attempts were made to rebuild the economy of the Land, and to reduce the horrendous 32 million Guilder debt. The population at the time numbered no more than 1 million. Artisans and traders were still organised in guilds, which permitted no competition or

lace rejoiced, but economically and financially the Land was in a bad shape. The final blow to Bavaria's power politics came in 1742, when the Prince Elector Karl Albrecht, at Prussia's instigation, in opposition to Maria Theresia, the Austrian Kaiserin (Empress), had himself crowned Kaiser. Once again, Austrian troops occupied the Land, and Karl Albrecht, disillusioned, noted in his diary, "So, I, fortune's fool, made myself out to be Kaiser, and made out that I had chosen Frankfurt as my residence, because it lay in the centre of my empire. But in reality, I was banned and homeless, for my

progress. So the rulers attempted to build up new businesses outside the traditional trade laws. In 1690, in the Au region, a princely cloth manufacturing enterprise was established. Later, in 1720, it was followed by a tapestry workshop and in 1764 a cotton manufacturer was established. With the exception of the Nymphenburg Porcelain manufactory founded in 1758, these businesses run by the state operated at a loss. There was still no question of any basic reform of the economy.

The Enlightenment came slowly to Munich. In 1702, a newspaper was published, gloriously entitled *Service and Pleasure for the Society of our beloved Neighbours of the Isar Valley*, and later, after 1750, the *Munich Weekly News* and the *State Learned and General News* were widely read in the city. In 1751 Wiguleus von Kreittmayr reformed the Bavarian legislation, but omitted to outlaw torture. The Bavarian Academy of Science was founded in 1759, and Max III Joseph, a truly enlightened ruler, introduced general compulsory education in 1771. During his regentship, the last traces of the Counter Reformation disappeared, the dra-

matic presentations of Christ's suffering ceased in favour of secular dramas. Schiller's *Räuber* (The Robbers) was performed in Faberbrau in Sendlingerstraße. Mozart often stayed in the city, and in 1781, the first performance of *Idomeneo* was held, but the young composer's wish to be employed at court was not granted.

The enlightened absolutism which Max

Left, the Sendling Peasants' Battle of 1705, copperplate engraving. Above, the Upper Gate at the end of Kaufinger-Straße, also known as "The Beautiful Tower".

III Joseph advocated, "Everything for the people, but nothing through the people", died with him. With him too, the old Bavarian Wittelsbach line died out. The Palatine line with Karl Theodor took the inheritance, and no Wittelsbach had ever been as unpopular as this Prince Elector. On the eve of the French Revolution, he was still toying with the idea of giving Bavaria to Austria in exchange for the Austrian Netherlands. The Duchess Maria Anna and her circle of patriotic Bavarians opposed this plan, but in the end it was the Prussian King Friedrich II who thwarted Austria's designs to annex Bavaria, in the War of Bavarian Succession. There was no actual fighting in this campaign, and so it became popularly known as "The Bavarian Potato War".

The Prussian king was, at this time, so beloved in Bavaria, that his portrait hung in almost every house. There was much feeling against Karl Theodor, and the more the ideas of the Enlightenment took hold among the intelligentsia and higher civil servants, the more censorship was enforced in Bavaria. By 1785 freemasonry was banned, as well as the Order of the Illuminati, a secret group of high officials led by Professor Weishaupt of Ingolstadt, who advocated reform of the body politic. Karl Theodor died in 1799, and the chronicle records that inns were full, and the people rejoiced.

For all his vanity and arrogance, Karl Theodor had considerably shaped Munich's appearance. He ordered the fortification walls to be razed in 1795, and the Karlsplatz, which was named after him, was promptly constructed at the western edge of the city. The people of Munich, however, obstinately still refer to it as "Stachus", after a certain Eustachius Föderl who once owned a beer garden there. It was also Karl Theodor who presented Munich with its beloved English Garden. In 1789, he commissioned Count Rumford, who was actually called Benjamin Thompson, and who had left America for Bavaria, with the court gardener, Sckell, to transform an erstwhile deer park into a beautiful piece of nature for the pleasure of the people of Munich.

THE ROYAL CAPITAL AND RESIDENCY

For almost 500 years, Munich's history was played out within the confines of the small square enclosed by the 14th-century city wall, an area with a periphery of about 5800 "ordinary paces", as Lorenz von Westenrieder recorded in his *Beschreibung der Haupt und Residenzstadt München* (Description of Munich—Capital City and Residency) of 1782. It was not until the 19th century that it burst its seams and, seen from today's point of view, that the good old days of Munich began with all the sentimental stories of humane kings, grumbling burghers and artists full of intrigue, of the casual live and let live approach to life for which Munich is still known today. It's all summed up in the local dialect, *"Wer ko, der ko"* which roughly means "Let those who can, get on with it" or the "Ja mei", one hears, an expression of resignation and wonder.

Royal Bavaria

For half a century Bavaria had kept out of European politics, so much so that the French Revolution of 1789 seemed a distant event, with no bearing on life in Munich. However, just after the new Prince Elector Max IV Joseph and his state chancellor Maximilian Freiherr von Montgelas (Baron of Montgelas) had moved into the city in 1799, French troops arrived, and by June 1799 they had occupied the city. The court fled to Amberg, while the occupying forces enjoyed a performance of the opera *Don Juan* in the Residenz theatre on their first evening of occupation.

There was no fighting. Bavaria aligned itself with France, and Max IV Joseph was crowned King Maximilian I by Napoleon. This step involved Bavaria, like 16 other German princedoms, in treason against the "Holy Roman Reich of the German Nation", and brought it to its end. Kaiser Franz II renounced the crown of the old Reich, and

Preceding pages, Schäffler dance in 19th century. Left, Ludwig I in coronation robes.

contented himself with the title of Franz I of Austria. Thus for the first and last time in its history, Bavaria became a sovereign state. Meanwhile its territory had doubled, and the population had increased to three times its former number, for in compensation for the loss of Palatine, partly annexed by France, was the acquisition of Franken (Franconia) and Schwaben (Swabia). The spiritual principalities fell to the new kingdom of Bavaria, and so Munich became the seat of the archbishop of Munich-Freising from 1821.

Building a Modern State

At the same time Napoleon's reforms began to change the medieval estates and the old social order in Bavaria, and in the other German states. The basis of a modern state was established. In Bavaria this was mainly the work of the Freiherr von Montgelas, who was originally from the Savoie. In a few years he had built up a modern state administration and had drawn up the Bavarian constitution, which was presented to the king in 1808, but not ratified until 1818, by which time Montgelas had gone, having quarrelled with the romantic-restorative Crown Prince Ludwig.

His basic reforms, however, by then could no longer be rescinded. Bavaria and the city of Munich had changed too much, if not always in ways popular with the citizens. What was unpopular, was less the the state reforms, the dissolution of the monasteries and the expropriation of the church's properties, but the changes in everyday life. Catholic Munich had had 124 public holidays in the year, with 52 Sundays, 19 mandatory holidays and 53 other holidays, when pilgrimages and processions offered a welcome break from the working routine. Montgelas forbade all these rituals, and even the monk on the city coat of arms disappeared for several years, for the Central Land Commissariat maintained that it was too much of a reminder of the old monastic way of life for the modern age. There were also,

47

too many newcomers from the territories of Schwaben and Franken and northern Germany, for the locals' taste. The equality of Catholics and Protestants in law was unpopular and lastly the rapid expansion of the city upset the inhabitants.

The Maxvorstadt (Max Suburb)

Despite all opposition, the city changed fundamentally during the 19th century. Monasteries were misappropriated or destroyed completely. The fortifying walls

a residential district between the Odeonsplatz and Stiglmaierplatz with gardens and squares, with neo-classical elements, a foretaste of later avenues in Munich.

"A New Athens"

It was Leo von Klenze too, who in the Odeonsplatz, created not only the lovely exit for the Briennerstraße, but above all, at the request of Crown Prince Ludwig, the Ludwigstraße, with its glorious buildings. Ludwig, who ascended to the regency in

were dismantled in 1805, and the only remaining part of the city wall is to be found in the Jungfernturmstraße. In place of the city moat, a wide tree-lined avenue, today's Sonnenstraße, extends in the western part of the city, from Sendlinger Tor, over the Maximiliansplatz of 1801, almost to the Schwabinger Tor (Swabian Gate) to what is now the Odeonsplatz. In 1807, King Max I held a contest for a design to unify the old city with the outskirts to create a harmonious entity. Architects Friedrich Ludwig von Sckell, Karl von Fischer and (from 1816) Leo von Klenze created the "Maxvorstadt",

1826, had been inspired by his journeys to Italy, and in Leo von Klenze, he found an architect able to transform his ideas into reality. Ludwig I had stated his aim of making Munich a city of such consequence, that no-one could say they knew Germany without having visited Munich. The citizens, however, were less than enthusiastic about the royal ambitions. There were complaints about the costs, the unprecedented width of the street, and there was general consternation at Leo von Klenze's uncompromising attitude. For the architect supervised everything, right up to the smallest details, until he finally clashed with the king himself, who noted, of his architect, "In artistic and technical matters, he is excellent, but his thirst for power is great, and everything of note must be authorised by him and overseen by him personally."

Klenze was a confirmed classicist. Apart from the Ludwigstraße, he was responsible for the Königsplatz (King's Square) with its propylaea, and the glorious Glyptothek. He built the Alte Pinakothek (The Old Picture Gallery) and completed the Residenz by building the Königsbau (King's building). The king, for all his love of the classical, was less singleminded than Klenze, and was also fond of medieval architecture. He was supported in this by his circle of friends who were of a more romantic disposition, referred to by Klenze as "a clique of abstruse mystics". In 1827, Friedrich Gaertner finally replaced Klenze. He softened Klenze's harsh style by neo-romantic accents, and created the Staatsbibliothek (State Library) and University, and completed the Ludwigstrasse with the Feldherrnhalle and the Siegestor (The Military Headquarters and Triumphal Arch). Contemporaries of the king remarked that a "New Athens" had come into being.

Even Heinrich Heine, the poet and writer, praised Munich for its wonderful buildings, but remarked drily that to call the city a "New Athens" was going a bit far. The new buildings were still rather isolated at the edge of the old city centre and in 1840, the city, with its 90,000 inhabitants, was not really large. But the city was growing, and through Ludwig's love of building, had acquired some wonderful landmarks on the outskirts. The neo-Gothic Mariahilf-Kirche (Church of Maria's Help) in the Au was built by Ohlmüller and Ziebland constructed the Newroman St. Boniface Church and the New Pinakothek. And it was thanks to this king that Munich received its enormous Bavaria statue, which greets visitors to the

Left, *Bavarians of Merit* in the Hall of Fame. Right, Aquarelle of 1810, in the background the towers of the Church of Our Lady.

Oktoberfest (October Festival), and in fact the festival itself was begun by him. In 1810, the marriage of the Crown Prince and Therese von Sachsen-Hildburghausen was celebrated by horseracing followed by a *Volksfest* (festival for the people) which was so popular that it has been held ever since, without the wedding.

Age of the Bourgeoisie

Munich was soon to become well-known for its merrymaking and festivals, particu-

larly in artists' circles. Gottfried Keller captured this *biedermeierzeit* (age of the bourgeoisie) in his novel *Der grüne Heinrich* (Green Henry) with its description of the artist's life and the carnival celebrations, also the terrible conditions of the many unknown artists and writers who waited in vain for success. Carl Spitzweg depicted the idyllic life of their dreams. He lies buried in the southern cemetery, next to Goethe's portraitist, Joseph Stieler, who, in 1823, with Domenico Quaglio, founded the *Münchner Kunstverein* (The Munich Society for the Promotion of the Fine Arts). It was appropriate, for in 1839, Spitzweg's picture *Der arme Poet* (The Poor Poet) received such savage criticism, that he never dared to sign his works afterwards. He was an outsider, self taught, and his pictures of everyday life in Munich stood out in contrast to the 19th-century Munich school of landscape painting of Georg Dillis, Wilhelm von Kobell and Carl Rottmann. As in no other German city, historical painting dominated the Academy of Fine Art, founded in 1807, with painters such as Peter von Cornelius, Wilhelm von Kaulbach and Karl von Piloty whose pathos and conventionality finally led them to be ridiculed by the younger generation of artists at the end of the century.

The attraction of Munich for painters, writers, sculptors and architects was due not only to Ludwig I and his love of the arts, but also to economic stability of the city. In the first half of the 19th century Munich was a city of trade, administrative authority and commerce. The university was moved from Landshut to Munich in 1826. The foundations of ministerial bureaucracy were laid and ministeries were expanded. All this was reflected in the novels of Ludwig Thomas and Lion Feuchtwanger.

Due to the fact that, unlike in Prussia, the uprising of the peasants did not result in their being driven from their farms, Munich only gradually acquired a proletariat, which found asylum in the Au and Giesing areas. By 1895 there were still no more than 38 enterprises employing more than 200 people, among them the locomotive factory of Krauss and Maffei, as well as the cart manufacturer Rathgeber. So for a long time the city was moulded by the bourgeoisie and perhaps that explains how in Munich, originality and provinciality, artistic avant-garde and general ignorance, political radicalism and proudly acknowledged conservatism go hand in hand, giving the city its special character, even today.

Storming the Arsenal

During the 1830s, Ludwig I turned towards the restoration, by recalling the Capu-chin and Franciscan orders and in 1832 by reintroducing press censorship. At the university, a romantic movement of spiritual renewal grew up around the philosophers Görres, Baader and Schelling, and the neo-absolutist ideals of the Regent were less and less acceptable to a society demanding civic freedom. When uprisings broke out in 1848 throughout Europe, the students in Munich rose up too, and on 4th March the citizens stormed the arsenal on Jakobsplatz.

Perhaps more than general political unrest, it was the infamous affair of the king with a dancer named Lola Montez, which caused uproar and threatened the dynasty. As the minister Abel wrote to the king, "The affair of your majesty and this adventuress has given rise to a situation which puts the good name of the monarchy in jeapordy, and threatens the power and respect due to a beloved king and even his future happiness." In the end, Ludwig abdicated in favour of his son Maximilian, and Lola Montez emigrated to Mexico.

Beginning of the Modern Age

The accession of Max II brought liberal times to Munich. The day to day political affairs were left to the civil servants, for his interest lay in science and the arts. In 1855 he founded the Bavarian National Museum, appointed the historians Giesebrecht and Sybel, as well as the chemist Justus Liebig to the university, and brought the writers Emanuel Geibel and Paul Heyse, two north-erners, to Munich, where they became the centre of the "Crocodile" circle of writers. Heyse, although the first German to win the Nobel prize for literature, is today forgotten, as a writer, but his name lives on in the underpass from the main railway station.

Like his father, Max II built an avenue in Munich, the Maximilanstraße. He organised the largest architectural contest of the 19th century, and the winner was Wilhelm Stier, an architect of the Berlin Schinkel School. But the greatest buildings there, the Regierung (Government) Building of Upper Bavaria, and the Bavarian Parliament Building, the Maximilianeum, are by Friedrich Bürklein. Apart from the Ludwigstraße, this lovely street lined with gracious buildings is the most beautiful in Munich.

During the regency of Max II the suburbs of Haidhausen, Au and Giesing were incorporated into the city of Munich, so that the expansion of the city eastwards would give it a basis on the further bank of the Isar. Between 1861 and 1870, in the south of the city, the Gärntnerplatzviertel (Garden Square area) was created. After the incorporation of Sendling (1877), the following suburbs

built in the Old Botanical Gardens, where the General German Industrial Exhibition of 1854 was held. This building burnt down in 1931. In a way that no other monarch did, Max II promoted the technical innovations of his time, and offered the world famous hygienist Max von Pettenkofer a chair at the university. The king also promoted education for his subjects, and established the Maximilianeum from his own private means, where until today selected high school students receive free education. The Maximilianeer students still board in the

became part of the city, Neuhausen (1890), Schwabing (1890) by then a town in its own right, Nymphenburg (1899), Laim (1900) and Thalkirchen (1900). The modern era set its mark on the city.

In 1839 the railway came to Munich, as the line from Lochhausen was opened. The main railway station begun by Friedrich Bürklein was continually expanded until 1884. It was destroyed in World War II. The Isar was crossed by a railway bridge at Großhesselohe in 1857. The Glass Palace was

The revolution of 1848.

Maximilianeum on the Isar, which is also the seat of the Bavarian parliament.

The Bavarian "Fairy-Tale King"

On the death of Max II in 1864, power fell almost entirely into the hands of the ministerial bureaucracy. Ludwig II, the Bavarian "Fairy-Tale King" realised his dreams of a beautiful, truly royal life outside the city, through the romantic castles which he had built all over Bavaria. He lost all interest in Munich itself after the city prevented the building of an opera house for his friend

Richard Wagner. The architect of the Dresden Opera House was to have built the opera on the site of today's Friedensengels, but the estimated cost of the project was 6 million Guilders, which caused not only the project to fall through, but led to the end of the friendship between king and artist. As the composer had attracted attention to himself through some rather unskilled intrigues, and had made his opinion of the people of Munich known, that he found them phlegmatic, priest ridden and devoid of artistic sense, he was asked by the king to leave the city where

1806, only the postal system and the railways remained *koeniglich-bayerisch* or royal Bavarian. Bismark only obtained Ludwig's consent to this by secretly giving him money to build his castles. Perhaps it was just because of his dreamy nature, that Ludwig was loved as no other monarch, and when in 1886 the Munich cabinet legally incapacitated him, and he drowned in the Starnberger See (Starnberger Lake) with his doctor, Gudden, in circumstances which have never been fully explained, the Land mourned a king whom no-one had ever had

his operas made their debut, *Tris-tan und Isolde* (1865), *Die Meistersänger von Nürnberg* (1867), *Rheingold* (1869) and *Die Walküre* (1870).

The king had little interest in the affairs of European and German politics, and it was not only this aspect of Ludwig's somewhat obstinate character which endeared him to his subjects, they also shared his distaste for the power politics of Prussia. There was no great enthusiasm in Munich for the Unification of Germany in 1871 under the leadership of Bismark. Bavaria lost its status as an independent state, which it had held since

to fear. At his funeral in the Michaelskirche, the chroniclers relate, there was a terrible storm, and lightning hit the church, "…did not set the church on fire, but flung members of the congregation against the wall. It was a heavenly finale to an earthly tragedy."

His successor, Prince Regent Luitpold, who ruled for Ludwig's mentally disturbed brother Otto, was long plagued with rumours that it was he who, out of lust for power, had instigated the proceedings to relieve Ludwig of his position.

Munich blossomed into a cultural city during the time of Prince Regent Luitpold. It was the time of painters such as August Kaulbach and Franz von Lenbach. The latter was a renowned portraitist and the leader of the *Künstlergesellschaft* (Artists' Society) founded in 1873. He even managed to have rivals such as the portrait painter Wilhelm Leibl thrown out of the city, until the Munich Secession of 1892 took against him, with artists such as Max Slevogt of Landshut and Franz Stuck. Max Liebermann enjoyed working in Munich, as did Wassily Kandinsky, who with Franz Marc, Gabriele Münter and Paul Klee, founded *Der Blaue*

traffic planning and land speculation. Schwabing, once a "placid village with a nice church" as Ludwig Thoma wrote, had been discovered by the nobility as a summer retreat, and towards the end of the 19th century artists settled in the area between Türkenstraße and Schwabinger Kirche. It was less the elite circle around the lyricist Stefan George who moved in, but the colourful bohemians, who were a constant source of wonder and disapproval for the staid burghers of Munich. A legendary figure of Schwabing was the Countess Franziska zu

Reiter (The Blue Rider) group in 1911, which influenced the development of abstract art in Europe.

Schwabing - A State of Mind

The centre of artistic life in Munich from 1890 to 1914 was Schwabing. Its reputation lives on today, but the charm of those years has been lost through the effects of war,

Munich at the turn of the century. Left, the railway station. Right, the Marienplatz looking towards the Old Town Hall.

Reventlow, emancipated and selfconfident enough to enjoy the scandal her lifestyle caused. In 1913 she published a novel about Schwabing, and was often at the offices of the satirical magazine *Simplicissimus*, which was started by Albert Langen in 1889. Its symbol was the red bulldog, and all the best known authors of the time contributed, Thomas Mann, Karl Kraus, Frank Wedekind, Rainer M. Rilke, Hermann Hesse and Heinrich Mann.

Artists such as Olaf Gulbransson, Karl Arnold, Thomas Theodor Heine, Alfred Kubin and Eduard Thöny illustrated the articles with caricatures. Another feature of Schwabing life at the turn of the century was the famous group of artists known as "Simpl" around Kathi Kobus, who met in the Türkenstraße, where the resident poet Joachim Ringelnatz held court.

In the Türkenstraße, the Café Grössenwahn (Café Megalomania) —it was actually called Café Stefanie—was once located, and was the haunt which the anarchist writer Eric Mühsam used to frequent. In Zum Goldenen Hirschen (The Golden Stag), also in the Türkenstraße, was a cabaret group *"Elf Scharfrichter"* or "The Eleven Executioners", to which belonged Th.Th.Heine, Olaf Gulbransson and the authors Heinrich Lautensack and Frank Wedekind. In the course of time there came to be a kind of secondary population in this area. "The indigenous population was spiritually dead and beer sodden," according to Theodor Fontane, and the newcomers mixed all kinds of artistic ideas and forms and created their own original lifestyle.

In 1890 Georg Hirth founded the periodical *Jugend* (Youth), the bible of the Jugendstil or Youth Style, the architecture which gave the prewar city its coloured facades. Most of these buildings were destroyed during World War II, apart from the Müllersche Volksbad, one of the most beautiful of the buildings of this period. The Jugendstil was a reaction against the historicism of Munich architecture of the late 19th century as manifested in Prinzregentenstraße (Prince Regent Street), the last of Munich's great avenues.

Gabriel von Seidl, the most famous architect of his time, designed the National Museum as well as the Künstlerhaus (Artists' House) in Lenbachplatz and the Lenbach Villa. Adolf von Hildebrand created the loveliest fountain in Europe with the Wittelsbacher Brunnen in Lenbachplatz. Building on the Neuen Rathaus (New Town Hall) went on until 1903. It took the place of the old landscaped houses on Marienplatz, and its Gothic style still seems out of place in this oldest square of Munich.

At the turn of the century, Thomas Mann,

who had lived in the city since 1894, wrote *München Leuchtete* or "Munich sparkle". But this now famous characterisation of the city had originally been meant ironically. The authorities had never been able to come to terms with all that was produced in the way of art in Schwabing. In 1895, for example, Oscar Panizza was sentenced to a year's imprisonment for blasphemy because of his play *Das Liebeskonzil* or "The Council of Love", and Th. Heine and Frank Wedekind were detained for their caricature of Kaiser Wilhelm II in *Simplicissimus*. Social

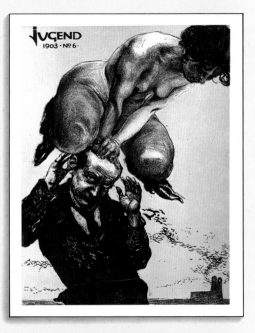

tension was increasing. The population of the city had grown to over half a million by the end of the century, and at the same time the number of unemployed had increased. The average life-expectancy was 25 years and tuberculosis was rampant, particularly in the neighbourhood where the workers reside. Many houses remained unoccupied, their cost beyond the reach of the ordinary people. In the damp, overcrowded districts of Au and Giesing, there was little trace of "the good old days".

Cover of *Jugend* (Youth) Magazine.

THE WITTELSBACH DYNASTY

The Dukes

1180-1183	Otto I
1183-1231	Ludwig I, of Kelheim. He founded the towns of Landshut and Straubing and in 1214 married his son to the daughter of the Count Palatine of the Rhine. Beginning of the Palatinate line of the Wittelsbachs.
1231-1252	Otto II, The Noble. He was the first Wittelsbach to rule over Munich.
1253-1294	Ludwig II, The Stern. The first Wittelsbach to build himself a residence in Munich.
1255-1340	Division of the Land into Upper and Lower Bavaria.
1294-1347	Ludwig IV, The Bavarian. In 1314 he became the German King, 1328 Roman Kaiser and conquered Brandenburg, Tyrol and the Netherlands, territories lost under his successors.
1347-1349	Ludwig V, The Brandenburger, and Stefan mit der Hafte.
1349-1353	Ludwig V, The Brandenburger, Ludwig VI, The Roman and Otto The Lazy. They ruled together until 1353; then Land divisions until 1505 in Brandenburg, the Netherlands, Upper Bavaria—Tyrol, Lower Bavaria—Landshut and Lower Bavaria—Straubing.
1353-1361	Ludwig V, The Brandenburger.
1361-1363	Meinhard
1363-1375	Stephan II, mit der Hafte; 1363-1392 Reunification of Upper and Lower Bavaria.
1375-1392	Stephan III, The Parer, Friedrich The Wise, Johann II The Godly. They ruled together until 1392; then the Land was divided into the dukedoms of Lower Bavaria—Landshut, Upper Bavaria—Ingolstadt and Upper Bavaria—Munich.
1392-1397	Johann II, The Godly.
1397-1435	Ernst The Courageous and Wilhelm III
1435-1438	Ernst The Courageous
1438-1460	Albrecht III The Good
1460-1463	Johann IV The Black and Sigismund
1463-1465	Sigismund
1465-1467	Albrecht IV The Wise and Sigismund
1467-1508	Albrecht IV The Wise; 1505 final reunification of the Land, but the area between Kufstein, Kitzbühel and Rattenberg taken by the Tyrol.
1508-1516	Wilhelm IV The Steadfast
1516-1545	Wilhelm IV The Steadfast and Ludwig X
1545-1550	Wilhelm IV The Steadfast
1550-1579	Albrecht IV The Magnificent
1579-1594	Wilhelm V The Pious
1594-1597	Wilhelm V and Maximilian
1597-1623	Maximilian I; in 1623 he received the electorship.

The Prince Electors

1623-1651	Maximilian I; Bavaria extended its territory to include Upper Palatine
1651-1679	Ferdinand Maria
1679-1726	Maximilian II. Emanuel, The "Blue Prince Elector"
1726-1745	Karl Albrecht (1742-45 as Karl VI, German King and Roman Kaiser)
1745-1777	Maximilian III Joseph The Well-Beloved; with his death the Bavarian line of Wittelsbach ended.
1777-1799	Karl Theodor (from the Palatine-Sulzbach line of Wittelsbach); 1799 Bavaria lost the Inn area to Austria.
1799-1805	Maximilian IV Joseph (from the house of Palatine—Zweibrücken); Napoleon crowned him King.

The Kings

1806-1825	Maximilian I Joseph
1825-1848	Ludwig I
1848-1864	Maximilian II
1864-1886	Ludwig II
1886-1912	Luitpold; he ruled as Prince Regent for King Otto I, who was mentally ill.
1913-1918	Ludwig III

Munich's "good old days" ended in 1914 with the outbreak of World War I. The miseries of war took hold of the city. "There was hunger, even in the well-off areas. Hunger was the catchword at every beer table and became an invisible and ubiquitous presence. Yet in Munich many people had things which had long been unobtainable in the north of Germany. Everyone hoarded as much as they could. Exclusive items could be purchased on the black market and deserters were no longer anything unusual," as Oskar Maria Graf remembered.

The Red Flag over Munich

Graf, a baker's son from Berg on the Starnberger See (Starnberger Lake), was one of the most penetrating chroniclers of the 20th century. He was an eye witness of the 1918 revolution, which grew out of demonstrations and strikes which had broken out even during the war. After the war, the workers' plight remained desperate. On 7 November, more than 100,000 people made their way to the Theresienwiese, where Erhard Auer of the SPD (Socialist Party of Germany) and Kurt Eisner of the leftist USPD (Independent Socialist Party of Germany) advocated a new constitution. While the SPD merely wanted to issue a proclamation, the majority, lead by Kurt Eisner marched back into the city. The barracks were occupied without the use of force, and when the guards of the Residenz went over to the side of the rebels, Ludwig III had little choice but to flee the city in the night. The regency of the Wittelsbachs over Bavaria, which had endured since 1180, was coming to an end. At the break of dawn, red flags fluttered from the towers of the Frauenkirche (Church of Our Lady). Kurt Eisner was elected premier of the land, now to be known as Freistaat Bayern (the Free State of Bavaria), by the *Revolutionary Workers'*

Preceding pages, the "Stachus" before World War I. Left, Theatinerstraße before World War II.

Council which were formed by the various groups of workers in Munich .

Although the Bavarian revolution began peacefully, the situation soon got out of control. Bitter conflicts sprang up between left and right wing social democrats, and between anarchists and communists, on the organisation of the takeover. Eisner recoiled before a radical system of government by commissars, and left most of the officials in place. He failed to persuade the folks from the countryside to provide the town with food supplies. By 7 January 1919, demonstrations broke out again, and three people were shot. The elections of 12 January resulted in a debacle for Eisner's party. The worst happened to Eisner a month later. On the way to parliament to announce his resignation, Eisner was killed at the Promenadeplatz by an angry young nobleman Graf von Arco auf Valley.

Power then fell into the hands of the Central Council of the Bavarian Republic, which comprised the SPD, USPD and the Revolutionary Workers' Council. On 17 March, they elected the social democrat Hoffmann as new premier. However, his ideas of a democratic republic were not radical enough for the majority of the workers. In Augsburg, there was a general strike against Hoffmann, When the writers Gustav Landauer, Erich Mühsam and Ernst Toller proclaimed a republic to be governed by commissars in early April, Hoffmann's government officials fled to Bamberg, and called out the *Reichswehr* (military) to help them.

The political scene in Munich was so fragmented that the republic did not last. On 14 April, led by Eugen Leviné and Max Levien, the communists seized power. A food blockade had been organised against the city. From another end, the army and volunteer corps led by Franz Xavier Ritter von Epp approached the city. Unlike any other uprising in Germany, the Munich republic had an utopian feeling about it. Oskar Maria Graf related how a Lieutenant Sebastian Wigelberger, who as an officer of the hastily formed Red Army declared war through a delegate's pronouncement at the approaching troops before any shot was fired. At the Stachus, the shoecleaner Asli, with only four men, amazingly managed to hold off two regiments for several days. Shortly before the end of the fighting, nine prisoners were accidentally shot in confused circumstances in the Luitpold Gymnasium (Luitpold Grammar School). The revolutionaries immediately went on a hunt for the culprits. When they entered the fray, the Freikorps literally soaked the Munich revolution in the

The parties of the left in Bavaria never recovered from their defeat in 1919. The SPD regime under Johannes Hoffmann fell immediately. A period of economic leadership by Bavarian notables began, described by Lion Feuchtwanger in his novel *Erfolg* (Success). It told of the groups who gathered in the backrooms of the Hofbräuhaus, suspicious of the leftist groups and the media, and well disposed towards radical right wing circles. Until 1933, the BVP (Bavarian Peoples' Party) held power under Heinrich Held and led the land, as one highly res-

Der bayr. Ministerpräsident Kurt Eisner (1) u. Minister Auer (2), welche im Landtag in München Revolver-Attentaten zum Opfer fielen.

blood of mass killings. Most of the leaders of the republic were bestially murdered and only few escaped quick death with lengthy prison sentences.

Hitler's Putsch and Inflation

No other event in Munich's history has been so quickly forgotten as the republic. There is hardly an inscription to remind one of it. But when Eisner's murder could no longer be ignored after World War II, a memorial had to be kept from sight at the scene of the crime.

pected Bavarian historian Karl Bosl wrote, "on a monarchist-conservative and nationalist course revolving around associations of the Fatherland, combat groups and activist groups. The politics of public order in Bavaria, as practised by the conservatives, helped to prepare the ground for Hitler's putsch of November 1923."

From 1919 on, Munich became a hotbed of reactionary movements. It was here that Julius Streicher founded his anti-semitic German Freedom Party. In the backrooms of the Vier Jahreszeiten (Four Seasons) Hotel, the obscure *Thule-Gesellschaft*, an association of the anti-semite Dietrich Eckart would meet. Hitler also lived in the city after 1919. He became a member of one of the newly founded splinter groups, which later became the NSDAP (National Socialist Workers' Party of Germany) and which was well-known for its mass meetings in the Hofbräuhaus. National dishonour due to the Treaty of Versailles, unemployment, inflation and anti-semitism—these were the themes on which Hitler exploited to gather the combat units of the various right wing groups around him, and in 1923, to attempt

cheered him on from the roadside, but he was stopped by the armed police before he reached Feldherrnhalle.

The subsequent legal proceedings degenerated into a judicial fiasco, as Ludendorff was acquitted and Hitler was sentenced to five years imprisonment. It was during this time that Hitler wrote *Mein Kampf* (My Struggle). He was released in 1924.

The times were ripe for Hitler's inflammatory tirades not only in Munich, where he had established the headquarters of his movement, but also beyond the city. It was mainly

to oust the government. With his SA troops, he stormed through a meeting of national associations in the Bürgerbräukeller on Rosenheimer Berg. All the prominent Bavarian politicians were present at the meeting, and Hitler personally declared the regime overthrown. With General Ludendorff and his SA troops, he marched towards the Feldherrnhalle on 9 November 1923. The people

Left, Kurt Eisner (far left), premier at the time of the Socialist Republic, with Erhard Auer (far right), minister of the interior. Above, Hitler's putsch of November 1923, crowd in front of Old Town Hall.

comrades in arms during Hitler's reign in Munich and Bavaria who later took charge of his NS (National Socialist) dictatorship. Heinrich Himmler's father was the headmaster of the Wittelsbach Gymnasium (Wittelsbach Grammar School); Hermann Göring was from Rosenheim. Hitler also had the support of the industrialists, as well as easy access to the aristocrats in Munich. His followers, however, were drawn mainly from the lower middle class and the working class groups who had suffered most during the unemployment of the 1920s. During this period, more than 20 percent of

61

Munich's population had risen to 700,000 and was dependent on welfare. Moreover, the impact of inflation in 1923 was such that a short tram ride from Stachus to Marienplatz cost 230 billion Marks!

During the 1920s

The economic and political situation gradually stabilised in Munich and throughout Germany. The city of Munich developed its economy through its own efforts. In 1925, the Deutsches Museum (German Museum)

was constructed by the entrepreneur Bernhard Borst on Dachauerstraße, and was called the *Borstei*, and to this day it is a highly desirable address in Munich.

There was by then very little trace of the "wild years of the 1920s" in Munich. Films such as Eisenstein's *Battleship Potemkin* were banned, as was the dancer Josephine Baker. Young budding artists and musicians were leaving the city. The conductor Bruno Walter, like the authors Brecht and Zuckmayer, left for Berlin. Only a handful remained, and they included the writers Tho-

was opened, an event broadcast directly from the Bayerische Rundfunk (Bavarian Broadcasting Corporation), which had been operational for a year by then. On the Oberwiesenfeld, today's Olympiagelände or site of the Olympic Games, Munich's first airport was opened. New estates were built to alleviate the housing shortage, the Alte Heide (Old Heath) in Freimann and roomy and contemporary model districts in Neuhausen and Ramersdorf. New suburbs grew up on the outskirts of the city, Daglfing (1930), Perlach (1930) and Freimann (1931). The most pleasant residential area

mas Mann , Lion Feuchtwanger, and Otto Falckenberg whose *Kammerspielen* (intimate plays) were moved from the Augustenstraße in 1926 to their present location in the Maximilianstraße. They remained the exceptions in a city which clung to tradition and whose cultural authorities were sceptical of the enigmatic sketches of Karl Valentin as well as any avant-garde art from America or the Soviet Union. Munich was not even the least moved when Thomas Mann gave a powerful speech in 1926. He chastised the widespread undemocratic and anti-semitic spirit, saying that the city of

Munich had become a stronghold of reaction, a seat of obduracy and intractability, a city without outlook.

"Capital City of the Movement"

The little openmindedness remaining in Munich was finally eradicated by the advent of the National Socialist dictatorship in 1933. The National Socialists had no difficulty in the power takeover in Munich. The Bavarian government under Heinrich Held was dissolved by the Reich governor Epp.

established. The *Völkische Beobachter* newspaper faithfully reported the fact to the public. Within a few weeks, the city was firmly in National Socialist hands. In the Wittelsbach palace, formerly the seat of the Munich city republic, the Gestapo set up their torture cellar. After the *Röhm-Putsch* of 1934, Hitler got rid of anyone who opposed him within his inner circle. The rebels were taken to Stadelheim Prison for execution— the period of terror for the Jews had begun. In 1938, the synagogue in Herzog-Max-Straße was closed. Of the more than 10,000

The lord mayor of Munich, Scharnagl, stepped down upon the ultimatum given by the Gauleiter Adolf Wagner, and in the Reich elections of 5 March 1933, the National Socialists won a majority in the city. From the summer of the same year, they remained unopposed in the city council; anyone who opposed them earlier had either fled, or had been deported to Dachau. There the first concentration camp in Germany was

Left, the erstwhile synagogue in Herzog-Max-Straße, destroyed in 1938. Above, parade of National Socialists on Königsplatz.

Jews in Munich, only 200 survived the war.

Hitler himself always held the city of Munich with special affection. He had lived in Prinzregentstraße (Prince Regent Street) for 16 years, and the party headquarters Das braune Haus (the Brown House) was at the corner of Arcis and Brienner streets. Monumental buildings were planned for the *Capital City of the Movement*. The main railway station was to be moved to Laim, and a broad thoroughfare was to lead from there to the Stachus, past a huge Hitler monument. The plan did not materialise. What happened to the appearance of the city was already bad enough. In the Englischer Garten (English Garden), the Haus der deutschen Kunst (House of German Art) was established. The latter is now simply known as the House of Art. It was opened in 1937 with the infamous exhibition of "degenerate art". To create an imposing approach to this building, the closed frontage of the Ludwigstraße was reopened and the Von-der-Tann-Straße rebuild . It was a move welcomed by the post-war town planners, who were able to locate the Altstadtring (Old City Ring Road) there. The Königsplatz was taken over as a parade

Unsuccessful Resistance

But this anecdote cannot conceal the fact that in Munich, as well as in the rest of Germany, the National Socialists had widespread support. The attempt on Hitler's life in the Bürgerbräukeller in 1939 by the Swiss artisan Eisner, was greeted with horror. There were very few who dared to voice open opposition. "Shall we sacrifice German youth to the base instincts of power of a party clique? Never!" was written in the publication issued by the *Weissen Rose* (The White

ground and was neatly paved with granite slabs which were not removed until 1988. The Führer's buildings on the Arcisstraße survived the war, and today house a musical college. It was within these premises that Hitler and Chamberlain signed the *Munich Agreement* of 1938. There was a memorial for National Socialist combatants who were overthown in 1923 at the Feldherrnhalle. Anyone passing the monument had to raise one arm in the Hitler salute, while those who wished to avoid doing this, took an alternative route via the Viscardistraße, which became known as Dodge Street.

Rose), but the members of the group—Hans and Sophie Scholl, Christoph Probst, Alexander Schmorell, Prof. Kurt Huber, Willi Graf and Hans Leipelt—were executed in February 1943 in Stadelheim.

No organised resistance could be formed, as the parties of the left had been vanquished in 1933. Some priests did preach against anti-semitism and dictatorship. The Jesuit father Alfred Delp was hanged after the unsuccessful attempt on Hitler's life of 20 July 1944, and Pater Rupert Mayer, since beatified, suffered many years imprisonment in Dachau. The institution of the church, however, generally managed to come to terms with the regime, and even the popular Cardinal Michael Faulhaber of Munich, referred to the 1944 assassination attempt as cowardly attempted murder. Shortly before the end of the war, a Freiheitsaktion Bayern or Bavarian Freedom Campaign tried hard to bring about an early capitulation. But on 29 April 1945, two members of this group—Lieutenant Roth and Major Caracciola-Delbrück—were shot. The arrival of the American troops in Munich on 30 April 1945 brought World War II to an end.

their lives in the air raids. Out of a pre-war population of 700,000 there were only 470,000 survivors in 1945.

Ruins and Rebuilding

The war left a landscape of ruin. Munich was unrecognisable and uninhabitable. The first task was to feed and house those who had remained in Munich, or who had returned. The American military regime reinstalled the pre-war mayor Karl Scharnagl to his post. Under his leadership, and that of

Like so many German cities, Munich was disfigured beyond recognition after the war. The city had suffered countless air raids since 1940, and the worst attack was in 1942. By the end of the war, almost 45 percent of the buildings had been destroyed, including the historical buildings and memorials. Twenty-two thousand Munich soldiers fell during the war, and over 6,000 people lost

Far left, the Bavarian Lion in post-war debris. Left, Lord Mayor Thomas Wimmer doing the *Rama dama* (clearing up). Above, the Karlstor after the war.

his representative, Thomas Wimmer, the great clean up began. Heaps of rubble formed the *Schuttberg* on the Oberwiesenfeld. As early as 1945, the first edition of the *Süddeutschen Zeitung* newspaper appeared. The first free elections in 1946 were won by the CSU, a newly formed party of Christian Conservatives. Public life gradually began to gain stability. Soldiers returned, and during the next three years, the city was continually rebuilt. The Federal Republic of Germany was founded in 1949, with Munich as the capital of the Federal Land of Bavaria.

As an economic centre, Munich gained

much from the division of Germany. With the loss of central Germany, cities such as Nürnberg and Regensburg lost their strategic economic position. The main routes shifted, and Munich took up its new role as the centre of European north-south trade. The city grew rapidly to become the largest industrial city of the Federal Republic. BMW and MAN, MTU and Siemens, MBB and Dornier, the crème de la crème of German industry, moved to Munich, or rebuilt manufacturing plants which had been destroyed. Industries ranged from automobile construction to high-tech microelectronics. Munich also became the largest publishing centre of Germany, and was the hub of a thriving film industry. Less admirable but still important for its economy, the city developed the largest industrial base for manufacturing weaponry .

Modernisation

With this slogan, Munich was given the actual or supposed attributes of the 20th century. By 1957, the inhabitants numbered over a million. And in Neuperlach from the east to the west, around the Arabellapark and in Hasenbergl, faceless hideous satellite towns are built. It seemed that the post-war city planners wished to make Munich a city fit for cars. It was an idea popular at the time, when Munich had only barely recovered from the wounds it carried. All over Bavaria, Munich is taken as an example of just how a city can be "planned" for the car. The Austrian cabaret artist, Helmut Qualtinger, wrote that "In the middle of Bavaria where the motorway stops for no reason, Munich begins. Just as war is the continuation of politics by other means, Munich is therefore the continuation of motorway traffic, by other means."

It was not until the late 1960s that people came to their senses. A plan to sacrifice the west bank of the Isar to a motorway complex was eventually scrapped. The vociferous protests by the people of the city and the press stopped the project. It is said that a visit to Los Angeles by the lord mayor, Jochen Vogel, led him to believe that a city fit for cars would mean the end of the city itself.

And so it came to pass that, during the preparations for the Olympic Games of 1972, the *Innenstadt* or inner city area was transformed into a pedestrian precinct free from traffic. Outlying districts were connected to the centre by the mass transportation systems of the U and S Bahn (train) service. Since then, the traffic situation has somewhat eased. However, it is still advisable to use public transport when going to the centre of town. It was not only damage from the war and the denuding of the streets for traffic convenience which disfigured the city. Department stores and insurance companies need space, while many old office complexes and affordable apartment buildings fell to the whims of speculators. However, by the 1970s, many old buildings had been restored—the Alte Rathaus (Old Town Hall), and the Frauenkirche, the Residenz (Palace) and the Ludwigstraße. Even the Pinakothek and Alte Peter, which had been very badly destroyed after the war and seemed irreparable, were saved. But what the architect Erwin Schleich termed "the second destruction of Munich" had already just begun.

Many buildings and complexes were demolished. Only the Renaissance tower of the glorious Maxburg remained; no-one knew why. The Neue Pinakothek disappeared, as did the Marstallplatz and the Allerheiligen-Hofkirche (All Saints Palace Church), which Klenze had built for Ludwig I. Many bourgeois houses and palaces which once belonged to the aristocrats had to make way for new buildings, and were therefore not repaired. It was these losses which led Schleich to conclude that no other city in Europe had lost so much in the war. The multi-lane Altstadtring took over the well proportioned facade of the Maximilianstraße right to the Maximilianeum on the banks of the Isar. The harmonious ensemble of the Ludwigstraße and the Siegestor are overshadowed by the prominent black highrise of a department store. However, this scenario is expected to change soon. At the

Deutsches Museum, the modern Europaeischen Patentamt (European Patent Office) encroaches on an old residential area, and even on the outskirts of the city, the Mittlere (Middle) Ring suffocates all the streets with noise and fumes. The streams which once ran freely here were covered by tarmac. In the inner city and areas like the Lehel, legal offices, banks, trading houses and insurance companies only help to drive the man in the street away. Pedestrians are banned and restricted to old underground squares such as the Stachus.

though the proceedings were marred by the terrorist attack on Israeli competitors.

Today, Munich is a city of superlatives. It is the largest university town in the Federal Republic, the largest industrial city, the city with the most leisure opportunities, the most beautiful city in the Republic (even though there is some disagreement over this claim by the locals of Hamburg), the city with the best theatres in the Republic, not forgetting the widest range of cultural activities. And even if all these superlatives mean nothing to you, an evening in a beer garden, a walk in

"Metropolis with a Heart"

Even though Munich has lost much of its charm, it is still one of the loveliest cities of Germany, and by far the best loved. A survey held among Germans revealed that 35 percent would rather live in the Isar-metropolis than in Hamburg or Berlin. The press dubbed Munich "the secret capital of Germany". The city gained much affection through its staging of the 1972 Olympic Games, the so-called "Happy Games of Munich", even

Munich fashions of the 1950s.

the English Garden or an afternoon of sunbathing on the banks of the Isar will easily compensate for the astronomical rents and the relentless show-offs by those who fancy themselves as part of Munich's "in-crowd", for the traffic chaos in the streets and for the fact that the city's cultural events are almost always packed. And should you find the town too cramped, it's conveniently easy to escape to the lakes and mountains and seek out one of the resorts. Whichever the case, it is on days like these when you realise that life in Munich is lived to the full and that nothing else really matters.

THE LOCALS—AN UNKNOWN ENTITY

The composition of the world famous football team *FC Bayern München* is symbolic. For all its rich tradition and success reflected on Munich, the team is made up almost entirely of non-locals. Since the days of Franz Beckenbauer (who was from Giesing), team players have come from Belgium, Denmark, Sweden and even Prussia. This elite team is trained by a Rhinelander. It is not a strange coincidence that the "foreign element" in the coach is typically so much of Munich. A well-known journalist from the *New York Times*, on his search for the secret capital of Germany and its origins, discovered that the city was Prussianised!

James M. Markham, the puzzled American searching for the real Munich local was quite bewildered by Bavaria: for many years, an important "Minister of Culture" in the Rathaus but now retired, Jürgen Kolbe—from Saxony; the illustrious general manager of six theatres, August Everding—from Westphalia; the editor-in-chief of a Bavarian newspaper with an international reputation, Dieter Schröder—from Berlin! So where would you find a true born-and-bred local? Surely if you were to meet one, you would recognise him at once, just as the first Munich explorer, Lorenz Westenrieder remarked in 1782, that the real local is easily distinguished from anyone else. But it's a case of finding him first!

Grim reservedness and wariness towards strangers are traits of the Munich local. He is known to occasionally mumble to himself about the iniquities of the world in a kind of basso continuo—*granteln* it's called. Many have settled in Munich and the invasion has led the local to feel that he is being pushed to the wall. As Westenrieder remarked, "Whoever visits Munich will want to make it his home." He then gave the impression of the local as being indifferent. Basically, the inhabitant of Munich is anything but a city

person, even after several generations. "The dwellers of the land have always been peasants and farmers who are hostile to towns. Munich was a town with a village atmosphere," wrote Lion Feuchtwanger in his novel *Erfolg* (Success).

This village mentality is evident in the way some of them can't even see beyond the city border. For them, there is no Munich local as such, there are only people from Laim, Giesing, Schwabing or the Maxvorstadt. There is

clan warfare (acted out, in not always playful "cops and robbers games" by kids on the street) between, for example, Westend and Schwanthalerhöh. Neither street is exactly salubrious, but the inhabitants of the one seldom mix with the riff raffs of the other.

Thus, the Munich local is difficult to define. There's also the *Zugroast'n* (newcomer), and even people who have already been in Munich for five years, exclude themselves from that category.

There have always been prominent foreigners in Munich. During the Counter Reformation, for example, the city of the Prince

Preceding pages, Munich waitress at the *Oktoberfest* ; Munich beauty. Left, local stallholder. Above, holding on to sweet memories.

Elector was the centre for intellectuals from many different places. The ducal librarian and later Ecclesiastical Council Secretary, Aegidius Albertinus, who became one of the founders of Southern German literature with his 50 publications, arrived in Munich from the Netherlands at the age of 33!

After the war, the influx of countless refugees came from the East (Sudetenland, Egerland and Silesia) who were taken into the city. Today, it is the big high-tech companies and the weapon factories which entice newcomers. Then, of course, there are

Market) or use the public transport system. By his very nature, the real local is a villager who is fascinated by the city's mechanised transport that he is more often than not a bus conductor! You may just catch the soft tones of the local dialect over the loudspeaker of an S-Bahn (city train) announcing the next stop, or bemoaning the slow progress of the train.

You will meet a man of very few words, who mumbles an apology which sounds more like a monologue, and who feels uneasy at giving long explanations. His dialect is difficult even for Germans to understand.

the *Gastarbeiter* (foreign workers). Where, then can you find the true local?

In a city where foreigners besiege the residents' registration office, where each new semester sees freshmen with rucksack and sleeping bag coming from abroad to occupy seats at the university, where in this sea of human beings can you spot the local? This elusive person seems to assume a mythical outfit like the strange Wolpertinger creature in the Jagd und Fischereimuseum (Museum of Hunting and Fishing).

Walk through the streets, mix with the crowd in the Viktualienmarkt (Victuals

Introspection is anathema to him, and questions probing his innermost thoughts would embarrass him. The local is not in the least interested in what he is. When he finds too much religious or psychological probing, he comes out with "*Mei Ruah mecht i hom!*" (Leave me in peace!)

So we'll do as he asks and leave the Munich local in peace, and let those interested seek him out for themselves. It should be an experience in itself.

Above, beer drinking—the Munich pastime. Right, steadily steering an Isar raft.

KARL VALENTIN LIVES!

"I don't remember exactly, was it yesterday, or on the fourth floor."

- Karl Valentin

Forty years after his death, a letter from the Munich Tax Office, addressed to a certain "Dear Mr. Valentin", requests that he clarify his tax situation. Maybe this is some kind of revenge by the officials, against whom Valentin inveighed, with the words "Down with the Tax Office, long live devaluation."?

Der Firmling (The Confirmand) of 1934 or *Im Schallplattenladen* (In the Pop Record Shop) of 1934.

Karl Valentin lives. Not only in his films, which are shown at special times (e.g. for the Oktoberfest or October Festival) at the Film Museum at 1 St.-Jakobs-Platz, not only in the Valentin Museum at the Isartor (Isar Gate) where you'll find the famous "stolen nail" on which he hung the joiner's profession he had learned. And not only in the

Karl Valentin, who died on Carnival Monday, would have loved it! And he would have made up a scene or dialogue all about it, just as he did in *Valentiniaden, Ein buntes Durcheinander, Stürzflüge im Zuschauerraum und Die Raubritter von München* (Valentineana, A Lively Muddle, Nose Dives in the Auditorium and The Robber Barons of Munich). His legacy for the cinema would have been richer by another film strip, which would, without doubt, have been up to the standard of *Der neue Schreibtisch* (The New Desk) of 1913-1914,

minds of the city officials, who pay their most famous grumbler homage with exhibitions, floral tributes and strong beer festival speeches. On the edge of the Viktualienmarkt (Victuals Market) he stands, the figure of the fountain, not far from the Gedenkbrunnen (Memorial Fountain) of his erstwhile comic partner, Liesl Karlstadt. At the feet of this unique comic couple, and even the figures reflect Valentin's nonsensical nature, the visitor will still always find a fresh bouquet of flowers.

No less a man than Bert Brecht said of the

"skeletal fop" as Valentin called himself, "When Karl Valentin, totally serious, made his way through a crowded beer restaurant, through the noise of beer tankard lids, singers and the scraping of chair legs, one had the impression, that this man wasn't joking. He actually was a joke ... a complicated, bloody joke. He had a very dry sense of humour. One could listen while smoking and drinking, all the while shaken by uncontrollable laughter. But it wasn't lighthearted laughter. In his

he answered, "When I saw the midwife, I was speechless; I'd never seen her before in my life." His birthplace at 41, Zeppelinstraße, has been bought over by the city of Munich. Hopefully, the place will be used in a sensible way, in the nonsensical sense of Karl Valentin, which means in keeping with his *Sinn für Unsinniges* (Sense of nonsense), which he so masterfully exposed in his encounters with the German language.

For Valentin himself, there was no happy

scenes and dialogues, he takes what seems to be familiar everyday life, and by taking things seriously, too literally, and with acute observation, he exposes the situation as illogical and contradictory. His figures take accepted social and linguistic habits apart, and through relentless hair-splitting, reduce them to a hilarious yet tragic absurdity."

Asked for his earliest impression of life,

Left, Karl Valentin Fountain on Viktualienmarkt. Above left, film scene with Karl Valentin. Above right, a Munich folksinger—WeißFerdl.

ending. After the war, the people no longer wanted their "Vale" and ignored him, as what could have been one of his own tragicomic scenes. In 1947, somewhat embittered but not without his customary humour, he wrote to the folksong collector Kiem Pauli, "I've really got to know the dear people of Bavaria, and particularly those from Munich. Everyone else , apart from the Eskimos, is more interested in me than the people here. But one can't blame a fellow for not wanting to know his compatriot, after all." Long live Karl Valentin!

OF POLITICS AND BEER-DRINKING

In Bavaria, politics is a matter for the stomach. If your stomach is full, and you've got a job, everything's all right. Epicureans like the Bavarians, are most concerned with the matter of food, and with what is even more important—drink.

For many Bavarians, the whole matter can even take on political significance. "When we started to brew lager, World War I broke out. While we kept drinking more lager, Hitler came to power. When we drank al-tained that dumplings and thick beer were the cause of the stupidity and the phlegmatic nature of the dwellers of the Alpine foothills. But it's not mere stupidity, rather the wisdom born of experience which characterises the Bavarian : You can't alter the course of the world, all you can hope to do is keep body and soul together. When a Bavarian opens his mouth, it's not to elaborate upon the uncertainties of life, but to provide for his physical comfort.

most nothing but lager, the world nearly ended with World War II." That's how the problems of the world were summed up by the author Georg Lohmeier, in answer to a question about the malt and alcohol content of beer. In othere words, had more dark beer been drunk, the world would have been a better place.

Just how far all this can be taken seriously is hard to tell. Politics in Bavaria is often said to be a matter for crooks. And perhaps Friedrich Nicolai wasn't mistaken, when on his journey through Bavaria in 1781, he main-

In the novel *Filserbriefen* by Ludwig Thomas, a newly elected member of the Bavarian Parliament wrote to his wife telling her about his new role. To his great relief, in his new capacity, all he needed to do was to hold his tongue and not make speeches. He discovered that had others taken on the task of governing in his place, he would have only needed to vote as instructed and to keep quiet. Also, he had managed to sell all those thick piles of official documents, which would only have given him a headache, to the butcher, for two sausages.

So it seems no mere coincidence that the most famous of all Bavarian politicians, one who was always identified with the Bavarian people and their idiosyncracies, was the son of a butcher. With such a background, former Bavarian Premier, Franz-Joseph Strauss could be relied upon to take care of the practical aspects of life. With him, his fellow countrymen felt they were in safe hands. And so, quite simply, they handed the reins of power over to him for as long as he lived,

almost making him an ersatz monarch.

The headquarters of that kind of politics is the pub. From speeches round the beer table, to the highest level of discussions, the rule is, for politics you need good solid food and plenty of beer. An example of this was the Franzens-Club, the political local of the former Premier. This Male Club was founded in 1973 at the Oktoberfest, with the then still

Left and above, politics flowed freely in the Town Hall and in the beer garden. (Caricature from *Simplicissimus*)

uncontroversial grilled chicken king Friedrich Jahn. Joseph März, proprietor of a meat export business, was one of the inner circle, and Strauss was able to smoothen the path for him and his business. In return, März put his *Nussdorfer Hof* at the disposal of the Franzens-Club. It was here that credit in milliards of marks was managed for the German Democratic Republic. It was here too that Strauss and Wilfried Scharnagl, the chief editor of the *Bayernkurier*, the *Pravda* of the CSU, would pore over their statements to the Bavarian people. There has rarely been such harmony between "independent" journalism and and State government. Strauss often admitted that "Scharnagl writes what I think, and I think what Scharnagl writes."

Thomas Wimmer, Folk Hero

Whether the average Bavarian, rather a rustic sort of character, is at all interested in matters of such importance is questionable. He is more concerned with his immediate surroundings and the bread and butter issues of life. Thus it is that some *Sozis* (Social Democrats) have almost become folk heroes in Bavaria, something quite unthinkable on a national scale.

One such figure was the Lord Mayor after the war, Thomas Wimmer. He was loved dearly by the people of Munich. Most, if not all, of them felt that he really was representating the people. The influence in the man became most apparent when the local residents rallied to his *Rama dama* call to clean up the city after the wartime destruction. His weekly meet-the-people sessions, during which anyone could see him personally to discuss problems, have never been forgotten. Wimmer's innate qualities thus contrasted markedly with the regal posturing of some later incumbents to that office. When the people of Munich look back to the early days of communal politics, it is with a certain nostalgia that they think to themselves, "There'll never be another Wimmer".

MUNICH, A CAPITAL OF WELL-BEING?

The Bavarians! Apart from Texans and overseas Chinese, there can be no other people who so consummately live up to the cliched image others have of them, with their *Schuhplattln* dancing and mugs of beer.

According to one of Munich's old grumblers, Herbert Rosendorfer, in an autobiography, the Bavarian conception of himself as playing the fool. And it's often not easy to draw the line between ironic posing and self deprecating mimicry. This fool may turn up in the guise of Seppl in leather shorts or appear as a real prince, a false baron, a fat industrialist with an ever open wallet or a high-flying film star, picking at a cold buffet. The alarming thing about these stereotypes is that they do exist in Munich and are easily recognisable. So the two myths overlap: that of the naive native, and the sophisticated know-all. If the Bavarian is the "nigger of Germany", then Munich is like an African state in the hands of elegant colonials.

Respect and Stupor

"At last I've reached the wondrous land" exclaimed the Swiss poet Gottfried Keller in 1840, but thereby hangs a tale. Newcomers can be driven to distraction by the lifestyle in Munich. Two years later, Keller, completely broke, could only manage an unfinished curse over Munich, beginning,
"A slovenly, immoral nest,
Of fanaticism, coarseness and cowherds,
Of holy pictures, dumplings and women on bikes."
But then his ideas run out, and all he can say was that he was toying with a "sonnet on Munich, struggling with a stubborn rhyme". After his departure, further attempts to capture the essentials of the city in poetry were abandoned. To a Munich local, whether or not he is a new arrival, Keller's departure is

a mystery. He must have fallen prey to the fate of many an "outsider" who failed to realise that when it comes to the clichés of Munich, you have to join them if you can't beat them. The Munich search for pleasure has even reached encyclopedia status! In last century's Brockhaus, it was stated that "The inhabitants of Munich, of which newcomers outnumber the indigenous people, are cheerful, given to social gatherings, preferably over something to eat or drink, ... not satis-

fied with cheap pleasures, frank and unrestrained, not given to new ideas, ... but living comfortably. ... The foreigner soon feels at home, and then enjoys living in this attractive and lively city which has much in the way of art and the beauty of nature to offer."

Money, pleasure and grandeur without end. The conclusion is always the same: Life in Munich is better than in any other capital city in the world. It's just less than six hours to the Mediterranean and only one hour to the Alps. One can go to any of the dozen or so lakes for a half-hour swim. Or one can visit the Englischer Garten (The English Garden)

Preceding pages, pretty girls of Munich chat over a drink at a street café. Left, a mannequin evinces the link between fashion and culture. Above, a morning ride in the English Garden.

which is right in the city. There is so much to explore at every corner in the city of Munich.

At weekends, the visitor may get the impression that Munich opens up to become one of the largest cities in the world. However, the converse is also true. The *Föhn* brings not only the Adriatic breeze to the city, but also the optical illusion that the Alps are next to the Isar. Nevertheless, people do not need to leave the city merely because of the weather.

For those lucky enough to live in Munich, they can easily have all the comforts of life of posers goes on and on. Then, there are the legendary beer gardens. Their existence does not detract reality from myth. The fact that the temples of culture are somewhat behind the times, does not make the slightest dent in the royal Ba-varian complacency.

Beer and Kir Royal

One of the first documents relating to life in Bavaria dates from the 15th century, and it was written by the humanist Aventinus. He stated clearly and concisely, "The Bavarian

within reach. Isn't Munich a cosmopolitan city, but with a village atmosphere, or more than that, a village of a million? Isn't it situated in one of the loveliest parts of the world, despite it being a developed city? Doesn't it offer a combination of relaxed southern European lifestyle with central European efficiency? Don't the richest people and the most beautiful women make their home here? Aren't there more private theatres, stylish operas and excellent state theatres here than in the rest of the Federal Republic? Aren't there more galleries, fashion shows and cultural festivals in Munich? And the list people are much given to drink." Aventinus—a pale ale has now been named in his honour. In fact, statistics only support the myth of how the local folks hold their drink in Munich. There must have been quite a few Prussians who have had contributed to the Hofbräuhaus' profits. But Aventinus was certainly not wrong. For nowhere else is drinking widely heralded as the main activity for weeks at a stretch, and nowhere else is it enjoyed with such great fun and intensity.

Even the Prussian pioneer of progress, Friedrich Nicolai, travelling in the 18th century, noted that, "The Bavarians are coarse, but not hard; blunt but not cruel; bold and cheeky but not daring. They are superstitious of course, and the ordinary man is lazy and given to drink." Let's just take going to a beer garden for example. This is no mere pastime, but a serious undertaking, requiring correct and careful preparation. For you do not just nip a quick one. That would not be keeping with local tradition. The combination of sun, the obligatory chestnut trees and the large mugs of beer make sure that you do not leave until the early morning air forces you to. Then, strangely somehow, you find

Festivals—Relaxation or Hard Work?

A contemporary of Nicolai made the point that leisure is attacked with grim determination, "The Bavarian disdains all repose in his time of rest." In other words, the Bavarian does not expend as much energy on any of his several other activities as on his relaxation. Nothing pleases him more than a festival, be it of any kind at all.

Munich festivals do not perish from lack of interest, but only from the hysterical success of which they are assured of. It hap-

yourself back at the same place the following day. The widely preconceived idea that barley juice is one of the staples of the Bavarian diet, has been reinforced rather than denied by a recent TV series in Germany, called *Kir Royal*. This programme elevated the mixture of currant juice and champagne to the national drink of Munich. But whether it's pure beer, or sweetened or adulterated champagne, it all adds up to the same compulsive love of pleasure, found only in Munich.

Left and right, shopper's paradise—furs, game, sausage and wine, everything you could wish for.

pened to the famous Theatre Festival. The Munich Film Festival has fled to the vast expanse of the Gasteig Palace of Culture, in order to hold its own against the onslaught of the masses. A similar fate awaits the bi-annual Contemporary Music Festival. In the metropolis of conservatism—where there is a considerable difference between politics and culture—the technique of "integrating" critical potential through frantic applause has been perfected.

It is almost impossible in Munich to undertake any other form outside this general entertainment. To make sure of that, the calendar of events is always filled with festivals which charge exorbitantly and yet manage to attract full houses. Then there's the so-called "fifth season". Vying for this title are not only the somewhat lame carnival (where masquerades are held all year round, so no carnival licence is needed) but also the *Strong Beer Festival*, to help with the fasting during Lent, and the *Oktoberfest* (October Festival) which is held in September. Lately, the various cultural festivals have come into contention too. No-one can escape this leisure time activity. Any human activity is,

Even basic bodily functions are included in the leisure time rituals. In Munich, you don't just eat. Even innocently chewing the famous, but rather tasteless white sausages is regulated by the most absurd historical eating traditions. And it's one of the greatest pleasures of the local resident to explain to the foreigner these rules (for example "*A white sausage mustn't hear the chimes of midday.*") with the indisputable "That's just the way it is!" and then remind him to adhere to the rules so as to understand Bavarian life.

Even ordinary groceries are sold with first-

wherever possible, included in leisure time in Munich. More than anywhere else, state visits, exhibition openings and theatre premiers belong to the world of making contacts rather than the world of culture. The tourist visits this wonderful city of Munich just as he would have come here to shop. Then again, he comes to Munich for his shopping just as he would have come here for the opera. The ever present entertainment applies even to anarchists. The autonomous group of the early 1980s, *Free Time '82*, staged a laughable bank robbery while elsewhere in the land, houses were burning?

class quality service in mind. A whole chain of institutions which couldn't be found anywhere else on earth, sees to that object. The vans of the well-known party caterer's named *Feinkost-Käfer* (Käfer Delicatessen) are part of the city scenery. The traditional delicatessen store of Dallmayr, and the Viktualienmarkt (Victuals Market) ensure that there's nothing which can't be found in Munich, in the way of food. There's a refuge from excess culinary democracy in the *Tantris* or the *Aubergine*, where gourmets insist that some of the best food in the world may be enjoyed. If that isn't good enough, there's always the roast pork ritual, and if all else fails, that notorious white sausage.

In Munich, even a leisure stroll can turn into a social occasion. If one can go to the opera in jeans, then conversely, the Sunday afternoon walk in the Englischer Garten (English Garden) can be hailed as a fashion parade. There's no stinting on make-up or perfume, the dog's coat is beautifully groomed, and his master is resplendent in his Burberry. However, in a kind of dialectical opposite to this, people in Munich are ready at the slightest opportunity to shed all this

and restrictions, but where their leisure is concerned, the matter is relatively more serious. The town council only allows nude sunbathing in certain areas on the Isar and in the Englischer Garten. The Nymphenburger Schloßpark (Nymphenburg Palace Garden) is, however, still out of bounds.

If you walk north from the Deutsches Museum (German Museum) along the Isar on a sunny day, you could be forgiven for thinking that people in Munich are all naked dog owners. And many a stranger, unable to decide whether to strip or to get himself a

finery, and lie naked on the grass. The Bavarian sun shines on, unembarrassed, while foreigners watch such a spectacle with either interest or bewilderment. From another angle, the female attractions of the city—which include the Frauenkirche (Church of Our Lady) and the statue of Bavaria—are enhanced by the presence of the local girls.

The nude sunbathing shows the true extent of Bavarian liberality. In politics, the Bavarians are prepared to accept certain guidelines

Left, Feinkost-Kafër—the gourmet's delight. Above, sunbathing naked on the Isar.

dog, has instead fled to the Flaucher Biergarten, or if in the Englischer Garten, to the Chinesischen Turm (Chinese Tower).

But the question still remains. "What is Munich all about? Residenz (Royal Palace)? Artists' city? Bolshevism, as it once was in May? Or white sausages?" This was the question posed by the artist Kurt Schwitters. No-one seems to know the answer. One thing is certain, and that is in this "Metropolis with a Heart", leisure isn't accompanied by liberating laughter, but more a muffled amusement which is kept to oneself, and which is probably rooted in complacency.

ARCHITECTURE AND TOWN PLANNING

Despite the rapid development of this "magnetic" metropolis of southern Germany, Munich has, remarkably, remained an attractive and pleasant city. However, for decades, the capital of Bavaria was in a different time zone from those of Frankfurt, Stuttgart, Düsseldorf and Hamburg. That, as anyone can clearly see now, worked to the advantage of this "village of a million". Politicians of Munich have always managed to ward off the excesses of industrial development—in particular when the well-loved old city skyline was to be drastically changed through the construction of high-rise buildings. Consequently, the advent of a relentless container architecture in the city has been maintained within acceptable limits, as compared to other population centres in the Federal Republic.

The City's Squares

Strangely enough, the city has problems with many of its squares. The empty space bordered by insignificant buildings in front of the Isartor (Isar Gate) has degenerated into a traffic junction, because the Altstadtring (Old City Ring Road) ripped open areas in the Forum of the Maximilianstraße and in front of the Prinz-Carl Palais which had once been closed.

Traffic dominates the Sendlinger-Tor-Platz (Sendlinger Gate Square) and the Stiglmaierplatz. The Feilitzschplatz does not focus on the centre of Schwabing, and in the Innenstadt (Inner City), the Jakobsplatz vegetates in isolated ugliness. Behind the Rathaus (Town Hall), one half of the Marienhof is a carpark, the other, a mass of bright flowerbeds. Lastly the square in front of the main railway station, evidence which tells of the hardship and poverty of the 1950s, must surely rank as one of the least attractive arrival checkpoints of any city in the Federal Republic.

So here too there's the provisional, the unfinished, the rough and the random all over the place. There is no recognisable,

coherent plan on the part of the authorities. Although incongruous projects, such as the Cultural Centre at Gasteig or the Europäische Patentamt (European Patent Office) on the Isar, were the objects of much competition, architects—who on professional grounds should actually be the ones to voice their criticisms—have transferred the task of protesting to the angry citizens. It is only when the opposition can no longer be ignored, do the more extrovert among them

join in the protest, and eventually come up with the most practical solutions.

Stephan Braunfels
and his Creations

Totally different, however, is one relatively young architect, Stephan Braunfels, who is a rare exception to the rule in his profession—he gets involved, throws himself into the breach, enthusiastically and tirelessly does drawings of alternatives to the official plans, and constantly tosses up new ideas for open discussion. With singleminded determination, Braunfels is attempting to beautify the city. In other words, he is constantly producing uncommissioned town planning schemes for Munich's main trouble spots.

Braunfels has turned his attention not only to the Hofgarten (Palace Garden) which was under threat from the State Chancellery (it was his initiative which gave the protesters the edge) but also to the Residenz (Palace), the Marstallplatz (Marstall Square), the Odeonsplatz area and the whole Altstadtring. In addition he has tackled the

Museum Ruin), the concrete bunker of Kaufhof on Marienplatz and the insufferable black glass colossus of the Hertie department store building in Schwabing.

Munich could do with more "cranks" like Braunfels. He has at last brought an aesthetic point of view to the discussions on town planning of the city of Munich. But of course, in actual fact, there have also been others who have taken over. Braunfels wanted to transform the banal Sonnenstraße into a boulevard like Düsseldorf's Kö; he would like to heal the wound inflicted on the

grave aforementioned problem of Munich's squares. He has produced delightful alternative plans for the Jacobsplatz, the Sendlinger-Tor-Platz, the Isartor, the Stiglmaierplatz, the Rotkreuzplatz and the Königsplatz. And his suggestion for a beautiful arcade for the Marienhof is, in fact, going to be carried out. He has also offered "transformation" ideas for notorious monstrosities such as the Armeemuseums-Ruine (Army

Left, the Armeemuseums-Ruine (Army Museum Ruin). Above, the Hertie Tower at Münchner Freiheit.

east of the Innenstadt by the Altstadtring with exacting and pleasing architecture…this genius who did not seem to wear himself out of offering a long list of suggestions, has never been given a commission in Munich. That really would have been a credit to the city.

But in the meantime a host of younger, progressive architects have sprung up, who in their own way have sought to move away from the outmoded stereotypes of functionalism while avoiding the dead end of unthinking adherence to post modern ideas, which combine nostalgia with the spirit of the age in cheap modishness. It is their immediate task to find the true symbiosis of experiences of the past and the demands of the present. There are, however, a few examples which show that Munich does have a role—albeit a modest one—to play in contemporary architecture.

A Caravel with White Sails

The high-rise complex of the Hypobank-Zentrale (Main Hypobank Bulding) in Arabella-Park is—apart from the spectacu-

slim towers, look like sharp and polished triangular prisms. As you approach the building, the wind-splitting edges of crystalline geometric form are actually round and sensuous. The shimmering glass and aluminium facade which envelopes the whole building exposes the graphic network of lines of the structure. The Bentz duo at one time said that their creation reminded them of a 15th century caravel with white sails billowing between silver masts.

There is a magnificent view from the top of the 114-metre-high Hypo Building over-

lar four-cylinder BMW Tower—the most original architectural contribution to the administrative buildings of the city. The Hypo towers, designed by Walther and Bea Bentz, managed to combine function and form to produce an attractive result, despite the many conditions and restrictions which they laboured under. Purpose did not hamper imagination.

The multi-faceted building seems to float majestically above the surrounding low-rise area. From a distance, the main parts of the BMW Tower which are of different heights and sizes and are slipped between the four

looking the old part of the German city and the Isar basin. From here it can be seen that the strategic locations of the Hypo Building and other administrative buildings in the Mittlerer Ring (Middle Ring Road) and the Arabella Park, just lying at the edge of the town, have had a positive effect on the preservation of the historical old city. As far as possible, offices and general pressure from the tertiary sector have been kept away. Moreover, the proposed U-Bahn (train) line will definitely shorten the existing five-kilometre distance between the service sector and the city.

In complete contrast to the Hypo Building is Uwe Kessler's elegant, unpretentious yet unusual design for the offices of the *Bayerische Rückversicherung* (Bavarian Reinsurance) in Tucherpark in the Englischer Garten. In the middle of a conglomerate of standardised, angular piles of office blocks and box-like hotels, are the modest (in size) but easily distinguished, four rounded buildings of the Insurance. Their graceful formation and detailed finish apparently stand out in stark contrast to their clumsy surroundings.

than in the conventional four- or six-cornered layout.

"Cathedral of Technology"

The facades of this high-tech architecture of human dimensions, are glazed throughout, clad in concrete balconies with the supports of the balconies giving an attractive "net-like" finish to the fine profiles of the huge windows. Only the more recent Printing Building of the Süddeutscher Verlag (South German Publishing House) in Riem

The "Rück" building was not rounded in order to distinguish it from its neighbours and surroundings. Rather the ground plan, consisting of three overlapping circles (the separate Casino building makes it four), is based on the reasoning that distances are shorter in round rooms, more economical use is made of space, lighting is more even, furnishing less restricted and division into hierarchical work areas is less of a problem

Left, the former Olympic Village which played host to the 1972 Olympics. Above, modern art in today's student village.

can compete with the "Rück" in terms of design and quality.

The team of Ekkehard Fahr and Partners, on the other hand, tackled the long-neglected task of the Munich Hauptbahnhof (Main Railway Station). They radically altered the particularly dull connecting hall by ripping off the roof and with the construction of an enormous skylight, transformed it into a "Cathedral of Technology". They used high grade steel, glass, perforated metal, brass and granite. A gallery level, formed by slim metal supports with bow-like alcoves, was created to give added height to the main area. One is constantly reminded of the enormous four-aisled station hall of the 19th century, which was demolished (rashly) after the war, because it had been damaged by fire.

The Fahr group also managed to clear up the untidy (and therefore unsightly) travel kiosks and create pavilions in painstaking detail, using the clear, industrial elements of construction which are consistent throughout. With their cross bars and attractive arc lights at the four corners of the roof, these kiosks easily stand out as islands of good

design, breaking up to some extent the enormous spatial area of the open hall. The futuristic, highly polished finish of the international press and bookshop shows how the architects have indeed given every possible consideration to the technical effects which succeeded in maintaining the overall ambience.

Unfortunately this transformation and upgrading of the Munich Station have not yet extended to the surrounding area, which has deteriorated, and the environs which are desperately in need of far-reaching improvement. Thus it is still the automobiles

in the multi-storey carpark of this station— probably the most boring of all the station buildings in the Federal Republic of Germany—which have the best view overlooking the city, and not the people who live and work here.

The Real Problem

By far, the greatest and most difficult task ever to be faced by Munich's city planners in the next decade—after the opening of the new airport at Erding—is the long-overdue and highly expensive transfer of the trade exhibition offices from the western side of the city to the plot of land left vacant at Riem, once the old airport is abandoned in 1991.

There has already been much argument among the politicians as to where exactly on the vast area of Riem, the buildings should be situated. The business sector is all for placing the buildings on the side of the town for convenience. However, a residential area has also been planned, and the people there would then be pushed behind an enormous commercial undertaking, so there are grounds for siting the buildings on the side further away from the town too.

Such disagreement typifies the current problems facing Munich's city planners. On the one hand they need to cater for the ever-expanding business sector, and on the other, they also have to cope with the attendant demands for residential areas.

So Munich is bursting at the seams, and the pressure on the surrounding areas is mounting. This surge is threatening the very quality of life which has made the city so attractive, both in the city area and in the environs, particularly if the Bavarian State Government realises its ambition of developing the new airport into the air traffic centre of the South to compete with the Rhein-Main complex.

Left, the impressive "cylinders" of the BMW Tower, a spectacular architectural contribution to the city. Right, in front of the Europäische Patentamt (European Patent Office).

MUNICH CULTURAL LIFE: ABILITY IS ALL

There's one thing which Munich does not want to be, and that is provincial. This is "Athens on the Isar", not some remote village in the Bavarian backwoods. So the old Bavarian expression "Wer ko, der ko" (Whoever can, can) is often quoted in relation to the cultural activities of the city because in Munich, you can see everything and do almost anything!

A Monarch of Culture

There's a monarch of culture in Munich. He's the director of the three state theatres, the National and Gärtnerplatz theatres and the Kammerspliele, as well as of the Marstall, Cuvilliés and Prinzregenten (Prince Regent) theatres. Not only does he live in a medieval castle (The Raubritterburg in the Grunewalder Isartal area) but he is also paid more handsomely than the Bavarian premier himself!

At the moment, this post is suitably filled by August Everding, who hails from Westphalia. He is not only a baroque figure himself, but also given to elaborate language, brilliant speeches and the grand entrance. In his capacity as director, he has represented the Bavarian lifestyle. His critics maintain that that is his main occupation. He is one of the most important figures of Munich's cultural activity, which can best be described in superlatives: Munich is the largest publishing city in Europe; the Geiselgasteig Bavaria Film Studio, which has already produced many million dollar movies, is the centre of the filmdom. The artistic metropolis was crowned with a monumental cultural centre built at almost ruinous expense a few years ago—the Cultural Centre at Gasteig.

After a laborious fund-raising campaign, Everding managed to breathe new life into the long vacated Prinzregententheater, which had been built to complement the Wagner Festspielhaus. Today the renovated building is ornate and resplendent, just as the

Left, Striving ever higher to the Olympus of art.

people of Munich would like their theatres to be, according to Lion Feuchtwanger.

That this lavish baroque style can be somewhat overwhelming, was felt long ago by the amateur artists who were trying to change things. Thus, in 1902, the sculptor Hermann Obrist in *Munich's Decline as a City of Art* wrote that the Isar metropolis, with all its cultural riches, was "being suffocated by its own fat...all good home-made Renaissance fat". There's no need to pursue culture, particularly anything unusual or experimental. One is constantly confronted by art, in glorious buildings and through theatres, museums, galleries and shops selling second-hand books.

It is said that you can see in Munich what you can only read or learn about in other places. Babies imbibe art with their mother's milk. Thus, there has always been a *kulturkampf* or cultural battle, between the innovative, the avant-garde and the existing, traditional values.

Munich's Kulturkampf

For the representatives of Munich's higher culture, this apparent Kulturkampf is merely the expression of a small minority. Yet, it is a smouldering fire which flares up occasionally. Thomas Mann declared in 1926, "This cultural and political battle, ladies and gentlemen, has not just been provoked, but has long been at the very heart and soul of this city."

Munich has always been a forum for radical new ideas. So Rainer Werner Fassbinder evolved his concept of the anti-theatre in his "action theatre" in Müllerstraße. At the end of the performance, the audience was washed out of the auditorium with a hose. Such public provocations and shocks administered to the bourgeoisie do not go down well with the Munich public in general. In fact, it takes very little effort to create a scandal, as remarked by Oskar Maria Graf. In his autobiography *Gelächter von außen* (External Laughter), an enthralling and lively picture of that chaotic period from 1918 to 1933, he recounted a telling episode: "Two painters rented an empty shop in the Türkenstraße. People could watch them at work through the large shop window. One of the painters created a group of dark blue horses, the other covered his canvas in a jumble of coloured lines and squares. A crowd of angry citizens soon gathered outside the window and commented, 'He's painting a blue horse! Must be colour blind, daft ape. Is that supposed to be a mountain, or guts? They're nutty.' When both paint-

1972, the art critic Laszlo Glozer suggested that the American object artist Walter de Maria should instal an "invisible sculpture", entitled *Hole of Thought* on the Olympic site. There was an immediate outcry; it killed the proposal. It seems well-known personalities have little influence here. When Joseph Beuys' Environment *Show Your Wounds* (it is now displayed in the Lenbachhaus Gallery) was bought for a handsome sum by the city, many citizens protested over the use of public funds to pay for such "junk". All they could make out of it was two worn-out biers.

ings were finished, they were carried, unwrapped, through the streets to a royal art shop, escorted by the police who had to keep thousands of angry, threatening citizens in check. The owner of the art shop did not order the paintings and was about to throw them away. Just then, an art collector spotted them by chance and confirmed that they were works by Franz Marc and Wassily Kandinsky, who are regarded as two of the most popular modern artists today!"

Sometimes, it's enough to simply announce an avant-garde art event to create a scandal. Just before the Olympic Games in

Pavarotti and "Culture Shops"

Obviously, there would be no such objections if an opera star were paid between DM 30,000 and DM 50,000 for a performance. As a CSU city counsellor once remarked, "When someone is world famous, there's no need to check whether you're getting good value for money." But with smaller artistic ventures, of which there are so many in this town, it's a different matter. The CSU parliamentary group in 1979 wanted to find out exactly what the budget for culture was spent on. The outcome was a new direction in the cultural battle of Munich, which was smugly commented upon nationwide at the time, and which showed another aspect of Bavarian cultural politics.

For while the subsidy for the Tölzer Boys' Choir was doubled—they are, after all, emissaries of Bavarian culture—the proposed grants for numerous smaller, private ventures ("classical" music businesses, theatre festivals, galleries) were stopped. But the main bone of contention was the "culture shops" which had sprung up in Haidhausen, Westend and Sendling. (There are such institutions in almost every part of the city.) The CSU group wanted to reduce the proposed DM 30,000 per shop to DM 5,000, maintaining that art could well be created without much money, a volteface by the same people for whom in the higher realms of art, money was not a problem.

It was really the concept of these "culture shops" which did not fit the bill. This was no sacrosanct art on display, but art for and by the citizens. This was in accordance with a Council of Europe idea of promoting art for the people, aside from the high-flown culture which was too expensive for many people. The theme here is towards a world of experience for the indivdual and the community he lives in. Culture of the laity was to be encouraged and promoted, and there were to be musical evenings and readings, as well as courses on photography and painting. The idea also included holding meetings with groups comprising war victims, pensioners and *gastarbeiter* or foreign workers.

"Is feeding the old folk cakes a cultural step we want to take?" asked Peter Gauweiler of the CSU. Apparently not. Every effort was made to starve the culture shops, for the DM 5,000 would not even have covered running costs. A rousing battle began in the media (particularly in the letters column). Only in conservative circles did all the commotion seemed much ado about nothing. In a typical commentary, Armin Eichholz of the *Münchner Merkur* paper, in his article entitled *Culture Cramp in Mu-*

The Bavarian State Opera (National Theatre).

nich, stated that "this progressive idyll, in which bread was handed out, and puppet carvings made should not be seen as a kind of culture at all. If only there wasn't all this talk of culture; social welfare would be a better way of looking at it, or plain farce."

Culture Palace at Gasteig

Evidently for some, caviar has to be served for an event to be culturally meaningful. There's no shortage of that kind of culture in Munich. Indeed, with reputation at stake, it seems that each new project has to be bigger and better than the previous one. An example of this is the Kulturzentrum (Cultural Centre) at Gasteig, that bastion on the Isar, which confronts the visitor as he approaches from the Ludwigs-brücke. The project had to be on a world scale, to be on par with the Centre Pompidou in Paris. However, this Bavarian version is not light and airy but a heavy angular brick building. The arch grumbler and Bavarian writer, August Kühn, described it as a penal institution for culture which cost a fair amount. The budget for the project was revised several times, but from the grand opening which took place, it was obvious that not enough had been spent on it. The world famous musician Sergiu Celibidache was the first to complain that the podium for the orchestra was too small. It must be admitted that even in the case of the Kulturzentrum, the adage *"Wer ko, der ko"* still applies, that although the money almost ran out, they did it in the end!

On the other hand, not wanting to do something is what stopped André Heller. He wanted to create a kind of fantasy world with the help of well-known artists (such as Salvadore Dali) on the Olympic site. The Munich city council couldn't work out what exactly this Viennese jack-of-all-trades wanted; it seems they lacked the imagination to picture this Hellerish fantasmagoria. His project was declined. With typical Viennese charm, Heller prophesied that the then lord mayor, Erich Kiesl, would be sentenced to two days imprisonment in the Last Judgement for breaking off the project.

STREETS AND SQUARES

Now that you have dipped into the history of Munich and have an idea of the city's unique charm and lifestyle, we can take you around the streets and squares and let you feel the atmosphere.

Our tour begins right in the very heart of the city. We start off through the pedestrian precinct—from the railway station to Marienplatz. From there you go *On the Trail of Old Munich*, around and about the historical parts of the city in the Marienplatz area. On your second day in Munich, we would suggest a walk round the city *From the Sendlinger Tor to the Odeonsplatz*. Here, you will have the chance to relax in Marienplatz again.

It's not far from the Odeonsplatz to the legendary area of Schwabing you have always wanted to see. We have devoted no less than four chapters to the largest and probably the most popular part of the city. Then, from the Feldherrnhalle, along the Ludwigstraße to the Siegestor (Victory Gate). On the left is the Maxvorstadt or Max Suburb, once the centre of *Art, Cabaret and Revolutionaries*. Schwabing from the Leopoldstraße to the Müncher Freiheit (Munich Freedom) is found in the article, *Modern Schwabing*. For those who have come to Munich for the art treasures of Athens on The Isar, *A World of Art* tells of the best of Munich's museums.

From almost anywhere in Schwabing, there are wonderful walks through the *Englischer Garten* (English Garden) into *The Lehel*, which stretches from the Haus der Kunst (House of Art) along The Isar to the theatre on Gärtnerplatz, or Gardener's Square. If you cross the river at the Deutsches Museum (German Museum), you are almost at the centre of the courtyards and the villas of Haidhausen, the "second Schwabing"—nowadays one of the centres of the Munich scene. It would be unforgivable to miss The Wies'n (The Meadows), as the people of Munich have affectionately named the Oktoberfest. Not far away, *The Stomach of Munich* "rumbles"—a slightly longer walk which begins in the Glockenbachviertel and leads over the Theresienwiese (Theresien Meadow) to the West end and Sendling. The article, *Of Beer Brewers and Princes*, takes you through the brewery area of Munich to the beautiful palace of Schloß Nymphenburg. *The Other Side of the Middle Ring* shows some sights worth seeing.

The last part of the book proposes a few *Excursions into the Bavarian Countryside* around Munich, to the beautiful lakes. Other tours are described in *Beer and Baroque*. If you want to venture into the area around Munich, then *Bishops, Princes and Imperial Cities* is the article for you. *Splendour and Misery of the Past* follows-up on the Schloß (Palace) Schleißheim and the memorial museum of the Dachau concentration camp. The crowning chapter, *The Fairytale King*, takes you on a dream journey to the castles of Ludwig II.

Preceding pages, roundabout on a merry-go-round; Bavarian lion in the Feldherrnhalle; view of the Church of Our Lady and Theatiner Church from the English Garden; Farmers' Festival in front of the Bavarian State Opera; cheers in the beer tent. Left, The Bavaria.

Munich

THROUGH THE PEDESTRIAN PRECINCT

Munich is a city of contrasts. This can be clearly seen in the Innenstadt, or inner city, where past and present vie for space in a densely packed area.

Grand palatial buildings of long ago contrast with the cold concrete castles of this century, and the traditional and indigenous defiantly faces the commercial and progressive. But that's not all. Going from the Main Railway Station over the Lenbachplatz, Stachus and Marienplatz to the elegant shopping streets around the Max-Joseph-Platz (Square), one follows a progression through the different social classes of the city. From the low dives around the station, through the middle-class department store and pedestrian precinct

to the string of elegant boutiques of the Maximilianstraße.

Munich's **Hauptbahnhof** (Main Railway Station), as it is today, dates from the 1950s. Its predecessor was destroyed by the bombs of World War II. The only reminder of the old station is a piece of stonework to the left of the main entrance, where there is a fruit shop under the arches now. Renovation work seems to be in progress continually inside the station. The visitor to the Isar metropolis is greeted by an elegant interior of marble, shining glass and polished aluminium. Perhaps it's time to spruce up the image of the surrounding neighbourhood. For south of the station square, where the tramps usually meet and sleep, lies a notorious area of the city.

Electronic and Erotic

Along the **Schillerstraße** and

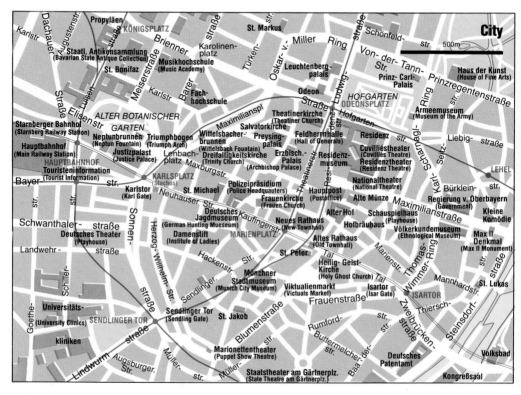

Goethestraße streets, commercial life has developed in a way typical of so many city station areas. Gaps between large and small town hotels have been filled by Italian, Yugoslavian and Turkish restaurants. There's a profusion of shop windows packed with electric appliances, some more exotic than others, coyly marked "Export Only", which the visitor to Munich wouldn't be able to find anywhere else in town. Behind the windows of snack bars, sausages sizzle and chickens are grilled. There are shops packed with all kinds of erotica. Clip joints and gambling dens, offices of exotic-sounding import-export companies and wage tax agencies selling their services to ignorant *Gastarbeiter* (foreign workers) complete the picture.

In complete contrast is the row of houses to the east of the station, where the **Kaufhaus Hertie** department store extends from the Prielmayerstraße and Schützenstraße corner almost to the Stachus. Behind the old but still lovely-to-look-at facade is the delightful perfumery department and a stately staircase crowned with a wonderful glass dome. The **Käfermarkthallen** (Käfer Delicatessen and Delivery Service), used by all Munich sophisticates, is well worth a visit, in the lavishly designed cellar of the store.

Schützenstraße, with its passages, is part of the pedestrian precinct of the inner city. Here, retailers of all kinds have set up shop, like in all major cities. However, only in Munich would you find something like the **Mathäser-Bierkeller** (Mathäser Beer Cellar), where impassioned drinkers arrange to meet very early in the morning, and where the police have to be called in as tempers flare from time to time. The Mathäser-passage, with its small boutiques is next to the Bierkeller. After the shopping area, the vista opens out as far as the

Watching the world go by at the fountain in Karls Gate.

Karlsplatz, simply and succinctly known as the **Stachus**. On the left is the Hotel Königshof and behind it, the monumental neo-baroque building of the **Justitspalast** (Palace of Justice) which was built at the end of the 19th century by Friedrich Thiersch.

Splendid Past

If you feel like a break from the hectic activity of the Karlsplatz, then turn left into the **Lenbachplatz**. Nineteenth century buildings fringe the square and in the centre is the **Wittelsbacher Brunnen**, a fountain (1883-85) by Hildebrand. The most imposing building, No. 2, dominates the square, and now houses the Deutsche Bank and Bayerische Börse (Bavarian Stock Exchange). The **Bernheimer Haus** (No. 3, built by F. Thiersch in 1887-1889) was one of the first residential-cum-commercial houses in Munich. Gabriel von Siedl

completed the **Künstlerhaus** (Artists' House) in 1900, and the luxurious interior design of the Prince Regent period can still be admired today in the Mövenpick restaurant. In similar vein, the **Venezianisches Zimmer**, or Venetian Room, has been retained most of its original setting.

In the Stachus

The traffic here is so bad that the square can only be crossed underground. The boredom of this subway passage is alleviated by an underground shopping centre. The square was named the Karlsplatz in honour of Prince Elector Karl Theodor, who has gone down in Bavarian history as the least popular of the Wittelsbach family rulers. Thus the people of Munich gave it the name "Stachus", after the far more popular owner of a beer garden there, Eustachius Föderl. In the mid-19th century an

Left, arcades in the shade. Below, the tricks which draw the crowd.

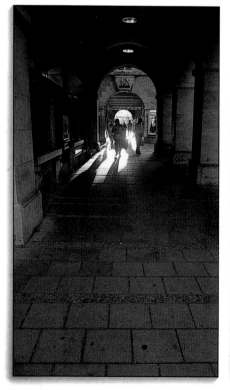

explosion in the house of the ironmonger Rosenlehner badly damaged the Karlstor (Karl's Gate) which led to its renovation, and subsequently with the addition of a memorial to four Munich characters in the arch of the towers.

Trends and Traditions

Behind the Karlstor, the **Fußgängerzone** (Pedestrian Precinct) begins in the **Neuhauser Straße.** Although much has been preserved, much of what remained has also disappeared. It is a sad fact that small shops are gradually being replaced by large department stores. This faceless anonymity is the same everywhere, and the result of chain stores and fast food outlets taking over from the old city traditions which few now remember. The name **Oberpollinger**, for example, which now hangs above one of the largest retail stores, is on a site where the very first beer brewer in Munich went about his daily chores in the 16th century. A hundred years later, the family Pollinger operated a brewery there. But only the name, slightly changed though, has survived over the centuries. On the same side of the street, is the **Bürgersaal,** which was built at the beginning of the 18th century according to plans by Giovanni Viscardi. In the basement is the grave of Father Rupert Mayer, who was deported to a concentration camp for his resistance to the Nazis, and who died in 1945 from injuries sustained while under detention. The priest was canonised in 1987.

The Augustinerbräu

Opposite, flanked by shops selling bedding, shoes and underwear, is a relic of Old Munich. Behind a proud Renaissance facade, is one of the finest and most congenial hotels in Munich, the

Right, *the* attraction for kids at the Hunting Museum. Below, a tourist checks his bearing.

Augustinerbräu. The entrance door on the left leads to a beer hall with cosy, dark rooms. The door on the right opens into the restaurant, the main attraction of which is the seafood room with its lovely stucco decoration. The Augustinerbräu, which dates from the turn of the century, is a veritable oasis in the bustle of the pedestrian precinct.

Directly opposite, is **Sankt Michael** (St. Michael's Church), which was built at the end of the 16th Century at the request of Duke Wilhelm V for the Jesuit population of the city. It was there too that Father Rupert Mayer preached his resistance against the Nazis.

Next door is the **Alten Akademie** building, which presently houses the Bavarian administrative office for statistics and data processing. Attached to that is the former **Augustinerkirche** (Church of St. Augustine) in which the **Deutsche Jagd- und Fischereimuseum** (German Museum of Hunt-

ing and Fishing) is to be found. There's nothing quite like this museum anywhere else in the world, certainly no exhibit which can compete with the legendary stuffed *Wolpertinger* or Bavarian primaeval creature.

Daily Life in Marienplatz

The pedestrian precinct leads from here as the **Kaufingerstraße** in the direction of the Marienplatz. On the left you can catch a glimpse of the mighty towers of the **Frauenkirche** (Church of Our Lady).

A few metres on, you come to the New Gothic facade of the **Neues Rathaus** (New Town Hall) which, apart from being the seat of the city fathers and administrators, also has many small shops on the ground floor. Despite the modern atmosphere of the city, around the **Kaufhof** department store, the *Krenweiberl* (horseradish women)

Left, the *Wolpertinger*, a Bavarian mythical creature. Below, relaxing at the Donisl.

dressed in traditional, colourful peasant dress still peddle their horseradish, as well as spices and tea, in marked contrast to the trendy fashions and modern department stores which surround them.

If the carillon of the New Town Hall isn't the focus of tourist attention, then the buskers are often the centre of attraction. They keep the atmosphere lively well into the night.

On the left hand side, the **Weinstraße** begins. No.1 is an old established address, which fell into disrepute in the past. It is the **Donisl** Hotel. In 1984, this former tourist attraction became a den of iniquity, as waiters used narcotic drops and other substances to render the guests senseless, so that they could relieve them of their possessions. However, those times are over, and a certificate near the entrance attests to the particular honesty and hospitality of the Verein Münchner Brauereien (Associa-tion of Munich Breweries). Local, hearty Bavarian fare is served.

Across the **Sporerstraße**, where the Frauenkirche towers are again visible, the pedestrian passes the long **Marien-hof** on to the **Maffeistraße.** During the day, the Weinstraße here is a mass of people, mostly office workers hurrying along and ambling tourists taking their time. It's almost always busy that one could easily overlook the tram, which makes an S-curve into the **Perusas-traße** from Maffeistraße.

Elegant and International

The Weinstraße now leads straight into the **Theatinerstraße**, which on sunny summer days is transformed into a street café as tables and chairs are set up outside. The establishments of sophisticated living are to be found here, and shop windows display designer names such as Burberry and Etienne

The New Town Hall and twin towers of the Church of Our Lady.

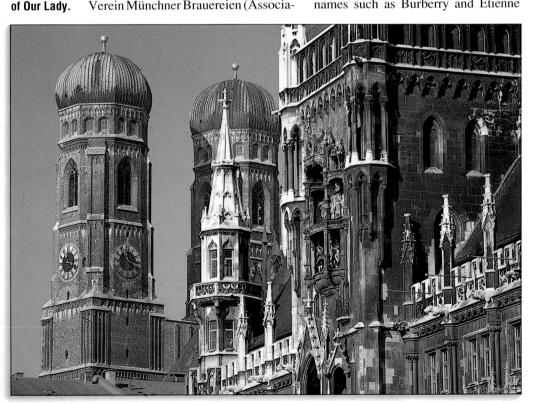

Aigner. The cuisine too is international, and in Restaurant **Boettner**, salmon and lobster are the order of the day. In keeping with this atmosphere is the **Hypo-Passage**, so-called because of the Bavarian Hypotheken- und Wechsel-Bank head office which towers above the other commercial buildings. The **Hypo-Kulturstiftung** gallery, established by the bank, is located here too; it holds major exhibitions.

On the same side of the road, just before the Theatinerkirche, you might want to steal a glance at the **Theatinerhof**, which is a courtyard with an elegant arched walkway lined by a handful of exclusive small boutiques. On a fine day, you can enjoy the atmosphere of this delightful courtyard at a table of the café **Arzmiller**, which is a favourite venue for the not-so-young generation; they come here for the wonderful cakes and pastry.

But for now, let's go back to the Theatinerstraße where several passages—the Theatinerpassage and the Residenzpassage, for example—lead us to the nearby **Residenzstraße.** Let's take the **Preysing-Palais** past the windows of the exclusive Residenz-Boutique, and then turn right into the Residenzstraße.

Between the two streets are numerous small shopping alleys, narrow passages with many nooks and crannies and little courtyards, where the finer things of life are for sale. Here the scent of expensive perfume mingles with the delicious aroma of fine chocolate. In the midst of these extravagant temptations is the courtyard of No. 13, from which a narrow passage leads to the **Eilles-Hof**, a small Gothic square with wonderful arcades. Over at No.11, part of a house which was built for one of the wealthier citizens, and which belonged to the Bittrich cloister in the 18th century, is the tea and coffee house of Eille. You

Fluttering flags in front of the Franziskaner.

must just take a look at the beautifully preserved interior.

Next door is the **Spatenhaus** where fine Bavarian dishes may be enjoyed. That brown and white sausage can be incorporated into haute cuisine, is proved by the well frequented **Franziskaner**, one of the oldest and most refined restaurants of its kind in Munich, on the corner of Perusa Street and Residenzstraße.

Boulevard No.1

Here the **Maximilianstraße** begins, to all intents and purposes the most elegant of all streets in Munich. It leads over the Altstadtring (Old City Ring) to the Maxmonument and ends at the Maximilianeum, just by the Isar. This is the place for those with expensive tastes. Here, one can spend days wandering through antique shops and fine art galleries, and shops where precious stones, fine fabrics, exclusive leatherware and the best furniture are found.

There are elegant cafés and restaurants too. In the centre stands the finest of all the hotels in Munich, the **Hotel Vier Jahreszeiten** (Four Seasons Hotel). Established in the mid-19th century, the hotel was generously subsidised by King Maximilian II. Even then, it was used as a guest house only for the rulers. Today visiting dignitaries still stay here, apart from the very few exceptions who are invited to stay in the Residenz. The hotel was famous for having a special kind of lift, a contraption for heaving a chair from floor to floor, as early as 1862.

There are several amusing anecdotes about the hotel. One relates to the King of Siam, who set a record for the amount of luggage he brought with him. He had 1,320 pieces, and history doesn't relate just how many rooms he needed for them all.

Hunting knives and tufts of chamois hair are the pride of true Bavarians.

HEAVEN IS HUNG
WITH HAM AND SAUSAGES

If one imagines Munich as a large house, and the Marienplatz as the elegant drawing room, Nymphenburg the reception room, Grünwald the private guest suite and the East end as the coal cellar, then the Viktualienmarkt (Victuals Market) is the larder of the house. Even though this pantry is stacked to the ceiling with good things, it doesn't give the impression that this is a millionaire's household. It has more in common with a well-stocked spick-and-span farmhouse.

This lively food market is more for good solid food than for elegant city fare, and is a gentle reminder of how Munich was, before it reached international metro-polis status.

To stand in the Viktualienmarkt today is to stand at the very birthplace of Munich. It was here in about 1000 A.D. that Benedictine monks founded the first settlement, and where the original St. Peter's Church was built in the 12th century. The site of today's Viktualienmarkt for many years lay outside the city of Munich. In the 13th century, a hospital for the poor and the sick was established here, and it was not until the Marienplatz became too small to cope with the growing market trading of the town, that the city fathers decided upon this temporary location for the food market. The recently abandoned cemetery of St. Peter's Church, despite its somewhat gruesome connotations, was chosen by the enlightened Duke of Montgelas, the founder of modern Bavaria.

In May 1807, the foundation stone for the new Viktualienmarkt was laid on the erstwhile site of the Heiliggeist-Kirche (Church of the Holy Spirit) hospital. In the course of secularisation, the hospital building was slowly adapted to its new function. Thus the meat was sold in what was formerly a hospital ward. One should not be carried away by talk of the "good old days" of the last century; standards of hygiene were deplorable. People waded ankle deep in mud to get to the stalls, and when they reached the vendors, the rotting produce often stank to high heaven. The specially formed Viktualien police force had a difficult time trying to keep law and order.

The history of the Viktualienmarkt, founded on a cemetery and poor house, in fact gives a clear indication that this is not a haven for gourmets, but more of a meeting place for the people of Munich. Nowadays, the people have a wider selection of culinary delicacies to savour than in those early days.

But this is still a place where money isn't everything, even though one does get the impression that there's nothing one can't have if one is rich enough. On the south western side of the market lies the cheap meat section, where meat from forced slaughters is sold in limited amounts at about three-quarters of the usual price, and only to end-users. Not long ago, those who bought their meat there were thought of as poor, and better families only bought dog meat there, Nowadays, people from all walks of life are happy to get a good bargain.

Here, on the steps of the tower shelter near the meat bargain section, an attempt was made to create a kind of Speaker's Corner, as in Hyde Park. Everyone was to have the right to air his or her grievances here. But the people of Munich have never been great ones for public speaking, and the grumblers' corner was never really used.

Another unmistakable sign that this place is rooted in the people is the memorial fountains. The Viktualienmarkt isn't just some kind of retail outlet; it's more like a village in itself, complete with village green, or in this case, beer garden, maypole and the small fountain, all of which is most inviting, for busy shoppers. It's all the more significant just whom these fountains commemorate—not some worthy Munich dignitaries—but local comedians such as Karl Valentin, Liesl Karlstadt and Weiß Ferdl. Perhaps one should remember that Karl Valentin, whose brand of misanthropic humour lost its appeal after the war, ended his days in starvation and poverty. Maybe his memorial, here in the midst of the gourmet paradise of ham and sausages, is reason enough for him to come back from the grave.

The Viktualienmarkt is there for the down-and-outs, for sad characters who could come right out of one of Karl Valentin's sketches and films. They can all get together here, and the tramps congregate just behind the meat bargain section. Even though the market may appear to be a huge delicatessen store, it does have something to offer to those on the bread line. For less than a Deutsche Mark, you can have a taste of the fare at almost any of the stalls. At the worst, there's always the beer garden in the centre of the market, where practically no one stops the city tramps from drinking up the dregs left in the glasses.

Last but not least, there are the market people themselves. Many of the stalls belong to the same family for generations, and a "race" of market people has grown up with

Left, Weiß Ferdl at the Viktualienmarkt. Right, a warm smile for service goes a long way!

its own legendary reputation. They're straightforward, the market ladies, who make no secret of the fact that they want to sell their wares, but not in bulk, preferably to connoisseurs. There's to be no arguing or haggling about the price or quality of the goods, and you mustn't touch ("Y'only touch what belongs to yer!") and their obscenities are legendary...or used to be. Many regret the slow disappearance of this rough peasant speech, and something of the atmos-

phere of this place will be lost, when these characters are no more.

But the market people don't only work and scold. Once a year on Shrove Tuesday, the whole Viktualienmarkt is transformed into a dance floor. Then there's a *gaudi* or celebration; the ladies at the market dance in a party which turns out to be so lively and noisy that it puts all of Munich's other carnival activities in the shade. The traditional activity is part and parcel of the Viktualienmarkt, which has its own life and place right in the heart of Munich.

ON THE TRAIL OF OLD MUNICH

What are the possibilities for a visitor who wishes to see the old Munich? There are two ways of discovering the city of the past. The first is the easier. Simply head for the Münchner Stadtmuseum (Munich City Museum) on St. Jakobs-Platz and visit the History of the City section. Of particular interest is a copy of the wooden model of the city, made by Jakob Sandtner in 1570, the original of which is in the Bavarian National Museum. With a little more effort, you can see the sights of Old Munich on foot. However, the points of historical interest are scattered far and wide throughout the city, with little regard for the fitness and stamina of the sightseer.

But before we set out, we would like to give you a brief historical insight into the layout of the city. In the days when Schwabing and Au were still country suburbs, the centre of the city was contained within a wide encircling wall, or more accurately within two walls. The inner wall dates from the 13th century, and the outer one from the 15th century and today the Altstadtring (Old City Ring) runs where the walls once stood. The enclosed area was divided into four Viertel or districts, with the Kreuzviertel area in the north-west, the Hackenviertel in the west, the Angerviertel in the south and the Graggenauer Viertel in the north-east. The dividing lines between these areas ran from east to west, from the Stachus to the Isartor (Isar Gate) and north-south from the Sendlinger Tor to today's Odeonsplatz.

From Marienplatz to the Hackenviertel

Let's begin right in the centre of Munich, in Marienplatz, which is anything but old and peaceful. The **Rosenstraße** leads off to the south, towards the Rindermarkt (Cattle Market). Here, we get a good view of the facades of the **Ruffini-Häuser** (Ruffini Houses).

We turn right into Sendlingerstraße, cross Fürstenfelder Straße and the Färbergraben. On the right, shortly after the **Süddeutschen Verlag** (South German Publishing House), where the Süddeutsche Zeitung and the Abendzeitung are printed, we come to No. 75, the **Alten Hackerhaus.** That this is a house full of tradition is attested to by the inscription above the door *Die Preustatt zum Hacker vom Jahre 1570,* which tells us that beer was brewed here by a member of the Hacker family as early as 1570. More historical information is given inside, on the back of the menu. Simon Hacker, a brewer, bought the place in 1738, and his daughter Therese married Josef Pschorr, from whom we get the name Hacker-Pschorr, which is still circulating today.

In 1825, the building was destroyed by a fire, but was rebuilt a few years later. In the early 1980s, extensive renovations were undertaken, and now it has become a very pleasant Bavarian restaurant with a lovely beer garden in the courtyard. There's a decorative family tree of the Hacker-Pschorr family on the wall. The neighbouring house, No. 76, known as the **Faberbräu**, was also involved in brewing, but is now affiliated to the Süddeutscher Verlag.

Soon after the Hackerhaus, the Hackenstraße branches off to the right. We are in the old Hackenviertel. Where the Hackenstraße meets the Hotterstraße is the **Hundskugel** (Dogs' Ball), the oldest restaurant in Munich. The gastronomic tradition of this house goes back to 1440. Since then, it has been taken over by the fashion designer Rudolph Moshammer, and its indigenous charm transformed into folkloric glamour. However, it's still worth taking a look at the interior of the building, particularly upstairs, to see the pine room and the Gothic room, two small but traditionally decorated guest rooms. How the

Preceding pages, view from the carillon to the Marienplatz with St. Mary's column in the square.

place got its strange name, is explained next door, in No. 10, a beautifully restored bourgeois house, which was acquired by the court sculptor Johann Baptist Straub in 1741, and renovated by him. Above the entrance is a relief which depicts six boisterous dogs playing with a large ball.

Where the Hackenstraße changes into the Brunnenstraße at the corner, stands the **Radlbrunnen** (Wheel Fountain), which, as the name suggests, is wheel driven. On the opposite side of the road is the **Radspielerhaus**. In the 17th and 18th centuries, this was the home of the noble family Rechberg, before the architect Métivier took it over in 1817. From 1827 until 1828, Heinrich Heine lived here; this is commemorated by a plaque on the house wall. In 1848 it was taken over by the Radspieler family, whose descendants run a furniture business. The showrooms lead to extensive gardens with

Italian charm lives in the alley.

fountains and sculptures, a veritable oasis in the centre of the city.

At the next crossroads, we turn right into **Damenstiftstraße** (Convent Street) which took its name from house No. 3. The former **Damenstift** (Convent) was built by the city master mason Mathias Widmann between 1784 and 1785, and served as a convent for the nuns of the Salesian Order. Today, the building, of which only the facade is original, houses the Salvator-Realschule für Mädchen (Salvator Girls' School).

The **St.- Anna-Damenstiftskirche** (Convent Church of St. Anna), built by Johann Baptist Gunezrainer in 1732-1735, also belonged to the Salesian Order and took the place of the Annakirche (Church of St. Anna) from the 15th century. The St.-Anna-Damenstiftskirche was heavily damaged during the last war, but extensively renovated during the 1950s. Across it stands

the splendid Rococo facade of the **Palais Lerchenfeld**, generally attributed to the master builder Ignaz Anton Gunezrainer. House No. 4, a well-preserved bourgeois house in the classic style of 1900, was in the possession of the city's master builders Balthasar Trischberger and Mathias Widmann.

At the crossing with **Herzogspitalstraße**, it's worth taking a look at **Altheimer Eck**, an address rich in tradition, but now part of the noisy pedestrian precinct. It seems almost an anachronism to read on the memorial plaque on the back wall of the shop, that this was the site of the birthplace of the composer Richard Strauss. His mother was in fact a Pschorr, of the famous brewing family. A left turn brings us to an archway leading into house No. 13. Here, in the rooms of the printer J.G. Weiß, is where the first German stamp, the famous "Schwarze Einser" (Black One) was printed. The premises of the **Deutsche Journalistenschule** (German School of Journalism) are to be found almost hidden in the backrooms of house No. 3.

We'll now turn back into the Herzogspitalstraße. On the right hand side is the **Weinhaus Neuner**, Munich's oldest wine tavern. It goes right back to the 15th century. During the 17th and 18th centuries, the building was the property of the Gregorian Seminary, and was the students' dining room. A quatrain, handed down from those days gives an indication of how the table manners of the day in Munich were seen: "Belching and spitting, picking one's nose, sneezing and scratching one's head at table is not good manners, but Bavarian." After its secularisation, in 1852, the Weinhaus was established, and the later clientele was no doubt above such vulgar behaviour, as regular clients included Richard and Siegfried Wagner, Carl Spitzweg, Hans Moser, Karl Valentin and Liesl Karlstadt. Today it is a venue for gourmets with a preference for fine Bavarian cuisine.

Are any of the local clients irked that the proprietress is Marianne Krukenberg, who's from Berlin? The house opposite, where the art and book shop Pfeiffer is to be found on the ground floor, was formerly the site of the Barth'sche Seelhaus, which was where spinsters and widows tended the poor and sick free of charge.

Over the Pedestrian Precinct into the Kreuzviertel

The longer way round takes us into the immediate proximity of the pedestrian precinct. So we turn right into the **Herzog-Wilhelm-Straße** which leads directly into the Neuhauser Straße. Brightly lit hamburger joints and jeans shops have little in common with the old Munich, so we'll bypass this commercial mile, to the BMW showroom with its gleaming vehicles, at the end of **Herzog-Max-Straße.**

The oldest inn in Munich.

Just before this building, on the right, is the **Gedenkstein** (Memorial Stone) in memory of the erstwhile synagogue. The area was developed by the Jewish community, which in 1883 began the construction of a large synagogue, then completed in 1887. In 1938, it was demolished by the Nazis. "Remember this, your enemy mocked you." is inscribed in the stone in Hebraic as well.

On the right is where Duke Wilhelm V erected the Herzog-Max-Burg fortress at the end of the 16th century. Today, only the tower remains. The building opposite is the seat of the archbishopric diocesan authorities, and was formerly a Carmelite church built by Konrad Asper in the mid-17th century. We now make our way northwards to Pacellistraße and come to the **Dreifaltigkeitskirche** (Trinity Church). This church was the work of Giovanni Antonio Viscardi, built between 1711 and 1718 to fulfil a vow made by the people of Munich at the time of the War of Succession. Following a prophesy by the mystic Anna Leidmayr, the church was built in gratitude for sparing the city by the approaching Austrian troops. Inside the baroque church, the cupola and ceiling frescoes are by Cosmas Damian Asam while the stucco work was by Johann Georg Bader. This was one of the few churches which was not damaged during the war.

To the left of the Dreifaltigkeitskirche, we continue into the narrow **Rochusstraße.** Where the street curves to the right, there is an old house on the left, with a memorial plaque to the Pilgerspital (Pilgrims Hospital). The church and hospital were established by Duke Wilhelm V in 1589 in honour of Rochus, and were exactly 300 years old when they were destroyed. The Rochusstraße soon leads into the historic **Prannerstraße**.

Opposite is the **Siemens Museum**, in which you can see telegraphic inventions by Werner von Siemens, who with Georg Halske founded the firm in 1847. Landmarks of technological invention, from the first electric train to the microchip, are on display here. Only a handful of people in Munich can recall that this row of houses, including the Tela-Versicherung (Tela-Insurance), was once the hub of Bavarian political life. In 1808 the Bavarian state acquired the former Redoutenhaus, and Leo von Klenze drew up plans to convert it into a house for parliament. The diet sat for the first time in 1819. From 1848 onwards, after the introduction of the new state voting system and the abdication of Ludwig I, the Bavarian parliament continued to sit here until the Nazis decided to dissolve it in 1933. The building was completely destroyed during the war.

The southern side of the street is graced by the classical facades of two palaces. At No. 9, is the **Palais Gise**, which in the 18th century was in the possession of Countess Arco and the

Cool spot at the Nürnberger Bratwurst (Sausage) Glöckl.

Count of Taufkirchen. In 1837, it was acquired by August Freiherr von Gise. The palace is attributed to the architect Karl Albert Lespilliez. The neighbouring **Palais Seinsheim** is from the same period, but underwent alterations in the neo-baroque style in 1900, and then further renovations in 1983. The project was wholly financed by the members of the Bavarian convention of municipal authorities, which has its seat in this palace.

During the morning, delivery vans and lorries are busy here, for this is the rear entrance to the **Hotel Bayerischer Hof** where all kinds of paraphernalia are delivered here for the comfort of the guests.

Opposite stands the **Palais Preysing**, not to be confused with the Preysing-Palais, in the Residenzstraße. As the wall plaque states, the building is attributed to François Cuvilliés the Elder and belongs to the Bayerische Vereins-

bank, which holds exhibitions on the ground floor.

We now come to **Kardinal-Faulhaber-Straße**. Take a look to the left at the Rococo **Palais Holnstein**, which was begun in 1733 and completed in 1737. Prince Elector Karl Albrecht commissioned François Cuvilliés the Elder to build this for his son Count Holnstein. Cuvilliés, a Belgian, came to the court of Max Emanuel when he was 21 years old. Because of his diminutive stature, he acted as the court dwarf, until the Prince Elector sent him to Paris to study architecture. On his return, Cuvilliés was named master builder at court, and eventually succeeded Gunezrainer. To the right of the Palais Holnstein is the **Bayerische Hypotheken- und Wechselbank** building. Also in the bank's possession is the **Palais Portia**, designed by Enrico Zucalli in 1693 for Count Fugger. It was later altered by Cuvilliés the Elder.

The world's most famous pub.

Round and About
the Promenadeplatz

In the Promenadeplatz (Promenade Square) area, one bank stands next to the other, since the area is now a well established financial centre. The history of this part of the city, however, began with trade of a rather more common nature. Until the mid-18th century, this was the centre of the salt trade, and was known as Kreuzgasse (Cross Street), which presumably is the origin of **Kreuzviertel**, as this part of the city is now called.

During the 18th century more and more aristocrats made their homes in this area, and the noise of the salt traders became a nuisance, so that eventually the salt market was moved to what is now the Arnulfstraße. The square got its name around 1800 when it was first used for military parades. Even today the name sounds appropriate, for in front of the Hotel Bayerischer Hof, where expensive cars are parked next to one another, people still parade. In the centre of the square is a garden with monuments commemorating the Bavarian writer Lorenz Westenrieder, Prince Elector Max Emanuel, and the composers Orlando di Lasso and Willibald Gluck.

Totally insignificant in comparison to monuments, is the memorial tablet on the eastern side, to the former Premier, Kurt Eisner. On 21 February 1919, he was on his way to the Landtag (State Parliament) in Prannerstraße to tender his resignation when suddenly, he was shot from behind here by Anton Graf Arco-Valley.

Now we'll take a closer look at the Promenadeplatz. At the corner with Kardinal-Faulhaber-Straße, is house No. 2. Between 1811 and 1813, the prominent politician Count Montgelas, had a palace built here as his official

The captivating "watering hole".

residence. Today the palace is an annex of the Bayerischer Hof. In 1807, a famous Bavarian was born in the neighbouring No. 4. He was Franz Count of Pocci. Also known as Count Punch, author of children's books, illustrator and composer, and best known for his invention of Punch and Judy. You can find out more of him in the Puppentheatermuseum (Puppet Theatre Museum) at the Stadtmuseum (City Museum).

The **Hotel Bayerischer Hof** dominates the Promenadeplatz. It is the only hotel remaining of those built in the Kreuzviertel during the 18th and 19th centuries. At the behest of King Ludwig I and on the initiative of the industrialist Maffei, the architect Friedrich von Gärtner constructed what was for its day an immensely expensive and luxurious hotel. The grand opening was held on 15 October 1841. Many other sparkling social occasions followed, as the establishment became very popular with the Munich upper class. Restored after having suffered much damage during World War II, the hotel soon regained its place in Munich society, and the gala functions and festivals held here are still major events in the city's social calendar.

As is usual in such cases, the surrounding shops reflect the expensive tastes of the hotel's clientele. The rest of the Promenadeplatz has little in the way of historical interest. The writer Ludwig Thoma once lived in No. 17 for a while in 1891, and established his legal practice there. House No. 13 is of some interest though; it was the former residence of the court master builder Johann Baptist Gunezrainer, who moved in 1730. Hotel Max Emanuel used to stand at the corner with Hartmannstraße. Today, this side of the street houses the offices of major credit institutions.

"White sausages have to be taken before midday."

Between Promenadeplatz and Marienplatz

We continue down Hartmannstraße in a southerly direction, and turn left at the "Schwarzwälder Probierstube" to the **Löwengrube** (Lion's Den). During the 19th century, this street was called the Knödelgasse (Dumpling Street) as dumplings were baked here.

On the left is the Munich police headquarters building. Behind that is the **Frauenplatz** with the glorious **Frauenkirche** (Church of Our Lady) which in the middle ages, was the second parish church north of the city, after the Peter's Church. Until the 18th century, the church was surrounded by a cemetery, which was in turn surrounded by a wall with five gates. When a child was brought for christening in the old days, gate money had to be paid to the sacristan. The old school house used to be on the northern side, where today the shops in Nos. 12 to 15 are found. During the 16th century, the same building was the School of Poetry which the Meistersinger (mastersinger) Hans Sachs attended for several months. Here he fell in love with a young girl and he recorded his emotions in a quatrain which marked the beginning of his creative life. At house No. 10 of the Frauenplatz, the much respected Ridler family founded in 1487, the **Reiche Almosenhaus** (Rich Alms House), where poor citizens were offered foodstuffs every Saturday. This custom continued until the institution was closed in 1806.

The neighbouring **Nürnberger Bratwurst-Glöckl**, a gastronomic attraction, a quirk of geography. However, we take the archway to its left into **Thiereckstraße** where we can peep into the courtyard of the Donisl and eventually find ourselves back in the lively atmosphere of the Kaufinger Straße and again in Marienplatz.

Marienplatz and the Town Hall.

MUNICH AFTER MIDNIGHT - DEAD!

It's after one in the morning, you've set the world right, made friends for life with strangers an hour ago, found a new love, and want another beer. That's when the going gets tough in Munich; to survive the night is a game. You have to keep the ball in play.

There is however, one haven which opens at five in the morning, and that's the **Café Frischhut**, known as *Schmalznudel* because of the delicious, fresh, deep-fried pastry they make there. It's in the Viktualienmarkt

a.m. and until 3 a.m. on Saturdays). This has been one of Munich's night spots for forty years, and the chinoiserie on the walls has never changed, nor has the music of the disco. Maybe just because of all that, or maybe because nowhere else serves you warm champagne in such a carefree way, this place is one of the first places to go when you're looking for somewhere to hang out.

But if you don't appreciate the bar's ironic cultural humour, you have to go for the

(Victuals Market) and has helped many a night owl get over it all. After the refreshing breakfast, there's nothing left to do but take a walk through the market, and watch the women busily setting up their stalls at the break of dawn. There's some comfort in seeing the normal day start, and in knowing that the night has passed and it's finally time to go to bed.

One o'clock is closing time in Munich. Perhaps the first stop for those who are looking for something different is the **Philoma-Bar** (Stiglmaierplatz, open until 2

smarter discotheques, which are not to everyone's taste. In Munich, these are reserved for *Stammgäste* or regular clients, as it says on the door. These regular guests aren't those who frequent the place, but those who look as if they do (and bags under the eyes seem to qualify one as much as correct dress). It's no use trying to talk your way in. The P1 in the Haus der Kunst (House of Art) once had the reputation of being "the most impenetrable door of Munich", and was for those who like to read on events at such haunts the night before, in the newspapers next morning. Another venue for the chic set is the **Parkcafé** at the Alter Botanische Garten (Old Botanic Garden). There the lease holders choose their clientele at the door, and have never made a secret of their aversion to walrus moustaches. Easier to get into is the **Far Out** (Am Kosttor 2), probably because of its longer opening hours.

Lovers of the bright lights of the big city, might just find themselves thinking of their wives at home rather more than they might

culture in a mix which offers very little of either, and leaves one wondering that something like that still exists.

Apart from these, there are a few other bars one can go to, the **Bodega-Bar** (Hans-Sachs-Straße 9), the **Wirtshaus am Platzl** (Am Platzl) or in Schwabing, the very first of the **Wienerwald** chain. The only good thing about these places is that they stay open longer. For a more refined atmosphere, there's **Iwan** (Josephspitalstraße 18) or

elsewhere—the night life is hardly hot. The railway station area is hardly more impressive than a sleepy provincial town. There is the fairly quiet **Leierkasten** (Ingolstädter Straße) and a row of establishments half way to the airport (Am Moosfeld), but the restricted traffic area makes them difficult to get there. On the other hand, the **Blaue Engel** (Blue Angel) in Wolfgangstraße is worth a visit, to see watered-down sex and Bavarian

Left, sex ads glow in the night. Above, Ringswandl - the Bavarian Django Edwards.

Schumann's (Maximilianstraße 36), both without doormen.

All these places take you through until 3 in the morning, possibly even until 4. Then it's not a question of where to have a drink, but how to pass the time until the Schmalznudel opens. Apart from the **Adam's City** (Pacellistraße 2), overpriced and lacking in atmosphere, there's the overcrowded **Nachtcafé** (Maximiliansplatz 5) which has good bar music. Or you can always drink at the **Mathäser Weißbierkeller** (Bayerstraße). On that note *Prost* or cheers and goodnight!

FROM THE SENDLINGER TOR TO THE ODEONSPLATZ

In the inner city of Munich, the contrast between old and new buildings, right next to each other is striking. Gaps blown into the city during World War II, were filled by modern functional buildings. Old buildings which remain, or have been expensively restored, seem like an anachronism.

Relics of the Past

The Sendlinger Tor (The Sendling Gate) which once led out to the trade route to Italy, is today one of the main traffic junctions in Munich. First mentioned in 1318, it was a component of the outer city wall which was built as the city expanded. Today, all that remains are two 14th-century octagonal side towers and a large archway which replaced the three original arches in 1906. On the far side of the arch, the **Sendlinger Straße** begins. It is in a lively shopping area but there are also a few features of historical interest, notably the architectural work of the Asam brothers. First of all there is the **Asam-Haus** (Asam House), No. 62. In 1733, Egid Quirin Asam created this Renaissance building with its stucco facade. Apollo, Athene and Pegasus with the arts and sciences adorn the portal.

Next to this is the Sankt-Johann-Nepomuk-Kirche (St. Johann Nepomuk Church) better known as the **Asam-Kirche** or Asam Church. Egid Quirin Asam established the building and was also the builder, with his brother Cosmas Damian. Egid Quirin was the plaster of Paris worker, and Cosmas Damian the artist. This rococo jewel was completed in 1746. It was

Preceding pages, silent worship in the Church of the Holy Ghost. Below, passing through the Sendlinger Gate.

only a few years before, that the patron saint, Johannes Nepomuk, had been canonized. The interior of the church is lavishly decorated. Countless motifs tell of the life of the saint: carvings on the door, ceiling frescoes and paintings on both sides of the highly ornate interior. At the end of the motifs stands the glorious two-storey high altar with the tomb of the holy Nepomuk. The right and left entrances to the sacristy carry portraits of the Asam brothers.

Opposite the church lies the **Singlspieler-Haus** a former brewery property which lately has been beautifully restored. A street of the same name leads over the busy Oberanger, to the **St.-Jakobs-Platz**. Once a marketplace, this is now a rather unattractive highrise carpark. On the left, the side facade of the **Ignaz-Günther-Haus** is visible: the famous rococo sculptor lived here until his death in 1775. Nowadays the restored building is used for exhibitions

Rococo splendour in the Asam Church.

and for the administration of the city museum. The half gable style, so typical of Munich, and referred to locally as *Ohrwaschl* (ear), is particularly attractive and an architectural delight.

Museums in the Museum

From here it is only a few metres to the extensive **Stadtmuseum** (City Museum). This building, originally a depot for grain and guns, became the city arsenal in the early 15th century. Today interesting exhibitions are held in the premises. The former ammunition hall of the city artillery, the ground floor, is now the Waffenhalle, a display of armour, helmets and breastplates. Also on display here are ten of the original sixteen **Moriskentänzer** (Morisk dancers) by Erasmus Grasser, They used to be in the Altes Rathaus (Old Town Hall).

The ground floor houses the **Filmmuseum** which, with its unusual retrospectives is an important component of Munich cultural life. You'll be able to watch silent movies with "live" orchestral accompaniment. While on the subject of film, the **Fotomuseum** on the first floor is well worth a visit. You'll also find a collection of exhibits from the Camera Obscura Laterna Magica through dusty studios of the early days, to the first dark rooms. There are all kinds of photographs giving an insight into the past, particularly the permanent exhibition of the *Bürgerliche Wohnkultur von 1650 bis zur Gegenwart* (Bourgeois Culture from 1650 to the present day). There are city plans from the days when Schwabing and Giesing were still suburbs, and a model of Munich's famous "Donisl" restaurant. For anyone interested in the history of the city of Munich, this place is a must.

On the third floor is the fascinating **Puppentheatermuseum** (Puppet Theatre Museum), which houses a collection of marionettes, puppets and curi-

osities from long ago. There are also all kinds of things from the fun-fair, like the metal figure with an oversized rubber head which the hotspurs of the old days used to measure their strength against. Punch is there too, and a bust of his inventor, children's author Franz Graf (Count) Pocci. The spacious **Musikinstrumentenmuseum** (Musical Instrument Museum) has a collection from all over the world, ranging from instruments made from African elephant tusks to the more conventional European orchestral types.

The Rindermarkt

The back of the museum faces the **Rindermarkt** (Cattle Market), with its contrasting styles of old and new so typical of the inner city. Between bare facades of an insurance office and the coloured windows of the shops, is the old 16th century **Löwenturm** (Lion Tower). Opposite, you can hear water gently splashing down the tiers of the **Rindermarktbrunnen** (Cattle Market Fountain) of 1964, with its modern statue of a shepherd and his flock, by Josef Henselmann. Behind the fountain are the traditional **Ruffinihäuser** (Ruffini Houses). This lovely old building, with its facade of filigree frescoe work was completed in the early 20th century by Gabriel von Seidl. On the far right is a representation of the old Ruffini Tower built in 1175 and demolished in 1808.

The Rindermarkt leads to one of Munich's landmarks, the **St.-Peter-Kirche** (St. Peter's Church) the city's first parish church. The oldest part of this prominent building dates from the 12th century. Since then, there have been many additions as a result of on-going renovation.

In 1327, there was a fire in the city which damaged the church. Later in

Facade of the City Museum.

1607, it was struck by lightning, following which the new tower, now called the **Alte Peter** (Old Peter) was built. The extent of damage suffered by the church during World War II is captured in photographs displayed at the northern entrance. Among the most interesting are the 14th century Gothic side altar of the Schrenk family, the high altar with Erasmus Grasser's St. Peter and the four church fathers by Egid Quirin Asam. The choir stalls on the right and the two side altars are designed by Ignaz Günther.

For those who brave the 300 steps up the tower, the reward is a spectacular view of the city, and of the Alps on a clear day. From up here, you can see not only the old and new landmarks of the city, but also many lovely hidden courtyards and colourful roof terraces of parts of the old city which are still inhabited. You can also hear music from the buskers in the pedestrian precinct.

Up on Old Peter.

Marienplatz

We are now in Marienplatz, which is and always has been, the heart of the city of Munich. In the days of the salt and grain trade, this lively square was known as Schrannenplatz (Grain Market). The **Mariensäule** (Column of the Virgin) which dominates the square, was erected in 1638 on the wishes of Prince Elector Maximilian I in gratitude for sparing the city during the Swedish occupation. The figure on the column is a crowned madonna holding sceptre and orb, on her arm the Christ child lifting his hand in blessing. On the base are four putties fighting the four miseries of the Thirty Years' War: lion, dragon, snake and basilisk, symbolising war, hunger, heathenism and plague.

Every day, at about 11 o'clock, crowds gather in front of the magnificent facade of the **Neuen Rathaus** (New Town Hall) to watch the **Glock-**

enspiel (carillon). Then the figures of the coopers perform the *Schäfflertanz* or coopers' dance, which was originally performed in Marienplatz in 1517 to commemorate the end of the plague. Then there is the performance of the tournament which was held at the wedding of Wilhelm II and Renata von Lothringen (Lorraine) in 1568. The coopers still perform their dance in Munich, every seven years at carnival time. Less well-known is the other Glockenspiel also on the facade of the Town Hall, which takes place every evening (at 9.30 in summer and 7.30 in winter) and shows a night watchman and the Münchner Kindl (Child of Munich). The Neuen Rathaus was built between 1867 and 1908 by Georg Joseph Hauberrisser, in Flemish Gothic style. This alleviated the problems of overcrowding in the **Alten Rathaus** (Old Town Hall) close by.

The first town hall was destroyed by fire in 1460, and the Gothic building of the Old Town Hall was constructed by the master builder Jörg von Halsbach alias Ganghofer, between 1470 and 1480. During World War II, the building was almost completely destroyed, and it was decades before the restoration was completed. The large *Tanzsaal* or ballroom is upstairs, where the Moriskentänzer by Erasmus Grasser used to be kept. These are now to be found in the Stadtmuseum.

Since 1983 the tower of the Alten Rathaus has housed the **Spielzeugmuseum** (Toy Museum) of the caricaturist Ivan Steiger. Under the arch, a spiral staircase goes up to the first floor, from where a lift takes you up to the fifth storey. Then as you go down the stairs, you trace the history of toys, from 19th century wooden toys, through steam engines, carousels, doll houses, die-hard cowboys and indians and wild animals of every description.

Catch this carillon at the New Town Hall.

The more modern one gets, the more technology dominates—with displays of railways, planes and warships.

The City's Landmark

The master builder, Halsbach, who was responsible for the Old Town Hall, also created the most famous building in Munich, the **Frauenkirche** (Church of Our Lady). Its distinctive domed towers in late Gothic style gives it an air of strength and solemnity. The foundation stone was laid in 1468 by Duke Sigismund. The five portals are the work of Ignaz Günther; Erasmus Grasser made the apostles and prophets; Jan Pollack was responsible for the paintings and Ignaz Günther for the relief work. In the crypt are the tombs of the Wittelsbach family, where many Bavarian dukes are buried. Most magnificent of all is the memorial grave of the Prince Elector Kurfürst Maximilian I,

View of the Old Town Hall, with Old Peter in the background .

which was erected in 1622 by Emperor Ludwig der Bayer (The Bavarian) in honour of his reign.

To continue our walk, we return to Marienplatz and just before the Old Town Hall, we turn right into **Burgstraße** (Castle Street). The Late Gothic house at No. 5 offers a good opportunity to combine a thirst for historical knowledge with more profane thirst. In the mid-16th century this was the house of the town clerk. Nowadays, one can relax under the trees in the garden of the wine bar.

We are in an interesting area rich in history. A plaque on the wall of the neighbouring No. 7, attests to the fact that Mozart lived in the house from 1780 to 1781, and completed *Idomeneo* there. These days people still combine hard work and art in that building, for the patrons of the **Caféandarbeiten** (Handicraft Café) are women who, are busy knitting while enjoying their coffee and cakes. Knitted tarts and pieces of cake in the window indicate this unusual combination of activities. Opposite, in No. 8, François Cuvilliés the Elder, the famous rococo architect, lived and died. In No. 6 lived one of the most famous lawyers of the 18th Century, Freiherr von Kreittmayr.

The First City Fortress

The Burgstraße leads into the **Alten Hof**, which was built in the 13th century by Duke Ludwig II, as the first Wittelsbach residence. Later it became the imperial residence. Today the former fortress serves as a venue for cultural events and also as a welcome resting place with its shady trees and fountain. From here one can see the well-preserved tower gate with its beautiful Gothic alcove. There is probably nowhere else in the city where one can visualise what Munich was like in the Middle Ages.

After the historical delights, it's back to everday life, as we return to the

Burgstraße and by Cafe Handarbeiten we go under a small archway where we'll find a door into the **Zerwirkgewölbe**. Since 1733, game has been sold and processed here. Today it is a delicatessen, and at lunchtime you can taste its specialties of venison and game birds. The house was originally built in the 13th century, and belonged to the first Hofbräuhaus during the late Middle Ages.

The World's Most Famous Pub

We cross the **Sparkassenstraße** into **Ledererstraße** where the old Munich is rapidly being replaced by souvenir shops, bars and cabarets. Tourists are drawn here by the proximity of the Hofbräuhaus—here commerce has taken over from culture. On the left and through the Orlandostraße, we come to perhaps the most famous pub in the world. The Hofbräuhaus was moved to the Platzl in 1644, and only after 1830 was it open to the public. The nearby **Platzl** People's Theatre used to be a famous theatre where locals like Weiß Ferdl, Blädel Schorsch and Michl Lang performed.

From the Platzl, we turn left into Pfisterstraße and come to the **Münze** (mint). This trapesoidal building was commissioned by Duke Albrecht V and built between 1563 and 1567. Until the 19th century, the ground floor served as stables for the royal parties. From 1809 it was taken over as the state mint. Today it is the seat of the **Bayerische Landesamt für Denkmalpflege** (Bavarian Administrative Office for the Upkeep of Memorials).

After the **Hofgraben**, we come to one of the finest areas of the city, the **Maximilianstraße**. To the left, the majestic **Max-Joseph-Platz** opens out, in the centre of which is the memorial to King Max I. The area is surrounded by the most glorious buildings. Firstly there is the **Nationaltheater** with its imposing classical columns, the work of Karl von Fischer. It was burnt down five years after its opening, and then later rebuilt by Leo von Klenze. This theatre, which can seat over 2000, is an important opera house today, and the high point of the season is the **Opernfestspiele** (Opera Festival) in the summer.

Munich's Treasury

The neighbouring **Residenz** (Palace), was modelled on the Palazzo Pitti in Florence, and built by Leo von Klenze between 1826 and 1835. This royal residence comprises many inner courtyards, halls and chambers. Ludwig I lived here with his wife. Today one entrance leads to the **Residenz Museum** (Palace Museum) and to the **Schatzkammer** (Treasury). The latter houses one of the most important collections of ecclesiastical and secular treasures in Europe. There are

Carnival time in the Innenstadt.

142

Entrance
to the
Residenz
with the
bronze
memorial
of the first
Bavarian
king, Max I
Joseph.

crowns, goblets, medallions, necklaces, crucifixes, altars, swords and of course the royal insignia of Bavaria—the king's crown, the queen's crown, the imperial orb, sceptre and sword and the seal chest.

There is the magnificent crystal shrine of Duke Albrecht V, Empress Marie Louise's exquisite filigree travelling set, a gift from the city to Napoleon I's second wife. The many knives, forks, scissors and small boxes and bottles fit neatly into the drawers and compartments of this beautiful set.

The **Residenzmuseum** offers a great variety of exhibitions and examples of Munich courtly art. There is enough to fill a book, but we will confine ourselves to the highlights. Above all, there is the **Antiquarium**, which is the largest Renaissance room north of the Alps, and today a venue for glittering state occasions. There is also the Wittelsbach **Ahnengalerie** (Ancestral Portrait Gal-

lery) by Joseph Effner, with an extensive family tree. Then there's the **Porzellankabinett**, a porcelain cabinet by Cuvilliés with Meissen and Nymphenburg creations. Or the **Reichen Zimmer**, rich rococo rooms also by Cuvilliés. There is an unending list of treasures. The Brunnenhof (Fountain Court) must not be forgotten, with the Wittelsbacher Brunnen (Fountain), and the neighbouring Alte Residenztheater (Old Palace Theatre) better known as the **Cuvilliés Theater**, a small but highly ornate rococo building. The **Neue Herkulessaal**, which was formerly the throne room, is now a glorious concert hall for classical music performances.

"Profane" Buildings

On the south side of the Max-Joseph-Platz is another imposing building which cannot compete with its neigh-

bours in terms of cultural importance. The **Hauptpost** (Main Post Office) was begun in 1747 and completed in 1758, and was the palace of Count von Toerring-Jettenbach. After alteration by Leo von Klenze in 1838, it became the main post office.

The Residenzstraße

The **Residenzstraße** leads past the entrance, with a marked contrast between the imposing Residenz on the right side, and a row of expensive shops on the left. At the corner with Viscardistraße stands the **Preysing-Palais**, not to be confused with the building of the same name in the Prannerstraße. Master builder Joseph Effner constructed this for the Count Maximilian von Preysing-Hohenaschau between 1723 and 1728. Immediately behind this palace is the **Feldherrnhalle**, (Military Commanders' Hall) a building in the classic style, modelled on the Loggia dei Lanzi in Florence. In the outer archway are two statues of famous generals, one of Count Tilly, military commander in the Thirty Years' War, and one of Prince Wrede, who was victorious against the French in 1814. Inside, the military theme is reflected in a memorial to the Bavarian army of 1870-71. In 1923, Adolf Hitler marched through the inner city to this Feldherrnhalle with his numerous followers, but his attempt ended in a shooting and considerable loss of life. Years later, Hitler erected a memorial here, with a guard of honour, to whom the famous Hitler salute was to be given. Because many people at that time preferred to avoid this street by taking Viscardigasse instead, it came to be known as Drückerbergstraße or Dodge Street.

In front of the Feldherrnhalle is the **Odeonsplatz**, the end of our walk. The square is dominated by the **Theatinerkirche**, which Prince Elector Ferdinand Maria had built in 1662 in gratitude for the birth of his long-awaited heir Max Emanuel. The church was consecrated in 1675 but the building, begun by Barelli and Zucalli, had to wait almost another century before it received its splendid rococo facade, by François Cuvilliés the Elder. Inside is the dark wooden pulpit, beautifully carved by Andreas Faistenburger; Maria with the infant Jesus at the high altar, and a glorious painting by Caspar de Crayer, a pupil of Rubens. In the crypt are buried several of the Wittelsbach rulers, among them being Prince Elector Max Emanuel and his parents Ferdinand Maria and Henriette, the first king of Bavaria, Max I Joseph and Crown Prince Rupprecht of Bavaria.

Back to the present day. From the Odeonsplatz, the visitor can look straight down the wide, imposing Ludwigstraße to the Siegestor (Victory Gate) towards the direction of Schwabing. But of course, that's another chapter altogether.

Left, traces of splendour in the fountain court of the Residenz. Right, the imposing Theatiner Church.

BEER GARDENS

Mention Munich, and people think of beer gardens. Beer has been brewed here for centuries, in accordance with the Law of Purity of 1516, from barley, hops and water. A bit of yeast is added too, but nothing else. Normal beer, light beer, that is, has a little less alcohol than the north German beer, or the English. That's why it is drunk out of the world famous *Maß*, or litre beer mug. And you don't stop at one *Maß* either. If you are going home by bicycle, then you can have a *Radlermaß* or (mug for the bike) which is half beer, half lemonade. Then there's a *Russe*, a mixture of weiß beer and lemonade, which got its name from the Munich Red Guards, who first introduced the mixture in 1918. There's dark beer too, and even, paradoxically, dark *weiß* beer. *Weiß* beer is what the people of Munich call *Weizenbeer*, or wheat beer, which is usually light and sparkling. Then there's *Pils* and *Märzenbier*, *Bock*, and in the spring, the *Doppelbock* (Double Bock), which has 20 percent wort. You can even have non-alcoholic beer, but that's hardly ever served in the beer gardens—it just wouldn't be the same. For the people of Munich, the beer garden is a serious matter, almost like Sunday mass.

Why beer gardens? Well, you need them because of the climate. As the cultural philosopher Wilhelm Hausenstein remarked in 1949, "the heavy air brings on a terrible thirst, which cannot be quenched by wine or water, only by beer." Beer and air and there you have it, a beer garden. That's all you need. Brass bands have no place in a real beer garden. Nor do you need sun umbrellas, concrete floors or paper plates, and as every true Bavarian knows, there's definitely no place in a real Munich beer garden for a small beer. "Come back when you're thirsty." is what you'll be told by the barman if you ask for anything less than a *Maß*. A *Maß* will cost between DM 5.40 and 7.50, and then you can have pretzels, sausages, radishes or snacks as well. But you don't need all that. Since the days of Ludwig I, it has been the custom that

you can bring your own snack with you to the beer garden. All you have to buy from the landlord is the beer itself. When you order a Maß, what you get is a litre of light beer although since 1970, there has been a watch dog association to ensure that the measure is correct, the Maß is in fact not always full. This isn't cheating. During peak periods, a 200 litre barrel is emptied in twelve minutes. After all, five million hectolitres of beer is what the Münchner Bräuerei (Munich Brewery) gets through during a season. So sometimes when things are really hectic, the Maß might be a bit less full than on a quiet autumn afternoon. But who's going to complain? If you do say something, you're likely to be asked why foam wasn't part of the beer too. You don't want to rub the locals up the wrong way after all, so relax and enjoy the shade beneath the chestnut trees, and say *Prost* to your neighbour. Take time to sip the beer, and maybe one of the locals will tell you how it all started.

He'd say it all began because the brewer had to keep his beer cool. So cellars were dug, on the sloping right bank of the Isar, and on the hilly part of the city near the station. So that the sun didn't turn the beer in spite of the underground storage, chestnut trees were planted above the area. People sat under the trees because it was too hot in the sun, when you had your first *Maß* of the day. Ten in the evening was closing time. It still is 200 years later. No beer garden—no real one —is open after eleven at night. But nowadays a real beer gaden can't have the cellar below. It soon became obvious just how popular a beer garden was, and more and more of them were set up. The largest is the Hirschgarten (Deer Park) which can seat 8,500. In Neuhausen there's the Taxisgarten, the Concordia-Park and few smaller gardens. One of the most popular with the locals is the garden at the Chinesischer Turm (Chinese Tower) in the Englischer Garten (English Garden) which seats 7000 and has a merry-go-round for the children. Near the "Turm" is the Kleinhesseloher See (Lake) with the Seegarten (Lake Garden). Then it's not far to the Osterwaldgarten and the beer garden in Hirschau. For those who like to walk or cycle, do what Thomas Mann did and go to Aumeister. On the other side of the Isar is the Sankt-Emmeramsmühle or the Haidhauser Hofbräu-Keller on Wiener Platz, the Salvator-Keller on the main road or the Menterschwaige. Of course there are lovely beer gardens outside the city, but you don't have

Pasing, in the Fasanerie or the Flaucher in the Max-Emanuel behind the university, or in the Neue Schießstätte in Obersendling or in the garden at the Perlacher Forschungsbräuerei (Perlach Research Brewery). And we've only mentioned the main ones. In fact you only go into one beer garden a day. You have to fight for a place sometimes but once you're settled, that's it. The city with all its noise and bustle seems far away; the first *Maß* tastes good, but the

to go that far. Right next to the station is the Augustiner-Keller, which has room for 5000 drinkers and the Löwenbräu-Garten is not too far away.

If you're in the Innenstadt (inner city), you can simply sit in the Viktualienmarkt (Victuals Market), and then move on to the Hofbräuhaus. But you can get a *Maß* just as well in Obermenzing at the Altr Wirt (Old Innkeeper) or at the Landsberger Hof in

Men, women, Prussians and locals all together in the beer garden.

second even better. Even class distinctions become unimportant, as men, women, Japanese, Americans, even Prussians and locals drink together. Black and white, yellow and brown, all drink together, as the children run around. The atmosphere gets cozier, the service gets better, and you need another beer. Pity those who live nearby and complain about the noise. But there's nothing else the residents can do because in 1985, the Administrative Court of Munich decided that beer gardens were in the interest of the public. You can't argue with that!

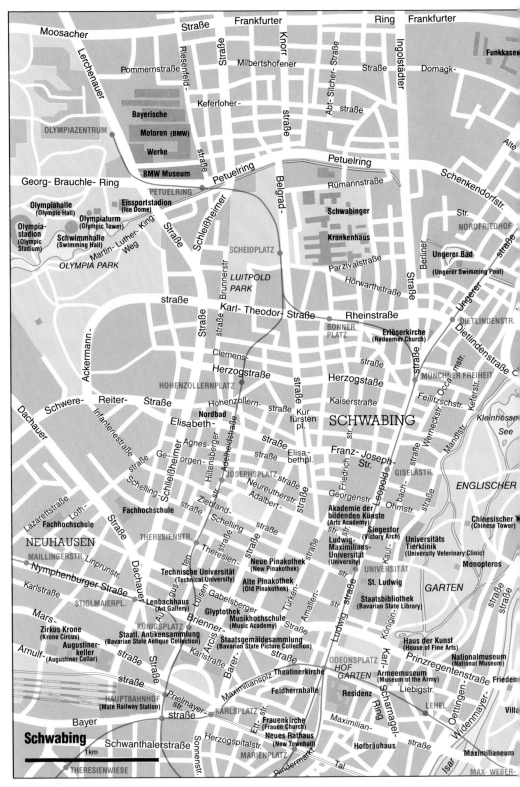

Moosacher

Straße Frankfurter Ring Frankfurter

Straße

Lerchenauer

Pommernstraße Riesenfeld- Milbertshofener Knorr Abt- Stlcher- Straße Straße Ingolstädter Domagk- Funkkase

Keferloher- straße

straße

OLYMPIAZENTRUM

Bayerische

Motoren (BMW)

Werke straße

BMW Museum Petuelring Petuelring Schenkendorfstr.

PETUELRING Belgrad- Rümannstraße Str.

Georg- Brauchle- Ring NORDFRIEDHOF

Olympiahalle Eissportstadion Schwabinger alte
(Olympic Hall) (Ice Dome) Berliner

Olympia- Olympiaturm Schleißheimer Krankenhaus Ungerer Bad
stadion (Olympic Tower) SCHEIDPLATZ (Ungerer Swimming Pool)
(Olympic Schwimmhalle Martin- Luther- King- Parzivalstraße Ungerer
Stadium) (Swimming Hall) Weg Straße

OLYMPIA PARK LUITPOLD Hörwarthstraße DIETLINDENSTR.
Straße PARK

straße Brunnerstr. Karl- Theodor- Straße Rheinstraße Dietlindenstraße
Straße BONNER Erlöserkirche MÜNCHNER FREIHEIT
Straße PLATZ (Redeemer Church) Occamstr.

Ackermann- Clemens- straße Keferstr.

Schwere- Reiter- Straße Herzogstraße Herzogstaße Feilitzschstr. Wenckstr. Kleinhesse
HOHENZOLLERNPLATZ Kaiserstraße Mandlstr. See

Dachauer Infanteriestraße Hohenzollern- straße Kur SCHWABING
Nordbad fürsten Wenckstr. Leopold-
Elisabeth- pl. Friedrich- bach- ENGLISCHER
Ge- orgen- Elisa- Franz- Joseph- Ohmstr. straße
Lazarettstraße Loth- straße bethpl. Str. Georgenstr. GISELASTR.
Schleißheimer straße JOSEPHSPLATZ straße Akademie der Chinesischer T
Fachhochschule Hiltensberger Neureutherstr. bildenden Künste Siegestor (Chinese Tower)
Adelheidstraße Adalbert- (Arts Academy) (Victory Arch) Universitäts-
NEUHAUSEN Fachhochschule Ziebland- Str. Ludwig- Tierklinik
Schelling straße Maximilians- (University Veterinary Clinic)
MAILLINGERSTR. THERESIENSTR. Schelling Universität Monopteros
Nymphenburger Straße Theresien- (University) UNIVERSITÄT
Karlstraße Luisen Türken- Amalien- St. Ludwig GARTEN straße straße
Technische Universität Gabelsberger Staatsbibliothek
Mars- (Technical University) (Bavarian State Library)
Zirkus Krone STIGLMAIERPL. Lenbachhaus Alte Pinakothek Ludwig
(Krone Circus) Augustiner- (Art Gallery) (Old Pinakothek) Haus der Kunst
Augustiner Brienner- Glyptothek Musikhochschule König- (House of Fine Arts)
keller KÖNIGSPLATZ Neue Pinakothek (Music Academy) Nationalmuseum
Arnulf- (Augustiner Cellar) straße Staatl. Antikensammlung (New Pinakothek) (National Museum)
straße Arcis- (Bavarian State Antique Collection) Staatsgemäldesammlung Prinzregentenstraße Frieden
Karlstraße (Bavarian State Picture Collection) ODEONSPLATZ Armeemuseum
straße Straße Barer- Theatinerkirche HOF (Museum of the Army)
straße Maximiliansplatz GARTEN Liebigstr. Villa
HAUPTBAHNHOF Prielmayer- Feldherrnhalle Residenz LEHEL
(Main Railway Station) str. Elt- Scharnagel-
Bayer Frauenkirche Maximilian- Oettingen- Maximilianeum
Schwanthalerstraße (Frauen Church) Ring straße Widenmayer-
Schwabing Herzogspitalstr. Neues Rathaus Hofbräuhaus Isar MAX- WEBER-
1km Sonnenstr. (New Townhall) Pindermarkt Tal
THERESIENWIESE MARIENPLATZ

150

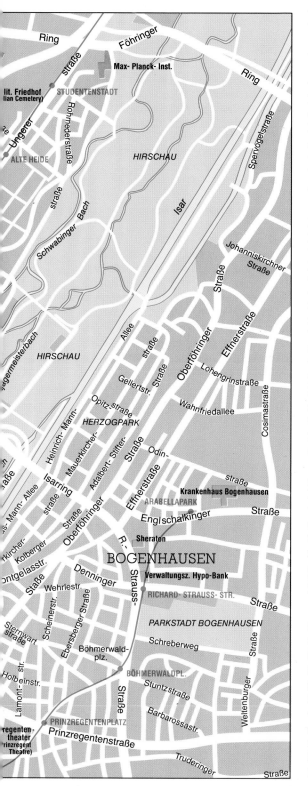

LEGENDARY SCHWABING

No other part of Munich has been written about as much as Schwabing. Never mind who lived, wrote, painted or agitated here. Whether it is Thomas Mann or Lenin, Paul Klee or Trotsky, all agree with Countess Zu Reventlow who said "Schwabing is much more than part of a city; Schwabing is a state of mind", just before World War I.

Contemporary columnist Siegfried Sommer opines: "Schwabing isn't the heart of the city, it's the belly." The poet P.P. Althaus, who remembers the old Schwabing, refused to go out of his house on Leopoldstraße, as a protest against what was going on outside his front door. Still, it's true to say that no road leads past Schwabing, and in fact the erstwhile village has grown. The only clear delimitation of Schwabing is that given by the postal service. According to those officials, Schwabing, or District 40, stretches from the Englischer Garten (English Garden) in the east to Schleißheimer Straße in the west, and from Ungerer Bad in the north to the Siegestor (Victory Gate) in the south.

Schwabing's greatest contrast may be seen at the junction of Ludwig and Leopold streets, where two different worlds meet. If Ludwigstraße represents the 19th century royal Munich, then Leopoldstraße is the epitome of the modern city. Schwabing actually begins after the Siegestor. But the gate can hardly be taken as a boundary, as Karl Valentin said "It's open day and night."

In legendary Schwabing, the centre for artists, revolutionaries and writers used to be in the Maxvorstadt (Max Suburb), near the university. The actual Schwabing had its origin in the narrow streets behind the Münchner Freiheit (Munich Freedom). Also part of Schwabing are the residential and business districts in the north, the Englischer Garten and the Königsplatz (King's Square), where the great museums of Munich are found.

THE LUDWIGSTRASSE

Leaving the Feldherrnhalle, Theatinerkirche (Theatiner Church) and the old city of Munich behind, you look towards the **Ludwigstraße** as far as the Siegestor (Victory Gate), which looks near enough to touch. But that's an illusion, for the Ludwigstraße is over a kilometre long. With its uniform facades, it was innovative of 19th century city planning. On fine days, you could feel as if you were on an Italian torso.

Until he began his reign in 1825, Ludwig I regarded this street as his private project—begun under his father Max I. Joseph—to further the expansion of the city. The Maximiliansplatz was then known as the "Sahara". In those days, it was simply the beginning of what was later to become the new suburb, the Max-Vorstadt.

In 1816, Ludwig I commissioned Leo von Klenze with the planning and completion of all the main buildings. What Schinkel was to Berlin, Klenze was to Munich. With Friedrich von Gärtner, he designed these glorious buildings between 1816 and 1852 to create one of the most important and harmonious architectural ensembles in Europe.

Rome of the Future

Klenze was fascinated by the enormous planned cities of ancient Rome and the Renaissance. He preferred geometrical form and with architecture of austere strength, he attempted to realise the king's idea of a street of modern times. It is true that this monument of city planning, remains rather uninviting today, even if one imagines it without traffic. Shops and restaurants were never part of the plan for this

Preceding pages, view from the Leopold-straße to Victory Gate. Below, The Feldherrn-halle.

street. In the Odeonsplatz, there is the **Hofgartencafé**, the cinema and a few shops to soften the cold atmosphere of the street. The tiny **Cafe an der Uni** has nestled in between the Ludwigskirche (Ludwig's Church) and the university. But apart from those shops, ministerial and administrative buildings dominate in contrast to the side streets where the pompous style had no place. However, these great edifices stood alone when they were first constructed.

An indication of the southern-end style of the Ludwigstraße was given in one of Klenze's earliest works, the **Leuchtenberg-Palais** (Odeonsplatz 4), which is now the Bavarian Ministry of Finance Building. Next door is the **Innenministerium** (Ministry of the Interior), both heavily guarded by security police. Eugéne Beauharnais, the original owner, was clever enough to build his palace in such a way and in such a central position, that it could

easily be converted into a hotel in times of revolution. In front of it is the Ludwig I memorial of 1862. Directly opposite is the **Odeon** (Odeonsplatz 3), built after the other buildings had been completed and was modelled after Leuchtenberg-Palais. Grand concerts and lavish balls were held here until World War II.

The Hofgarten

The park behind the Odeon stretches out to the heavily damaged hall of the **Armeemuseum** (Army Museum) of 1900-1905, where a house of Bavarian history and the chancellery of the Premier are planned. There has been much opposition to these plans, as the buildings would ruin the park. The enormous cupola of the Armeemuseum is on an axis with the small **Hofgarten-Tempel**, the centre of this symmetrically-designed park, which was laid out in 1613-1617 on the lines of an Italian formal garden.

During the 18th century, vegetables for the court were grown here, and it was not until 1780 that it became one of the first parks to be opened to the public. On the cupola of the twelve-sided pavilion, now covered with verdigris, is a copy of the **Bronze-Bavaria** figure of Hubert Gerhard (the original is in the Residenzmuseum). The Hofgarten itself is surrounded by archways. On either side of the entrance are **Klenzes Arkaden** (Klenze's Arcade), with frescoes of the history of Bavaria and the Wittelbachs, designed by Peter Cornelius. Karl Rottman's frescoes used to be here too, before they were transferred to the Residnezmuseum.

Following the arcades to the left, one passes display windows of some of the best shops in town. On the northern side is the **Theatermuseum** (Theatre Museum) at Galeriestraße 4, which houses an interesting collection of documents relating to the history of the theatre: manuscripts, libretti, historical records, sketches for costumes and sets, as well

Entrance to the Bavarian State Library.

153

as the largest Wagner collection after Bayreuth. A few steps further, you are confronted by Richard Seewald's **Ideallandscahften** (Ideal Landscapes), which were executed in weather resistant colours in 1961. Beneath are verses from Homer, Pindar, Sappho and Hölderlin—which nobles oblige—bring the Hofgarten to a stylish end.

Fascist Alterations

The **Galeriestraße** is often the last (vain) hope for motorists desperately searching for somewhere to park. But even this great street did not survive the fascist period unscathed. In the 1930s, in order to make an imposing approach to the **Haus der Kunst** (House of Art), the **Von-der-Tann-Straße** was cut through the Ludwigstraße. The Zentralministerium (Central Ministry) building replaced Klenze's two apartment buildings of 1820-1825. Today,

the **Landwirtschaftministerium** (Ministry of Agriculture) is housed in this building. In the courtyard of the building on 25 May 1945, two members of the *Feiheitsaktion Bayern* (Bavarian Freedom Movement)—Lt. Roth and Major Caracciola-Delbrück—were shot by the SS. Sadly, there is still no memorial plaque to commemorate that tragic incident.

After crossing the Von-der-Tann-Straße, one passes the **Geschwister-Scholl-Institut**, the Political Science Department of the University. In the next building, one can look out through a window onto the small but exquisite building of the library of the **Institut für Bayersiche Geschichte** (Institute of Bavarian History), built by Klenze in 1827-1830, which was once the Ministry of War building.

These institutes of learning, and the many students on bikes, indicate that one is now in the university area of

View from the Hofgarten Temple to the Theatiner Church.

Munich. The wider pavement near the Staatsbibliosthek (State Library) is always full of students. But not all these features alter the character of the Ludwigstraße at this point. In 1832, Leo von Klenze had to leave after quarrelling with his employer Ludwig I. His successor, Friedrich von Gärtner, completed this monumental street. He created the Staatsbibliothek, the Ludwigskirche (Ludwig's Church), the University and the Siegestor (Victory Gate). He loved the architecture of the Middle Ages, with its round and pointed arches, and thus the stretch of the Ludwigstraße from the Von-der-Tann-Straße to the Siegestor turned out more sophisticated without losing its bright atmosphere.

Friedrich Gärtner's Bowl Fountain in front of the University.

Book Exhibitions

Easily recognisable from afar is the **Staatsbibliothek** (Ludwigstraße 16) with its statues of the ancient thinkers, Thucydides, Homer, Aristotle and Hippocrates. Despite the tumult of traffic around them, they maintain their pose of deep contemplation. The facade of this 1832-1842 building was modelled on the Palazzo Strozzi in Florence and inside, the immense staircase is a copy of the Scala dei Giganti in the Doge's Palace in Venice. This leads to the reading room, which one may enter after showing identification papers. Book exhibitions are held in the foyer and their schedules are sometimes listed in the calendar of events.

For those with little or no interest in the written word, there's a café in the basement, where one can sit outside if the weather is fine. The Bayerische Staatsbibliothek was founded on the collection of Wilhelm IV, and the building itself was a result of the dissolution of the cloisters of the Land in 1806. In order to keep the various collections together, this building was constructed.

With almost seven million volumes, it is now reputed to be one of the largest libraries in the world.

Next to the library is the **Ludwigskirche** which was consecrated in 1844. With its bright twin-tower facade, its wide gabled-front, niches with figures, and round arch windows, it is a hodgepodge of neo-romantic and New Gothic styles. The two slender towers contrast with the baroque style of the Theatinerkirche (Theatiner Church). Inside, the second largest fresco in the world, takes after Michelangelo's in the Sistine Chapel. The *Last Judgement* was painted by Peter Cornelius and took him from 1836 to 1840. Ludwig I proudly asserted that after the masters of the Italian Renaissance, there was no painter like "his Cornelius". Nevertheless, any comparison with Michelangelo's paintings must be one of size for in terms of quality, there can be no real comparison.

The University

In 1826, Ludwig I moved the University of Bavaria from Landshut to Munich. While study continued in the Alten Jesuitenkolleg (Old Jesuit College) in Neuhauser Straße, Gärtner built the university buildings on either side of the Ludwigstraße. On the side of the Englischer Garten (English Garden) is the **Georgianum**, initially a seminary for priests but is now the Law School. Opposite, on Geschwister-Scholl-Platz (Scholl Sibling Square), is the huge main building of the university. It was on this square with its two bowl-shaped fountains that large groups of restless students gathered and staged demonstrations for weeks in the late 1960s. Fortunately, those dark days are of course gone, though not forever.

Through the main entrance, we get to the Lichthof (patio) of the university, which is worth seeing. There is a memo-

In the Lichthof of the University.

rial plaque to the Scholls, Hans and Sophie, who with other students, Christoph Probst, Alexander Schmorell, Willi Graf and the Professor of Music, Kurt Huber, made up the resistance group called *Weiße Rose* (White Rose). On 18 February 1943, the caretaker spotted them distributing pamphlets from the upper storey to the patio and reported to the Nazis. The propaganda was uncovered, the resistance members were sentenced to death and thereafter executed.

Today, the university is one of the largest in the Federal Republic of Germany with about 60,000 students who study here despite all the disadvantages of such a massive campus. The authorities tried to attract some of the students to other Bavarian universities, but it was in vain. Each year the number of students in Munich grows. Although the university brought life to this part of the city, its presence is a mixed blessing. In-

Winter in The Monopteros.

stitutes sprang up all over the area, and rooms and apartments were rented to acquire more space. Even the new buildings in Theresienstraße and Schellingstraße 3 failed to offer a long-term solution to the problem. Fortunately, the stream of students has of late become manageable for the concerned authorities.

The Ludwigstraße ends at the Siegestor (Victory Gate) which was built in 1843-1850 without, in fact, a victory to commemorate. Ludwig I was no supporter of the military, and this memorial to the army was more a gesture of reconciliation, as much more had been spent on construction than on cannons. The Siegestor was a replica of the Roman Constantine Arch, which had been badly damaged during World War II and only provisionally restored. It served as a reminder of zero-hour and of the ruined city, out of the ashes of which modern Munich arose.

In The Englischer Garten

Crown Prince Ludwig commissioned Franz Schwanthaler in 1803 to create a statue of a youth for the Englischer Garten (English Garden. It is now in the arcade of the Hofgarten, and the inscription below it read something like a park rule: "Wander innocently here, then return to your duties refreshed!"

One may well doubt whether those who planned and completed this "Volksgarten" (People's Park) have in fact been entirely successful in achieving their aim. For some

It was wholly the idea of Lieutenant General Sir Benjamin Thomson, later known as the Count of Rumford, who came from America to make Munich his second home. He had the idea of creating a kind of allotment for the soldiers, who in peacetime had nothing to do. Each soldier was supposed to tend his own cabbage patch. But the soldiers had other ideas, not being too keen on the hard work entailed by the creation of the garden, and so the planners widened their

people don't find what goes on here "innocent" at all, as the "wanderers" refresh themselves before they return to their duties. Some of them find it necessary to take off their clothes and sunbathe completely naked, to regain strength for work. The "nudists" in the Englischer Garten are an inevitable part of the summer tabloid tittletattle. Are they natural figures in a kind of idealised Bavarian-Greek grove or simply a public nuisance? The fact remains that this nude sunbathing is the most controversial activity in the Englischer Garten.

concept to a "People's Park...where people were able to enjoy one another's company, and those of different classes could draw nearer together in the bosom of nature."

However, the "natural beauty" had to be created first. This five-km long stretch along the Isar was still in its original condition at the end of the 18th century, and was used by the Wittelsbachs as a hunting ground, and a deer pasture (the name Hirschau or Deer Meadow is a reminder of those days). The court gardener, Friedrich Ludwig Sckell wanted to make a huge natural composition, with specially constructed landscape and secondary features, various bridges. Some ideas which were partly based on Thomson's original plans for a model farm were included, such as a sheep farm, a nursery and a veterinary school.

If you stroll through the Englischer Garten today, you'll find not only a wonderful place of natural beauty, but also some rather misappropriated "ideas on the education of the people" from the age of enlightenment. In for equestrians, and plenty of room for football matches and evening strolls.

What the sentimental and early Romantic founding fathers hoped to achieve with their ethnic buildings, such as the wooden *Chinesischer Turm* (Chinese Tower), namely familiarisation with foreign cultures, now happens spontaneously in the beer garden of the same name, where people of all nations mingle freely. Perhaps this excuses the people of Munich a little for their neglect of

the Monopteros, Leo von Klenze's Roman-style temple, the landmark of the garden, you can often hear a "jam" session by buskers. In the Sixties, it was the venue for hippies and "flower power" people from all over the world. But whether it was in the spirit of the founders, the Englischer Garten has truly become a people's park, where people do as they please. The angler can fish in the Kleinhesseloher Lake, there are enjoyable rides

Left, sipping beer by the Chinese Tower. Above, in good company on the Kleinhesseloher Lake.

the Japanese Tea House with its enactment of the famous tea ceremony, and their preference for a beer and a snack *am Turm* (at the Tower). But they do chat with the foreigners at the next table when they get a chance, not only to find out how other folks live, but also to extol the virtues of the Englischer Garten in particular, and of Munich in general.

That the odd *Maß* is consumed here under this Bavarian-Chinese-English sky is by the bye. Whether this has a beneficial effect on work in the afternoon, only the silent youth of Schwanthaler knows.

Dies Blatt gehört dem Staatsanwalt!

Jahrgang   **Preis 20 Pfg.**   Nummer

SIMPLICISSIMUS

Abonnement vierteljährlich 2 Mk. 25 Pfg.   **Illustrierte Wochenschrift**   Bayr. Post-Zeitungsliste: No. 88t

Billige Ausgabe   Billige Ausgabe

(Alle Rechte vorbehalten.)

Dies ist das Hundevieh,

(Zeichnung von Th. Th. Heine.)

welches so unsägliches Elend über unser Vaterland gebracht hat und von allen anständigen deutschen Wappentieren verabscheut wird.

ART, CABARETS AND REVOLUTIONARIES

If you don't want to wander along the Leopoldstraße from the Siegestor, and don't feel like lying on the grass in the Englischer Garten, you could try discovering a part of the old Schwabing in the area behind the University. Much of what remains of the reputation of this famous part of the city is now almost a cliché, and the area of Amalien, Türken, Schelling and Barer streets where the agitators of old once lived, is now populated mainly by students. Nowadays just a few historical places serve as a reminder of this district's fascinating past. During the week, the place is always lively with crowds of people in the streets. You'll find plenty of shops for new and second-hand books, and a good variety of pubs and cafés.

One of the most lively streets is **Sch-ellingstraße**. First you pass the modern concrete complex at No. 3, where you'll hear a babble of different languages, as the university philologists share the building with foreign bookshops. Then you'll come to a pub which has been kept exactly as it was in the 1970s, the **Atzinger** at No. 9. **Kitsch und Kunst** (Kitsch and Art) is what you'll find a bit further on and then English and American literature in **Words' Worth** in a lovely renovated 1888 courtyard house. If you like old books and engravings, you will enjoy browsing in **Hauser** (No. 17) and **Kitzinger** (No. 15).

Billiard Tables and Roast Pork

The **Schelling-Salon** has a natural relaxed atmosphere, with its billiard tables and roast pork, is a home away from home for many an unattached student on Sundays. You can get a real insight into the life of a 1900 Schwabing

Preceding pages, *Almanac of the Blue Riders* group; cover of *Simplicissimus.* Below, playing billiards in the Schelling Salon.

162

artist in **Kaffeehaus Alt Schwabing** (Old Schwabing Coffee House) at No. 56 with its Viennese style and stucco. On the other side of the road is the **Münchner Buchgewerbehaus** (Munich Printing House) at Nos. 39-43. Where the Völkischer Beobachter was once printed, is now where the Bildzeitung is produced. During the anti-Springer demonstrations here in the 1960s, two people lost their lives.

A few houses along, at No. 49, is the birthplace of the Bavarian politician Franz Joseph Strauß. "Osteria Bavaria", a little further on, was Hitler's local. It has changed its nationality (thank goodness!) and is now the **Osteria Italiana** (No. 62), easily one of the best Italian restaurants in and around Munich.

From here to the Schleißheimerstraße lies one of the largest residential areas of Schwabing. The abandoned **Alte Nordfriedhof** (Old North Cemetery) in this neighbourhood now serves as a recreation area for the young and the old.

National Socialist Buildings

If one turns from Schellingstraße into Arcisstraße in a southerly direction, one passes the **Technische Hochschule** (Technical High School) at Arcisstraße 21, which was first opened in 1868 and then later extended between the wars. The naked horsetamer by Bernhard Bleeker still stands next to the main entrance of the university, a relic of National Socialist aesthetic ideals. In the 1930s, his nudity caused outrage in the Catholic Church. Today, despite their hideousness, he and his companion on the other side of the road do not bother anyone. Also of National Socialist origin are the two buildings further down the Arcisstraße, divided by Briennerstraße. The **Staatliche Hochschule für Musik** (State Musical High School)

The *Basis* bookshop in Adalbertstraße.

was built in the 1930s as a Führer-gebäude (Building for the Führer) for Hitler. It was here that the Munich Agreement of 1938 was signed. The NSDAP ruled in those days from where the state graphic collection, the **Staatliche Graphische Sammlung**, is housed today at Meiserstraße 10.

From Alten Simpl to Max-Emanuel

We'll turn back to the lively atmosphere of Türkenstraße. There are many inviting streetcafés here where students patronise in the summer between lectures. There are the cinemas and the shopping bazaars. Some of the shops here sell the Indian ethnic clothes and handicrafts of the Woodstock era. If the noise of the Türkenstraße is too much, you can enjoy the peace of one of the three inner courtyards of the **Amalienpassage**, a rare success in modern city planning. Also in Türkenstraße is one of the best cinemas, the **ARRI**. But if the weather is too good for a film, you can always head for the shady beer garden of the **Max Emanuel-Bräuerei** (Max Emanuel Brewery) and listen to the folksongs of the *Münchner Volkssängerbühne*.

The Akademiestraße is dominated by the **Akademie der bildenden Künste** (Academy of Fine Arts), which opened in 1886 and attracted foreign students to Schwabing. Opposite, in house No. 15, Bertolt Brecht lived with his friend Arnolt Bronnen during the 1920s. Brunnen was the dramatic adviser then at the Kammerspiele (Little Theatre) in the Augustinerstraße, where Brecht's *Trommeln in der Nacht* (Drums in the Night) was first staged.

Still worth a visit is Kathi Kobus's pub of 1903, **Zum alten Simpl**, which was the centre of bohemian life in Schwabing. Joachim Ringelnatz was for a long time the house poet here. One day,

The *Alten Simpl* in better times.

however, he opened his own Taback-haus zum Hausdichter (Tobacco House of the House Poet) at 23 Schelling-straße. His main attraction was a skeleton lying in the window. This must have frightened his clients away, for business turned out bad. In grief, Ringelnatz left his business. The shelves were still stocked full, the door wide open, but he simply walked out.

Bohemian Life in Schwabing

The name "Simpl" given to Kathi Kobus's artists' meeting place came from a satirical periodical named *Simplicissimus*, founded in 1896 by Albert Langen and Th. Heine. It attacked prudence and intolerance with mock caricatures and sharp satire. Almost every author of that period who lived in Schwabing and who fought against narrow-mindedness, wrote for the paper. Some of the writers later became well-known,

Solitary figure at the old north cemetery.

like Thomas Mann, Rilke, Wedekind and Ludwig Thoma, who was thought of by some as the Bavarian Homer. Otherswere less well-known, like Otto Julius Bierbaum, whose quote "Humour is when in spite of it all, you laugh", epitomises the intellectual climate of Schwabing at the turn of the century. Wilhelm Schulz, Eduard Thöny, Olaf Gulbransson and Karl Arnold drew caricatures for *Simplicissimus* which have remained famous to this day.

However, a satirical poem about the Kaiser (Emperor) in 1898, unleashed a scandal which led to a lawsuit. The publisher, Albert Langen fled to Switzerland for three years, while Wedekind and Heine were put behind bars for several months. It was Heine who designed the cover of the magazine, a stumpy red mastiff, baring his teeth, to symbolise that Schwabing was no mere grove of muses, but a political place

where historic events would not pass unnoticed or uncommented upon.

Legacy of the Eleven Executioners

To take the typical German down a peg or two, that was the aim of the *Elf Scarfrichter* (Eleven Executioners) who made up a cabaret in the neighbouring *Zum goldenen Hirschen* (The Golden Stag). They modelled themselves on Aristide Bruant's *Chat Noir* in Paris, with its colourful mix of satire, parodies and songs. To avoid censorship, they declared themselves a society, with no entry fee, but they kept solvent by imposing a hefty cloak-room charge. Among the members was Schwabing's *Brettl-Diva* Marya Delvard, one of the first vamps of the century. Just then, Otto Falckenberg founded the Kammerspiele in a half-ruined house in **Augustenstraße**, thus beginning a reform of Munich theatre.

The *Elf Scarfrichter* no longer exists, but there are many similar cabarets in Schwabing today, who keep up the Off-Off-Theatre tradition. There is the **Studiotheater** at Ungererstraße 19; the **Münchner Lach- und Schießgesellschaft** (Munich Laugh and Shoot Company) at Ursulastraße 9, a cabaret which has become famous all over Germany on television; the **Rationaltheater** (Hesseloher Straße 18); **Tams-Theater am Sozialamt** (Haimhauserstraße 13a); **Theater Heppel & Ettlich** in Kaiserstraße 67 and Munich's oldest cellar theatre, **Theater 44** of Hohenzollernstraße 20.

But at the turn of the century, politics in Schwabing was not confined to the stage. In the autumn of 1900, four Russians came to Munich. They were social revolutionaries, wanted by the Russian secret police, and they slipped underground in the cheerful chaos of *Schwabylon*. Under the alias Meyer,

The Academy of Fine Arts.

Vladimir Ilyich Ulyanov rented a place in Kaiserstraße 46. With his compatriots, he published two periodicals, *Der Funke* (The Spark) and *Die Morgenröte* (The Dawn), and there for the first time he signed himself Lenin. In Munich he also wrote *What Is To Be Done?*", a theoretical precursor of the October Revolution.

Gründerzeit and Jugendstil
(Time of Expansion and Art Nouveau)

Lenin's hiding place was in a part of Schwabing which is still attractive, and worth a visit. In the western part of Schwabing, the centre of which is the **Elisabethplatz** with its market stalls, are some lovely houses of this period of expansion, which are comparable to those on either side of the **Kaiserstraße**.

Sandwiched between Theodor Fischer's magnificent building of the **Volks- und Gewerbeschule** (Techni-

Impressive Jugendstil facade in Ainmillerstraße.

cal High School) of 1901-1902 and the **Theater der Jugend** (Youth Theatre) of the 1950s, is the little beer garden in Schwabing's Viktualienmarkt.

There are two different but equally interesting routes to take through Schwabing. One can cross **Kurfürstenplatz** over to the colourful **Hohenzollernstraße** and visit the old but charming **Filmcafé** and the fascinating courtyard junk shops. Or one can look for the remaining Jugendstil or Art Nouveau facades which serve as a reminder that the style was centred on Schwabing after 1900.

When *Simplicissimus* was founded in 1896, a periodical named *Jugend* (Youth) appeared with such success that an international art movement was named after it. Georg Hirth, founder and publisher of the periodical, said he wanted no more decadence, but "spring, love, engagement, the joy of motherhood, play, sport, mummery, beauty, art and music." But the foundation of the paper was important in another respect; it created an atmosphere of departure. Although older than Munich, Schwabing felt itself rejuvenated through art, and saw itself as "Munich's most beautiful daughter". If one looks at the facades of **Ainmillerstraße 22** (1898) or **Römerstraße 11** or **Franz-Joseph-Straße 19**, one could feel that part of Schwabing at least had succeeded in that aim.

In Ainmillerstraße lived the founders of the *Blue Rider* group of artists—Gabriele Münter, Wassily Kandinsky (No. 36) and Paul Klee (No. 32). Rainer Maria Rilke lived in No. 34. In **Römerstraße 16**, the aesthete Stephan Georg collected a group of young writers around him. The houses at the end of Georgenstraße (No. 4 and No. 10), the **Pacelli-Palais** of 1880-81 (No. 8) and Munich's first rental block in the Jugendstil, **Friedrichstraße 3**, are proof that this area was not inhabited only by bohemians, artists and revolutionaries who rented cheap rooms.

GEISELGASTEIG ISN'T EXACTLY HOLLYWOOD

Even Dwarves Started Small was the title of an early film directed by Werner Herzog, and it could equally apply to Munich's reputation as a film metropolis.

How many people in Munich realise that it was none other than their own best known comedian, Karl Valentin, who set up the first film studio in Munich? In 1912, he rigged up a studio with artificial lights in the cheese store of the trader Bernbichler in Pfister-straße near the Hofbräuhaus.

Karl Valentin had invested all his hard earned cash in five newly developed flood-lights. But the first time he had painstakingly assembled them, through his own clumsiness, they collapsed in a domino effect and all were smashed. Despite this filmworthy beginner's bad luck, Valentin managed to make more than 50 films, half of which may be viewed at particular times and dates at the Filmmuseum on St.-Jakobs-Platz.

Nowadays, however, the Bavaria-Film-studio is one of Germany's largest studios. Its history began in 1919, when the film pioneer Peter Ostermeyer made *Der Ochsenkrieg* (The Oxen War), based on Ludwig Ganghofer's novel, in Geiselgasteig, outside the city gates. Folks preferred sentimental stories to Valentin's scurrilous slapstick in those days. Which was why *Der neue Schreibtisch* (The New Desk), produced by Ostermeyr in 1913, was Valentin's only film ever made in Geiselgasteig.

It wasn't until the 1970s and 1980s that films like the Oscar- winning *Cabaret* with Liza Minelli, Ingmar Bergmann's *Snake's Egg* and *Ace of Aces* with Jean-Paul Belmondo were made outside the Grünwald residential area. The breakthrough into international success came with the studio's own production of *Das Boot* (The Boat). The five-year shooting for Wolfgang Petersen's submarine war spectacular was worthwhile, because it led to the making of films such as *The Never-ending Story* and *Enemy Mine*. Today, the set for *Das Boot* is a tourist attraction. From 1 March to 31 October, the film set is open from 9 a.m. to 4 p.m., and hosts a two-hour tour.

But Geiselgasteig isn't exactly Hollywood. One can't watch stunts or see an actual film being made. But one can walk down the set of the legendary *Berliner Straße*, discover a few film-making secrets, and explore the submarine which was built exactly as the original. The trip to Geiselgasteig (tram 25 from the Hauptbahnhof or Railway Station) is well worthwhile, particularly for children

who love to act or direct, and are allowed to do so behind and in front of the camera. For that special occasion, they "triumph" over evil (grown-ups)—at least for a few moments on video.

The "New German Film" has been declared dead by the critics, but it is supposed to be resurrected in Munich, where in the seventies Rainer Maria Fassbinder, Wim Wenders, Werner Herzog, Volker Schlönddorff among others reached a peak. A new generation of directors with the talent of Doris Dürrie (her first major film *Die*

Männer [The Men] was the last great work to come from the Isar Metropolis) is just not there at the moment. Perhaps Alexander Kluge was right when he said that everything is ready and waiting for a film maker, but there is no one. Perhaps Geiselgasteig is indeed a second Hollywood?

The "event of the year" is the annual Film Festival, held every June since 1983. Under the direction of Eberhard Hauff, it has become an extremely popular event, quite different from the star-studded Cannes Festival. Unlike other festivals, no prizes are awarded. The programme is worth the scramble for tickets, as all kinds of genre films are shown and workshops are held by directors, actors and authors.

Without the Film Museum on St.-Jakobs-Platz, many film buffs would be quite homeless. Here, under the direction of Enno Pata-

las, all kinds of films are shown, retrospectives and special showings from cinematic history as well as modern films. Highlights such as the reconstruction of old silent film classics, like Fritz Lang's *Metropolis* with live orchestral accompaniment, are given pride of place for their world premiere in the Philharmonie in Geiselgasteig. The atmosphere is relaxed and unconventional. You can enjoy a Weißbeer in the foyer of the Film Museum after watching a film by Achtern-

busch, and in true cinematic style blaspheme against God and all the world.

There are over 50 cinemas in Munich, including a foreign language cinema, a children's cinema and several film clubs. Call at Rindermarkt 3-4, where you can get a free booklet listing Munich's film fare.

A final tip: a competition for European Film Colleges has been held at ARRI in Türkenstraße every November since 1980, and connoisseurs find it a fascinating alternative to the Film Festival.

Even dwarves started small.

Left, Karl Valentin and Liesl Karlsadt in their film studio. Above, the boat from the movie of *that* name.

Modern Schwabing

If you live in the outskirts of Munich, and have had enough of the countryside and you feel like seeing an asphalt jungle, an avalanche of cars and a surging mass of humanity, then Leopoldstraße is the place for you. For nowhere else in Munich do you experience so much of modern city life. On warm summer nights, crowds of people shove their way along the streets, past numerous cafés, cinemas and stalls where young artists sell their work and burnt-out students peddle their old books. But there's precious little of the atmosphere of old Schwabing here.

In the middle of the crush, one realises just what it means to be on the favourite street of a big city. It's the same in any metropolis. Take London or Paris, for example, where the main streets have undergone a simlar kind of transformation as the Leopoldstraße.

Little more than a century ago, this was an almost rural street in a pleasant suburb, where citizens could enjoy a gentle Sunday afternoon stroll. The lovely villas and gardens there, damaged during World War II, were not rebuilt. Instead, functional buildings of the 1950s and 1960s were erected. Visible from a distance is the black colossus of the **Hertie** department store building. Known locally as "Snow White's Coffin", it is due for demolition as no-one wants to rent it.

The place where Heinrich Mann lived for 14 years (No. 59), where Countess Zu Reventlow (No. 14) invented her scandalous stories at the turn of the century, has become a place for profiteers to make a killing. At least the **Buchhandlung Lehmkuhl** (Lehmkuhl Bookshop) at No. 45 has remained the same since it opened in 1903.

In the early 1960s, Leopoldstraße

Preceding pages, Munich brings out the very best in fashion. Below, mobile pride on the Leopold-straße.

172

was the scene of the *Schwabinger Krawalle* (Schwabing Riots). It all began around midnight, when there was still a lot of traffic on the road, and three street musicians began to serenade outside the Gaststätte Leopold (Leopold Inn). Some police officers arrived to arrest the musicians for disturbing the peace. Passersby came to their defence and prevented the officers from removing the buskers. For three days and nights, Leopoldstraße was the scene of a mini-civil war as the riots continued. That it all ended as suddenly as it had begun was due wholly to a sudden heavy downpour!

After the *Schwabinger Krawalle*, Munich policemen were given lessons in psychology. The so-called Munich line was developed as a soft approach to demonstrators. This gentler method of solving social conflict resulted in the 1968 riots being far less serious in Munich than in other German cities, but even so, two people lost their lives in the Anti-Springer-Demonstrations. After 1968 the beatniks and students retreated, and the communes which had sprung up in the area broke up. Commerce returned, and property prices soared. Old established cafés and pubs couldn't compete with fast food outlets and smart bars. Even the **Gaststätte Leopold** where Karl Valentin made his first appearance in 1908, and which later became Erich Kästner's base, is nothing like it used to be. However, the Bavarian food is just as good.

Tall poplars still line the Leopoldstraße, near the Siegestor (Victory Gate), where little remains of what it once was. A baroque city palace built in 1895 by Martin Dülfer, called the **Wohnhaus** (Residence) at No. 4, has survived. So has the **Verwaltungsgebäude der Rhein-Main-Donau-AG** (Administration Building for the Rhein-Main-Danube Co.) at No. 28.

Being watched...

On warm summer days, there's plenty of activity on the wide pavements, with pedlars and artists selling all kinds of knick-knacks and kitsch as well as paintings in oil and watercolour.

To see and be seen, that is the motto of Leopoldstraße, and there's plenty of opportunity for both. The ice café **Venezia** and the Italian restaurant **Adria** are favoured by the demi-monde of daydreaming writers, film makers and the black-is-beautiful brigade due to their somewhat dubious atmosphere. The **Domicile** (No. 19) is for jazz enthusiasts and **Café Extrablatt** (No. 7) is the venue for Munich's celebrities.

Münchner Freiheit

Münchner Freiheit (Munich Freedom) is a part of Munich which was once said to have a face, but now has only a visage, according to Peter Paul Althaus. Alexander von Branca, the architect who built the Neuen Pinakothek, warned in the early 1970s that if one single house was removed in this area, the whole lot would fall down.

Once, there was a lovely beer garden surrounded by wonderful shady trees. It was sacrificed to roads and the underground system. In its place a stone forum was built, in the form of a concrete pit. Not surprisingly, everyone was unhappy until one day, some Schwabing folks took it into their own hands and created an oasis of green. This was the beginning of the reclamation of the desert and slowly the Münchner Freiheit was restored. Now people meet there when the weather is fine, to play chess or table tennis, or just to drink and chat. At Christmas, there are the **Christkindlmarkt** stalls of the Christmas market which many prefer to the "official" one in Marienplatz, because the former is smaller and cosier.

Around the Hertie high-rise area are

Playing chess in Müncher-Freiheit.

many pubs, bars, discos and snack bars, of which about 20 have the owner behind the bar counter, as in the **Weinbauer** (Fendstraße 5) or the **Säge** (The Saw) at Felitzstraße 9.

Village Atmosphere and Entertainment

A short walk away from the thundering traffic of Leopoldstraße is the peaceful village of Schwabing, where this legendary part of Munich had its origins. Even today, one can enjoy the village atmosphere, although now mingled with the more private happenings at the villas set behind their walls.

Small houses in large gardens line the Werneckstraße and in Seestraße 3, the **Bäckerhäusl** (Baker's House) of 1800 may still be seen. Another picturesque street is **Mandlstraße** which is next to the **Englischer Garten** (English Garden). Alfred Kubin lived in No. 26 for two years. The resistance fighter Willi

Graf was arrested at No. 28. The writer and revolutionary Ernst Toller also hid here after the collapse of the socialist republic in 1919, but he was discovered and arrested in **Schloß Suresnes** (Werneckstraße 24). This small palace dates from the 18th century and is one of the few summer residences built outside the city. Paul Klee painted here in 1919-21.

On the corner of Feilitzschstraße and Gunezrainerstraße is the last farmhouse left in Schwabing, the **Viereckhof**. Named after its owner in 1635, the farmhouse gives a nostalgic insight into the past with its roof and maypole.

The **Wedekindplatz** was the former market place of Schwabing. Several small streets converge here, which in the 1950s became the centre of "new" Schwabing. Today it is an amusement park, attracting mainly the younger generation of tourists. There's a whole row of bars, pubs and fast food joints in **Felitzschstraße**. Thomas Mann once

Below, daily life in the Occamstraße. Right, stationers from way back.

lived in No. 5, and it was there that he completed *Buddenbrooks*. For those nostalgic about the 1950-70s, there are **Schwabinger 7** at No. 7, the **Käutzchen** at No. 23 and the **Drugstore** at No. 12. For those interested in contemporary decadence, the **Occamstraße** has much to offer. Some of Munich's small theatre groups have established themselves here, offering a contrast to the city's traditional culture.

Completely Modern Schwabing

North of the Münchner Freiheit is a huge residential and industrial area which is really of little interest. So we'll turn westwards into **Belgradstraße**.

Along the Kaiserstraße, we pass the **Kurfürstenhof** (Prince Elector Palace) which is a misnomer, for like the Amalienpassage, this is a very modern residential area, where luxurious apartments overlook bright courtyards.

Taking the Belgradstraße in a northerly direction, you arrive at the **Luitpoldpark**. At the northern exit of the park is the **Bamberg Haus** (Bamberg House), built in 1912 as a garden restaurant. Today, apart from holding art exhibitions, this lovely villa still offers good but expensive cuisine. The **Schwabinger Schuttberg**, the highest point of the Luitpoldpark, offers a good view over the **Olympiagelände** (Olympic Site) and the industrial area to the north, on the other side of the Petuelring. The most outstanding edifice is the **BMW-Verwaltungsgebäude** (BMW Administrative Building) which resembles four cylinders. This masterpiece was ready just before the 1972 Olympics, and is one of Munich's landmarks. Next to it is the "soup tureen" of the **BMW-Museum**, the best cinema in Munich screening almost exclusively BMW films. Other movies are shown at the Munich Film Festival.

Below, this grocer offers you a warm smile and the hospitality that comes along with it. Right, a motor-racing aficionado .

THE OLYMPIC SITE

Almost every child in Munich has heard of old Father Timofei. Father Timofei still lives with his little Russian church in a specially designed spiritual enclave. This enduring idyll can be found right in the heart of the newest and most modern parts of Munich: the Olympic Centre.

It was the decision of the Olympic Committee in Rome to nominate Munich as the venue of the XX Olympic Games of 1972. In the meantime the Olympic Site has become

senfeld in the north. This wasteland was used by the *Bayerisch-königliche Kavallerieregiment* (Royal Bavarian Cavalry) as an exercise ground, before it became the first Munich airport in 1945. That year, the rubble cleared from the city after the war was dumped here to form the basis of the hilly landscape of the Olympic site.

The main attraction of the site is the bold tent-like roof construction which soars above the stadium, the Olympic Hall and the

one of the city's landmarks, and is one of its main tourist attractions. And rightly so too. Here the enormous financial outlay for the immediate demands of a major sporting event were cleverly blended with the long-term needs of the city.

So the 1972 Games gave Munich a high school sports centre, an indoor pool, new student halls of residence and a modern pedestrian residential district, not forgetting the glorious Olympic Park, a recreation area.

The only open ground near enough to the city for the Olympic site was the Oberwie-

swimming pool. Responsible for this initially controversial design was the architectural firm of Prof. Behnisch and Partners.

Munich, which had no good sporting facilities then, thus gained one of the best sporting complexes in Europe. The Olympic stadium can seat 80,000, the Olympic Hall 14,000, while the Olympic Pool is one of the best swimming pools in the world.

The football team of FC Bayern Munich plays its matches in the Olympic Stadium, and the Olympic Hall is used for all kinds of events, from bicycle races to rock concerts.

The site of a man-made lake as well as the artificial hills of rubble already mentioned, and it is dominated by the tallest reinforced concrete construction in Europe, the 290-metre high Olympiaturm. A lift brings you up to the 180-metre high platform, with a spectacular view over the whole of Munich. Below this platform is a revolving restaurant which can seat 230 guests.

In the summer free rock concerts are held in the Theatron, a modern amphitheatre by and bungalows became a students' hall of residence, and also their dining hall. It's worth taking a look at these bungalows, for they are all brightly painted by their occupants. The dining hall, "Mensa", is where you can have an economical lunch (Mondays to Fridays 11 a.m. to 2 p.m.).

Architecturally interesting is the Men's Village, where the south facing terraced design serves the students as balconies where they can grow plants. It was here that

the Olympic Lake. You can take a tour ride on the little blue-and-white train, or you may prefer to walk to see the Olympic Village.

This is separated from the main site by the Mittleren Ring (Middle Ring Road) although there are footbridges across. It is on the north side of the site, and is the size of a small town, housing about 9,000 people. The former Ladies' Village with its high-rises

Left, FC Bayern plays a match to full house in the Olympic Stadium. Above, a swinging time at rock concert in the Olympiapark.

the attack on the Israeli team took place and spoiled the otherwise "Happy Games".

The press reported that this place was a ghost village for some time but after the Games, it has now come alive . Despite the underground traffic which made this a pedestrian zone, the synthetic landscape did seem to put people off for a while. Now, the place is a hive of activity and the bungalows of the former Ladies' Village are among the most sought-after hostels in Munich. The students ensure that there's plenty of activity too, down at the "*forum 2*" cultural centre.

A WORLD OF ART

Some of Munich's best museums are right in the centre of Schwabing. They stretch from the area north of the Old Botanic Garden to Theresienstraße.

Take a slow walk from the Odeonsplatz through Briennerstraße, past the palace designed by Karl von Fischer to the **Karolinenplatz**. From a distance, you can spot the **Obelisk**, a memorial for the 30,000 Bavarian soldiers who lost their lives in the Russian Campaign of 1812.

"Athens on the Isar"

The spacious **Königsplatz**, flanked by three huge buildings, has been restored to its former glory. In 1935 the original lawns were removed and a bare stone surface laid. Now the grass has been replaced. After all, Ludwig I

wanted a Platz der Kulturen (Cultural Square), not an army parade ground. The parked cars have been moved elsewhere, and now one can sit on the steps which lead up to the Antikensammlung (Antique Collection) or the Glyptothek and enjoy the majestic proportions of Leo von Klenze's square.

The classical **Propyläen** complete this imposing square. Originally conceived as a gateway from the city out to Nymphenberg, this portico by Klenze reflects Greek architectural ideals.

The **Antikensammlung**, built by Ziebland (not Klenze) in 1838-1848, was used for art and industrial exhibitions in the 19th century before it later became a museum of modern art in 1900. Badly damaged during World War II, the building was not repaired until the 1960s when it became a museum for Ludwig I's antique collection. A passionate lover of Greek art, he had sent emissaries to Rome and Paris to

Preceding pages, graffiti shows up in the village of a million, Munich. Below, green at last—the Königsplatz.

purchase Greek and Etruscan vases, jewellery and bronzes.

Among his acquisitions were the huge sculptures of the **Ägineten** (Aeginetan Marbles) from the temple on Aegina, which had been excavated by German and English explorers at the beginning of the 19th century. These muscular warriors were transported to Munich in pieces, and restorers had the task of matching arms, legs and torsoes. Any missing heads were sculpted by Thorwaldsen, a Scandinavian sculptor with a love for the heroic figures.

The "Ägineten" were the basis of the **Glyptothek** collection, which, with the Antikensammlung, make up the finest museum of antique sculpture and vases in Germany.

The Prince of Art

Past the Propyläen, on the right, is the **Lenbachhaus**. Franz von Lenbach was the most famous portrait painter in Germany, at a time when artists were revered like gods. From a humble background, he painted all the notables of his day was very successful. People would pay anything to pose for him—no price was too high for fame, even in those days. In fact, a portrait by von Lenbach was a sure sign that an aristocrat had arrived.

Like his colleague Franz von Stuck, the Prince of Art had a villa built as his studio and residence in 1900. The sumptuous luxury of the place reflected not only his success as an artist, but also his well-developed business sense. Upon von Stuck's death, the Lenbachhaus was passed onto the city and was then converted into a museum. Some rooms have been left as they were, merely to give an indication of the gorgeous interior of the house. The two long side wings of the building enclose an Italian garden with gravel paths,

Mother and child in the Glyptothek.

complete with niches formed by hedges, fountains and sculptures.

The Lenbachhaus

The museum of the Lenbachhaus has several sections. The first floor is devoted to Munich-based artists, such as Jan Polack, a famous painter of the Late Gothic period, and the artists of *Der Blaue Reiter* (The Blue Rider) group formed in 1900 and which included Kandinsky, Marc, Jawlenskee, Münter, Macke and Klee. Most of the pictures painted during the brief but productive period between the founding of the group and the outbreak of World War I are kept here, making the Lenbachhaus the home of the group's impressive contribution. Kadinsky's early works, as with all the others, are displayed within these walls for the benefit of students who delve into the origins of abstract painting.

Contemporary art is well represented in the Lenbachhaus too, with *Zeige deine Wunde* (Show Your Wounds), an installation by Joseph Beuys, which was a very controversial piece when first produced, but is now accepted as a modern classic. When the work was acquired by the city, there was much criticism from the art establishment of Munich.

Nine Hundred Years of Art

Near the Lenbachhaus are the Alte and the Neue Pinakothek (The Old and the New Pinacotheca)—Munich's most famous museums. The two buildings face each other with only a garden in between. The relationship between the two museums is enhanced by the nature of their exhibits which somehow complement one another. Together, the paintings tell a vivid story spanning the 900 years history of Occidental art from

Das Schlaraffenland by Pieter Breughel the Elder in the Old Pinakothek.

the medieval period to the 20th century.

As early as the 16th century, the Wittelsbachs followed the Italian precept of commissioning paintings, or buying works through emissaries. Thus in 1698, Max Emanuel spent an enormous sum which was not paid off until a hundred years later, on paintings from Antwerp. Works by such famous Flemish artists as Van Dyck, Breughel, Brouwer, Wouvermann and Rubens, with their opulent women and apocalyptically entwined figures formed the basis of this collection. One could almost say that the **Alte Pinakothek** was built around these great paintings. Later acquisitions were those by Dutch masters, Rembrandt and Frans Hals, and several Italians like Raffael, Titian Tintoretto and Veronese.

The Birth by Paul Gaugin in the Old Pinakothek.

Several small private galleries were established initially and were, of course, not for public viewing. It was not until the 18th century that paintings from various palaces were collected together and made available to the general public. The Wittelsbach collection was hung in the gallery of the Hofgarten, which was soon found to be too small. As a result, Ludwig I commissioned his architect Leo von Klenze to build the Alte Pinakothek.

Ludwig's Grand Collection

The foundation stone was laid in 1826, but it took ten years to complete. The Alte Pinakothek was the largest art gallery building of its time. The rooms were soon filled with works from churches and individual owners. From his own purse, Ludwig purchased works of German artists, notably Dürer and Altdorfer, as well as paintings from the early Italian Renaissance, from Giotto to Leonardo da Vinci and Botticelli. Proudly he exclaimed, "What a collection I have, gentlemen! But I

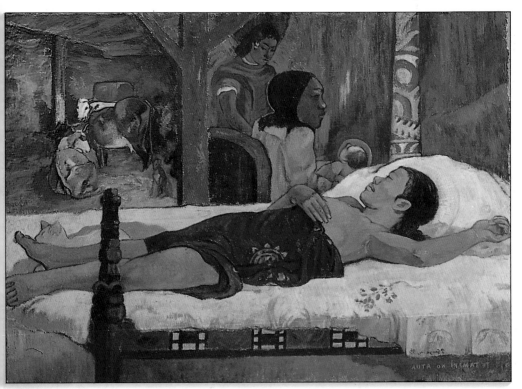

don't want it reported in the papers. For if a man loses money at the gaming tables or spends it on horses, it's taken as a matter of course, but to buy works of art, that, people will say, is a waste of money."

It is not easy to manage such an extensive collection. In some of the dark rooms, the paintings are either very close to one another or they are hung up so high that you will probably need opera glasses to look at the details.

On the other hand, the Neue Pinakothek, rebuilt only in 1975-81 after it was badly damaged during World War II, fulfils all the criteria of a museum building. The huge ceiling lamps give a well-lit interior through which the landscapes of the French Impressionists are revealed. The rooms of the Neue Pinakothek are looped round two inner courtyards. You will have to walk round corners, up and down narrow staircases and then finally through dark corridors which lead to a bright high-ceiling room. It is at this end of the winding passage that you find, under natural lighting, a collection of gloriously colourful pictures by historical painters such as Kaulbach and Piloty.

Well acquainted with the collection, Alexander von Branca was able to create a tailor-made environment for the paintings. The building looks very impressive from the outside too and might have attracted many an architecture student. The elaborate architectural forms, and the terraced ponds give it a post-modern slant. On the ground floor is a restaurant, with no less post-modern prices. On warm days, tables and chairs are neatly arranged around the pond to present customers with the better alternative. Like every other guest, you realise at once that you are in amicable surroundings. Over coffee and toast, you begin to cast your eyes upon Henry Moore's gigantic but admirable sculpture of a recumbent woman.

Right, a silent guest drops in for tea.

KIR ROYAL, LONG AGO

Frankfurt has its opera, Wiesbaden its casino, and the city of Munich its art galleries. At one time or another, everyone in Munich goes to a vernissage. Almost every week there's a new exhibition opening, where people like to be seen, drink champagne and look boringly stylish before the exhibits. Not long ago, the champagne was made into a *Kir Royal* by adding red syrup. But ever since a T.V. series by that name began, no one does that any more. For *Kir Royal* typifies the self-styled arty person who actually has no understanding of art, only money and a fondness for parties, and so has a say in Munich's arts circle. You might wonder why many folks live and let live, and why they yearn for New York's exciting life but are reluctant to leave the city. Perhaps the answer lies in Munich's history.

In the Neue Pinakothek is a picture of Crown Prince Ludwig and his artist friends. They are portrayed in Roman times, the atmosphere is unrestrained and Ludwig is ordering more wine. The message is clear: art brings people together, removes class barriers and above all, offers participants a chance to celebrate. An idyllic scene in an Italian inn on canvas comes to life. In 1840, Munich staged the famous Dürer Festival, where the local artists dressed up to recreate the period of Dürer in a colourful pageant. Other festivals—the Venice of the Doges and the Florence of the Medicis—followed suit; the city became a stage.

Little individual talent is called for to make life itself into a work of art. So less creative intellects have left their imprint on the artistic life of Munich, while more of those long-forgotten artists have come to the city in droves around the mid-19th century.

In the summer, it is simply wonderful to be in the country, to stay in an artists' colony, to paint outdoors in the day, and to enjoy the company of other artists at night. But it's not always so idyllic. An eyewitness recounts that in Dachauer Moos, a spot favoured by artists, "there was a painter's parasol every

fifty metres, and at the more popular spots, people had to wait for days for their turn. Some places were painted so often, that the locals were suing other parties for damages." In winter, it's back to the city where the tone is set by the princes of art, Lenbach and Stuck. They had grand palaces built in which to receive their admirers.

In his day, Lenbach was acknowledged the greatest portrait painter in Germany. From emperor to pope to Eleonora Duse, he

painted anyone of significance. And he never forgot to tell his famous models how he first arrived, young and innocent, and walked barefoot from his little village of Pfaffenhofen to see the treasures of Munich.

Less amiable was Franz von Stuck, who donned the mantle of grandmaster of the arts. He would greet his guests in the costume of a Roman emperor. He erected in his studio an altar of his works, to which his guests paid homage on bended knees.

In 1900, there were two possibilities if one wanted to study art in Munich. Paul Klee found himself in the "city of five thousand painters" and had to make a choice. He could either take private lessons or attend the famous Academy. The demand was great, the studios were full. So Klee took private lessons and attended the Academy where he met Stuck, then teaching there. That he was not overly impressed is evident from his diary, in which he wrote that the Princes of Art cannot foresee, even if proved to them, that their time is over; they have their peace,

Macke and Kubin. Their work belonged to the best of the Expressionist Movement, but more significantly, they were the trailblazers for abstract art. The group disbanded before the outbreak of World War I.

Munich has never fully recovered from the shock of World War I, and the onslaught of fascism. Thus much of the history of art stops at this point. The Artist's City of Munich, is it just a legend of the past? Maybe there's still hope: if you are lucky, you might just

their palaces, and royal Bavarian lifestyle. Klee was anyway more interested in life than in art at the time. He often spent the night drinking at beer gardens and invited pretty models to the nearby Isartal.

Groups of artists mushroomed and disappeared just as quickly. There was, however, one exception. In 1900 Kandinsky and Marc founded *Der Blaue Reiter* (The Blue Rider), and were joined by others like Klee, Münter,

Left, *The Tiger*, **by Franz Marc. Above,** *Pan Flute Player* **by Franz von Stuck.**

find yourself wandering through the narrow streets of Haidhausen or Schwabing, and then it begins to rain. So you take shelter at a doorway, and just after you've swept the raindrops off your body, you begin to notice the sign "Artist's Studio". Curious, you open the door. No, this is not some splendid artist's villa, but a big bright room serving as studio, gallery and living room—and there's no entrance charge. You are not greeted by a salaried guide or museum guardian, but by the artist himself. Thanks to the host, Munich may once again be called an artists' city.

THE LEHEL

Despite being part of the big city and like the Max-Vorstadt (Max Suburb) and Haidhausen, the Lehel has somehow kept itself apart and has retained its own particular charm. It is well worth taking a stroll through this area, especially along the left bank of the Isar between Frauenhoferstraße and Prinzregentenstraße. There are streets of lovely houses from the Gründerzeit (Time of Expansion). There are also some smaller dwellings which serve as a reminder that this was where Munich's poor raftsmen, artisans and petit bourgeois used to live in since earlier times. It is this extraordinary visual contrast of an almost idyllic small town atmosphere with an affluent class which gives the Lehel its unique charm. This picture of contrast is also evident in daily life: *Tante Emma* corner shops

next to exclusive galleries, sell everything you can think of; small family businesses next to giant retail concerns; old pubs next to smart restaurants; and village lindens next to video shops. However, this picturesque juxtaposition is slowly disappearing due to new urban architecture (e.g. The Bavarian Insurance Complex).

The **Prinzregentenstraße**, the southern boundary of the Englischer Garten (English Garden) was built between 1891 and 1901 as a fine avenue. Now it is a busy thoroughfare between Schwabing and the east of Munich. It begins where the road tunnel under **Prinz-Carl-Palais** surfaces.

In the nearby **Haus der Kunst**, at the top of Prinzregentenstraße, is the **Staatsgalerie Moderner Kunst** (State Gallery of Modern Art). This building was erected in 1933-37 as a splendid example of Fascist architecture. Apart from the changing exhibitions, there are

Preceding pages, The Maximilianeum, seat of the Bavarian Parliament. Below, The Prinzregentenstraße begins at the Prinz-Carl-Palais.

many works which were condemned as "degenerate" in the Third Reich, but are now classics of modern art.

Folk art and historical collections are to be found in the posh **Bayerisches Nationalmuseum** (No. 3). A must-see section is *Die Neue Sammlung* (The New Collection) with varying exhibitions of industrial and environmental design in the 19th and 20th centuries.

Just a few houses away, in the **Schack-Galerie** (No. 9) is a good collection of paintings from the 19th century including well-known works by Böcklin, Feuerbach and Lenbach as well as Schwind and Spitzweg. The building is also the seat of the **Bayerische Staatskanzlei** (Bavarian State Chancellory). Directly opposite is the house in which writer Frank Wedekind lived from 1908 to 1918.

The Isar Gate, home of the Karl Valentin Museum.

Turn into one of the side streets, and you'll find the real Lehel with its little streets and nooks and crannies. Sadly,

Sternstraße (Star Street) with its beautiful picturesque facades under a preservation order, is often filled with traffic. Long ago, a brook ran here, and the houses still support each other on the ground which were once river banks.

Away from the Bustle of the Big City

Through the narrow Gewürzmühlstraße, you get to **St.-Anna-Platz**, a haven of peace with trees, gardens and benches. However, there'll be no more peace after 1989, when it becomes the Lehel stop on the underground system. It was there in No. 2 that the writer Leon Feuchtwanger spent his early childhood. Feuchtwanger is best known for his classics *Jud Süß* and *Exil* (Exile) and for his novel *Erfolg* (Success) which is set in 20th Century Munich.

The **Pfarrkirche St. Anna** (Parish Church of St. Anna) is in the centre of

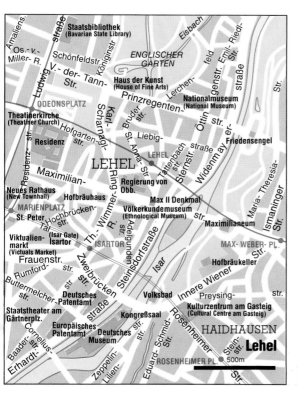

the square. It was built by Gabriel von Seidl in New Roman style, and consecrated in 1882. Inside, the enormous apse paintings and the high altar in the raised presbytery are of interest to the visitor. It became necessary to build the church, which now dominates the square, at the end of the 19th century when the old **Klosterkirche St. Anna** (Cloister Church of St. Anna) became too small for the growing congregation. This little church, built between 1727 and 1733 by Johann Michael Fischer, could be easily overlooked because it is at the edge of the square and is surrounded by the old monastery buildings. It used to house the monks of the Order of St. Hieronymus, and the Franciscans have lived there since 1827. The ornate interior was completely restored after it was damaged in an air raid in World War II. The treasures include the high altar, originally by the Asam Brothers, restored in 1970; the taber-

nacle by Johann Baptist Straub (1704-1784) which survived the fire unscathed; the paintings by Cosmas Damian Asam (1686-1739) in the front side altars and richly decorated pulpit by J.B. Straub.

After looking at the churches, you may want to wander through the side streets which have retained most of their original charm, and which surprisingly are not on the tourist trail. Before you reach the Maximilianstraße there's a delightful little inn at St.-Anna-Straße 2, called **Zum Klösterl** which is open every day except Saturdays from 6 p.m. and there you can enjoy good Bavarian food and Bohemian specialities.

The Maximilianstraße, which leads from the Residenz (Palace) to the Isar, is one of the loveliest streets created in the 19th century. The architect Friedrich Bürklein was responsible for this avenue which came into existence between 1852 and 1875. From St.-Anna-Straße

At the entrance to the Folk Museum.

one reaches the lower and wider end of the street, with imposing buildings on either side. Number 39, a Maximilian-style building, is the seat of the Upper Bavarian government. Opposite, in a New Gothic style building by Erich Riedel built in 1858-65, is the **Staatliche Museum für Völkerkunde** (State Museum of Ethnology). This museum is currently undergoing extensive renovation, will not be completed until the 1990's. However, the exhibits from Africa, Middle and South America and Asia may be seen in promotions which are specially organised from time to time. If you look down the Maximilianstraße towards the east, you'll see the magnificent silhouette of the **Maximilianeum**, seat of the Bavarian Parliament. At the foot of this imposing building, but on this side of the Isar, in the middle of the road, is the **Max II-Denkmal** (Max II Memorial), an allegorical representation of the four virtues of

Traffic at the Max II Monument.

power and the coats of arms of the four Bavarian areas (Bavaria, Schwaben, Pfalz and Franken).

A Whiff of Italy

South of the Maximilianstraße, the Lehel stretches on further. In contrast to the St.-Anna area, this stretch is more of a business district. Through Adelgundenstraße or Thierschstraße, you reach **Mariannenplatz**, with the **St.-Lukas-Kirche** (St. Luke's Church) of 1893-96 at the eastern side. It's not far to the Isar from here, and as you pass through Thierschstraße towards the Isartor, you will notice that the atmosphere changes completely. One shop stands next to the other without a care in the world. Boutiques, antique shops and cafés, each with its own original facade. They only add more colour to the street. As you look back from the Isartor, you feel this lovely street has an Italian touch,

Traffic at the Max II Monument.

despite the noise and traffic that comes and go every minute.

Museum of Giants

After turning left into Zweibrück-straße, you reach the extensive **Deutsches Museum** (German Museum). Proposed by Oskar von Miller and planned by Gabriel von Seidl, this Museum of Technology was first opened in 1925, and then rebuilt after World War II. With an area of 40,000 square metres, it is one of the largest of its kind in the world.

From mining to atomic physics, from typography to chemistry, from the abacus to the computer—you can trace the whole history of scientific development and technological advance. You can see what a computer looked like in Leibniz' day, and the original apparatus used by Otto Hahn and Fritz Straßmann when they first split the atom, and ushered in the nuclear age. You can experience an earsplitting crack of lightning in a metal cage, and watch the occupant of the cage come out unharmed. These and many other unforgettable experiences are offered here in Germany's largest museum. There are illustrations, historical experimental apparatus, films and demonstrations, and original exhibits, including awe-inspiring aircraft to gladden any boy's heart. Many grown-up boys and girls will certainly enjoy the interesting variety of hands-on exhibits and experiments in this fascinating museum.

One of the remarkable features of this huge museum, is the spacious layout, enabling music lovers to enjoy an extensive display of instruments while stargazers can peer at the sun, moon and Jupiter during the daytime in the observatory. However, if the weather is bad, the planetarium offers the clearest sky in Munich to study the heavens.

In the Aviation Gallery of the Deutsches Museum.

Taking the 16-kilometre length of exhibition walkway into consideration, there is no way you can see all of the exhibits in a day, unless of course you plan to stay in the neighbourhood for a few weeks.

In any case, after a visit, it's a good idea to take a walk along the Isar, and by way of contrast, enjoy the display of flesh as the ladies of Munich sunbathe on the river banks.

Gärtnerplatz

Either by way of **Corneliusstraße** or a little further through **Reichenbach-straße** we come to the beautiful **Gärtnerplatz**, (Gardeners' Square). This star-shaped square is surrounded by well-preserved houses built during the Period of Expansion. The **Theater am Gärtnerplatz**, which dominates the square for the present, was built in 1864-65, by Franz Michael Reifenstuel.

It was designed in Italian New Renaissance style, and was meant to be a theatre of the people. Nowadays, the programme includes operettas, operas and ballet productions.

In summer, the whole area is under shady chestnut trees, and look a mass of flowers. As in any recreational park, there are benches to laze on and watch the world go by. While relaxing at the square, it would be a good idea also to catch a view of the Reichenbachstraße up north. You would have realised then that you are at the centre of Munich. And to check on that bearing are the towers of the Liebfrauenkirche (St. Mary's Church) and the Alte Peter (Old Peter) just on the horizon. This would confirm your sense of direction is right. In fact it would also mean you are not far from the bustle of activity happening at the Viktualienmarkt (Victuals Market), and the never-ending crowd of the Marienplatz.

The Old Lehel, reflected in the post-modern facade of the new Savings Bank building.

THE ISAR: A TAMED TORRENT

In 1983, when the Münchner Stadtmuseum (Munich City Museum) organised an exhibition of the history of the Isar, the river was described as having been transformed "from an Alpine torrent into a tamed river of culture." In fact, if you look down from one of the Isar bridges at the gently flowing water, there is nothing to remind you of the ferocity of this former mountain river which caused chaos in the beginning of the 19th century. In 1813 this raging torrent smashed the Ludwigsbrücke (Ludwig Bridge) and drowned about a hundred curious onlookers, who were standing on the bridge.

The torrent was completely unpredictable. It was a long time before the first regulation work was undertaken and its course fixed. The branch channels wandered from year to year over the "rolling" surface of gravel. Then the river began to attract settlements and quickly developed into a main trade artery for the early Bavarians who settled in the area between the Alps and the Danube. These pioneers were a mix of Alemannian and Protoladinnians (found today in the Rhaeto-Romanic part of Switzerland and in South Tyrol). The areas around the Isar became centres of transport and attracted seigniories. Though older than Munich, Freising is very much in its shadow today. It was here that the salt route crossed the Isar and a cultural centre of Carolinian antiquity was established. Bishop Arbeo of Freising (764-783) developed the Klosterberg schools of writing into the first Bavarian centre for literature and education.

In times when a river was still an obstacle to movement, the bridge became a powerful factor. In the year 1100, Heinrich der Löwe (Heinrich the Lion) moved the bridge, then belonging to Freising, from Föhring to a place of monastic settlement upstream. Der Lowe then became the founder of Munich. With power over the river, the small settlement expanded rapidly and by the end of the 13th century, the Wittelsbach rulers and the

court made Munich their place of residence. The rulers of Munich then acted in a somewhat high-handed manner with regard to the river and and with what happened on and around it. For instance, the Raft Ordinance drawn up by the city council stipulated that any raft passing Munich was obliged to moor for three days and that the citizens faced a kind of refusal on all goods being transported. This *Stapelrecht*, or stock right, gave the city more control over the rafting trans-

port system, and made all kinds of things available to the people, in particular wood and stone for building.

But the Isar was not always an obedient carrier for the city of Munich. The river, which has its source in the Karwendel mountains, frequently burst its banks. As a result, much damage was caused to the land and incurred a long list of casualties. Even in the middle of the last century, the Englischer Garten (English Garden) was often flooded. But since then, a sophisticated system of dams, canals and reinforcements to the banks has tamed the Isar. Like historical romances, the wild torrents are now a thing of the past. Even the lovely open countryside where the river meanders freely in Ascholdinger and Pupplinger Au is fast disappearing. Now more and more freight is transported on the water, and the river provides the fresh water for the nuclear power stations, which are being constructed on its banks.

The industrial utilisation of the Isar really begins after the river has passed Munich. In to Thalkirchen on the *Gaudiflossen* (pleasure rafts) down the river through unspoilt countryside. People on the river banks, however, may be forgiven for thinking that it is due to the large quantity of beer consumed on board which causes the enchantment. These pleasure trips which began at the end of the last century (a time when "nature" was relegated to Sunday outings by city dwellers) have very little in common with the early rafters' experiences. Their lives were diffi-

the upper part of the river, the scene is still idyllic. In 1931, the author Julius Kreis wrote of a trip to the Isar valley of the Alpine foothills: "It is as if a magician had banished all the city noise and the difficult and godless times, and dissolved everything into timeless green waters, trees and heavenly joy."

This magician still seems to enchant people, as they float from Wolfrathshausen

Left, the Isar meanders, with the Angel of Peace in the background. Above, sunbathing on the gravel banks.

cult and dangerous. If they were to sip the wine from the cargo, they would lose their limbs. Today, rafters risk no more than falling into the water.

As you approach the city on the *Gaudiflossen,* you notice the romantic castle Burg Schwaneck in Pullach, an artificial creation set in unspoilt natural surroundings. It was built in 1842 by Ludwig von Schwanthaler. Apparently, Schwanthaler spent only one night in the finished castle—perhaps dream castles are not very comfortable to live in after all.

COURTYARDS AND VILLAS

Preceding
pages,
The
Philhar-
monic
in the
Cultural
Centre of
Gasteig.
Left,
parade of
traditional
costumes in
Maximilian-
straße.

Haidhausen poses a rival to Schwabing and has the reputation of being the new "in" place. Until a short while ago, this area was a shabby bourgeois district where students, foreigners, dropouts and impoverished artists lived in condemned houses. It is now suddenly going through a facelift. The old inns where labourers of the 18th century were housed are being turned into smart studios. On the erstwhile salt route where smiths and cartwrights once plied their trade, a luxury housing district has now emerged for people who like to combine the advantages of living in a metropolis with the village ambience. There is no other area in Munich which has retained its village atmosphere like Haidhausen. There are lovely shops and pubs frequented by the smart

set. In Haidhausen also lies a bohemian charm for which the new elites will move away from the city.

When you arrive in Haidhausen after crossing the Maximiliansbrücke (Maximilian Bridge), you will find the glorious **Maximilianeum** just ahead. It was built in the 19th century to complete the stretch of Maximilianstraße (Maximilian Street) and was to be an elite school. Today it houses the Bavarian Landtag (Parliament) and the Maximilianeum Stiftung (Foundation) where the best high school students in Munich are given free lodging and education.

Between the Maximilian and Ludwig bridges is the eastern bank of the Isar, which is now a lovely park. The clay from this area used to be made into Haidhauser bricks. If you don't feel like sunbathing, you can walk along to the Ludwigsbrücke where the salt route crossed the Isar to Munich in the 12th century. Here you'll find the lovely

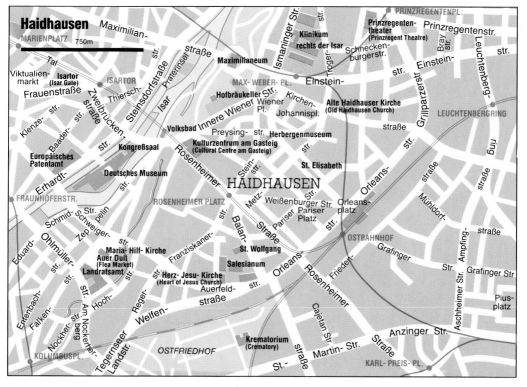

Vater-Rhein-Brunnen (Father Rhine Fountain), the work of Hildebrand in 1897-1903. This square opposite the Deutsches Museum (German Museum) has proved to be a wonderful place to relax in, as the tramps of the city discovered long ago.

Jugendstil

On the left after the bridge is the **Müllersche Volksbad** (Müller's Jugendstil Pool) of 1897-1901, a pool in the Jugendstil or art nouveau style. It is believed to be Germany's loveliest.

Less attractive is the **Kulturzentrum am Gasteig** (Cultural Centre at Gasteig), a building constructed of bright tiles and glass, and named the "Culture Bunker" by its detractors. This is home to the Philharmonic Orchestra under the direction of Sergiu Selibidache, to the Richard Strauss Conservatory and also to the largest city library in Germany as well as—a concession to less formal art—to the little theatre in the Black Box. Evening classes are regularly conducted here too.

After Gasteig, on the left, you arrive in the old part of Haidhausen. Here on **Inneren Wiener Straße** is the little chapel called the **Loreo-Kapelle**. This chapel is linked with the small **St. Nikolaus** Church which from 1315 was the church of the leprosarium on the outskirts of the city. It was rebuilt in Late Gothic style in the 16th century. If you continue along the Inneren Wiener Straße, the brewery buildings of the Hofbräuhaus are on the left side of the street, after they were moved from the Platzl in 1890. In 1987 they were almost completely burnt down. Was this fire an act created by the legendary Haidhausen mischief maker? Nevertheless, the **Hofbräukeller**, with its extensive beer garden, seems to be doing well.

You feel as if you are on a village

Cooling off in the Müllersche Volksbad pool.

green in **Wiener Platz** with its maypole and market stalls and the restored **Herbergen** (Inns) of the 18th century (Wiener Platz 4-6 and An der Kreppe 2a-d). However, the traffic and the smart **Café Wiener Platz** are a reminder that you're in a big city. **Kirchenstraße** (Church Street) too has retained some of its original charm from the time it was a small village street leading to the farming area of Haidhausen. But as can be seen from the inner courtyard of No. 15 and the new buildings on Seerieder-straße this area, once known as the broken glass district, is becoming more attractive. If the history of this part of the city interests you, visit the **Haidhauser Museum** (Kirchenstraße 24; Sundays and Mondays through Wednesdays, 2 p.m. to 6 p.m.).

The parish church of **St. Johann Baptist** (St. John the Baptist) at Kirchenstraße 39, has its origins as far back as the early 9th century and was the village

Below, village charm on Wienerplatz. Right, oasis of peace in Weißenburger Platz.

centre. It was damaged by the Swedes in 1640, then rebuilt and around 1700, Gunezrainer drew up the plans which made it a lovely Baroque church.

Through **Wolfgangstraße**, best known for the Blauer Engel, you come to Preysingstraße, where the fun is in Haidhausen. There's a whole spectrum to choose from, starting with the offbeat **Gasthof zum Kloster** (No. 77), typical Bavarian **Preysinggarten** (No. 69) and the modern **Kuczynski** where the yuppies gather for a superbrunch on Sundays. Between these are some relics of the past; opposite the **Kriechbaumhof** (No. 71) which was rebuilt exactly as it had been in the 17th century, you'll see some of those inns—used by the day labourers—which are now being renovated into smart studios and workshops. In the **Herbergenmuseum im Üblacker-erhäusl** next door, you can see what these places used to look like inside.

Financed by the *Beggar of*

Haidhausen Pastor Georg Walser, the so-called "Haidhauser Cathedral", **St. Johann Baptist** (not to be confused with the parish church of the same name), on Johannisplatz was built in 1852-1874. There is a perfectly preserved cycle of glass paintings of the Late Gothic style here. **Johannisplatz** itself with its little shops looks just like a film set from the 1950s.

The French Quarter

When the eastern part of Haidhausen came into being, the Bavarian army had just returned victorious from the Franco-Prussian War of 1870-71 and so the streets were named after conquered cities and successful battles. Thus the French Quarter was born.

Despite the cheap department stores which thwart all efforts to rid Haidhausen of its image as a poor area, many of the streets have retained their charm. It's worth taking a walk through the pedestrian precinct of Weißburger Straße, lined with lovely trees, to **Weißenburger Platz**. This is recognisable from afar by its three-tier fountain, all that remains of what was produced for the Glass Palace in 1853. This lovely square with its fountain and beautiful flowers and trees, is most inviting on lazy summer days and is very popular. Another square which is not far away is the **Pariser Platz** which retains some of its small town charm, but is not as idyllic as Weißburger Platz. At **Orleansplatz** the rails of the Ostbahnhof (East Station) mark the end of Haidhausen in that direction. If you still want to wander around Haidhausen itself, then stroll along Breisacher Straße on to Elsässer Straße. **Gasttätte Wiesengrund** (No. 15) offers good food at reasonable prices in a relaxed atmosphere. Bookworms can browse in the bookshop opposite, **Tramplpfad**. Live concerts,

Keeping each other company in the park.

usually of jazz, are staged—sometimes to a full house—in the **Unterfahrt** (at the junction of Kirchenstraße and Haidenauplatz).

From here, the No. 19 tram moves on to **Berg am Laim**. It is rather difficult to believe that there's actually anything worth seeing in this area dominated by traffic on the road and in the air. When you alight at the Baumkirchener Straße station and turn right into Clemens-August-Straße, you'll come to the old church of St. Michael. This was built by Johann Michael Fischer between 1738 and 1751. The interior deco were the combined efforts of Johann Baptist Zimmermann and the "father" of Munich rococo, Johann Baptist Straub. Incidentally, if you have made it this far, you've just earned yourself a drink in **Café Mahlerhaus** (Baumkirchener Straße 1) or in the old Munich beer house **Weißes Bräuhaus**.

The golden glow of the Angel of Peace reflects the well-being of those who live in the lovely villas behind the hedges here. The angel is at the end of a lovely terrace which leads along the banks of the Isar up some steps to one of the loveliest parts of the city. The bronze statue links the two parts of the **Prinzregentenstraße** which from the Haus der Kunst (House of Art) to the Prinzregentenplatz is lined with imposing buildings including a level apartment building from 1900.

The **Villa Stuck** is at the beginning of the street, built in 1897-1914 in accordance with the plans of the owner Franz von Stuck who, like Lenbach, was one of Munich's Princes of Art. The beautifully furnished building in the Jugendstil is a "unique and complete work of art" in which life and art are unified. Today this former artist's residence is the property of the city, and an object of constant cultural wrangling.

Also in keeping with the milieu is the

The Prinzregententheatre lights up.

delicatessen **Feinkost-Käfer**, a little further up. The historical atmosphere is preserved in the rooms and the most discerning gourmet is spoilt for choice.

Although Ludwig II—the great Wagner fan—was no longer living, there were plans to make the **Prinzregententheater** a Festspielhaus modelled on Bayreuth. Max Littmann completed the design and the building project was undertaken in 1900. After the war, the Munich State Opera moved in, but then the building was closed for renovation; it reopened in 1988.

Before he emigrated, Thomas Mann lived for almost 20 years at No. 10 of the Allee now named after him. Thus, Bogenhausen can lay claim to being the place of origin of several important literary works. After 1933, however, Mann was seen rather differently. There are quite a few famous names in the **Bogenhauser Kirchplatz** cemetery, among them Annette Kolb, Erich Kästner, Liesl Karlstadt, Oskar Maria Graf and Rainer Werner Fassbinder.

Nightmare of Modernity

How an economic miracle is translated into architecture, is shown by the enormous buildings erected in the 1970s in the **Arabellapark** area.

Apart from the Arabella House and the Sheraton Hotel, there is the **Verwaltungzentrum der Hypo-Bank** (Administration Centre of the Hypo-Bank), which is now very much part of Munich's skyline. This spectacular creation with its dematerialising glass and aluminium exterior, is seen by some as an architectural masterpiece, and by others as an oversized statement of economic power. If you want to know what it's like to be a worm, just take a walk through the Arabellapark, where architectural science fiction has become a reality.

Below, standing tall next to the Bavarian Hypo-Bank. Right, the Angel of Peace in winter.

208

WHICH WAY TO WHERE IT'S AT?

The manifold question is: where are the exotic cafés, the music and the action, and where do the beautiful women, hard drinkers and penniless artists hang out in Munich? Is the answer to life's mysteries found in a beer glass? Where is the Munich you've read about, which way to where it's at?

The question is a fair one, but the answer is elusive. You've heard of Schwabing, of course. Schwabing! That place which was haunted by the dreamers of the 1960s has

houses. The difference is that, in Munich, these places will be demolished. That is what happened to the legendary "Alabama Hall". The same fate awaits the theatre halls in Dachauer Straße where theatre and dance groups, musicians and variety artists are housed. Typically, these people are adept at staging festivals. They have learned not only to stage reputable festivals in Munich, but also to profit from them too. The result is that festivals of art which would otherwise be

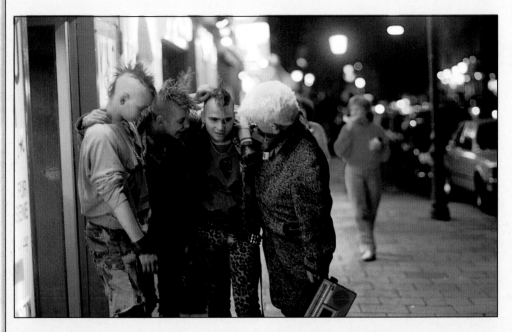

now lost all its charm. One thing is certain: Schwabing is definitely not where it's at these days. Thinking of Schwabing's past, in the **Café Extrablatt** of Leopoldstraße 7, you'll easily find the gossip columnist Michael Graeter—a journalistic phenomenon according to his colleagues who made it by quoting the rich and famous. There, he also entertains those who have that yearn to belong to the elite group.

The underground culture in Munich is, like everywhere else, played out in abandoned and condemned factories and ware-

neglected are held, like on Saturdays in the **Negerhalle** (Theaterhallen in Dachauerstraße 128). In the **Theaterfabric** (Theatre Factory) along Unterföhring (Föhringer Alley) and in the **Manege** of Steinseestraße 2, loud pop concerts are sometimes held.

For a while, it looked as if Haidhausen would succeed Schwabing as the "in" place. Exhibitions are still held in the **Galerie in der Lothringerstraße,** formerly a factory, which could not be relocated anywhere else. But the house is firmly in the hands of the city authorities, and is really nothing more than a cultural fig-leaf. After the pub licences in Haidhausen were severely curtailed, the scene now seems to have shifted to Gärtnerplatz, a former homosexual area.

Well, that's where you'll find various institutions which abhor good taste and manage to keep the rather sparse underground culture alive in Munich. The **Werkstattkino** (Workshop Cinema) at Fraunhoferstraße 9, which is hidden in a cellar behind the **Fraunhofer** an old beer hall, shows the most horrendous films and cheap Japanese monster thrillers, as well as the filthiest sex movies. There you'll find real hippies and noisy leather-jacket kids. You'll also find tasteless B-movies, among which are some of the most revolting things ever shown on screen. Because of the danger of violence in this area, beer is sold only in cans.

Incidentally, this neighbourhood owns the best underground football team—the annual winner of the Baader Cup. The organiser of this competition is the cafe with the same name, the **Baader Café** (Baaderstraße 47 around the corner). Here people stand around after concerts and drink, and find out what is happening in the local rock scene.

It's also here that the underground gossip writers find their material, to fill the pages of papers like the **Münchner Stadtzeitung** which offers its readers news on music and films, and an exhaustive calendar of events.

After the Baader, one usually moves on to the **Größenwahn** (Megalomania) in Lothringerstraße 11, where the beer is expensive. It is next to the Baader and the Werkstattkino, and although it has never really been "in", it is a place where one visits once a week. Old habits die hard in Munich.

The **Tanzlokal Größenwahn** (Megalomania Dance Hall) at Klenzstraße 43, named after a famous old bohemian café, is supposed to be a discotheque. However, it is more a place for standing around and look-

Left, punks planning a night out. Right, the executive set living it up.

ing cool. Anyway, it's a place where you know who everyone is—and each wants to be seen in—but don't actually speak to them and wouldn't dream of doing so.

From there you inevitably move on to the **Parkcafé** (Sopienstraße 7) or to the **Wunderbar** (Hackenstraße 3) where you all meet up again, and as there's nowhere else to go, you carry on through the night with the "Schickeria" or chic set.

Apart from these spots, there is really

nowhere else that people just meet up. There are drinking clubs, but those popular spots of the 1970s have faded from the scene. The Größenwahn Dance Hall, as a relic of those days, provides the beer for the hard drinkers, music lovers and shady characters.

What is it like to be "in"? Novelist Rainald Goetz, who with *Irre* (Mad) became the authority of the underground, put it like this: "I stood there, as I wanted to be a lone wolf, watching with arrogance. That was freedom! I drank to that. A lot of beer. I'm an outsider, but more 'in' than ever."

AUER DULT AND NOCKHERBERG

The two old quarters of **Au** and **Giesing** on the right bank of the Isar, are to Munich as Karl Valentin—who was born here—is to Thomas Mann, who found success on the other side of the river. It's here from time to time that you will most likely encounter that explosive mixture of native cunning, the smell of beer and scurrilous Bavarian anarchism.

The Isar is like a spiritual hurdle. There was once a 19th century saying, that the Au was where the good-for-nothings lived. Since the day labourers, season odd-job workers and tramps came to stay, this neighbourhood was often flooded by the Isar. It seemed the group of outcasts were not welcome inside the city. They lived cheek by jowl in *Herbergen* or inns, which they built themselves, and which you can still see in Nockherstraße as stark reminders of their lifestyle.

A Whiff of the Past

These inns have remained for two hundred years on the banks of the Isar, and seem to evoke a romantic past in the minds of the city dwellers. In essence, however, they resemble nothing more than stark post-war buildings.

The depressing, unredeemed side of the past is more evident here than elsewhere. The true vista of Munich is not what can be seen from the Olympiaturm (Olympic Tower) but what meets the eye when you walk along the Hochstraße between Gasteig and Giesinger Berg. There is no trace of the glory which King Ludwig I once bestowed upon the rest of Munich in the 19th century with his imposing buildings. When you look over the rooftops, your

Preceding pages, a snooze after hard day's work.

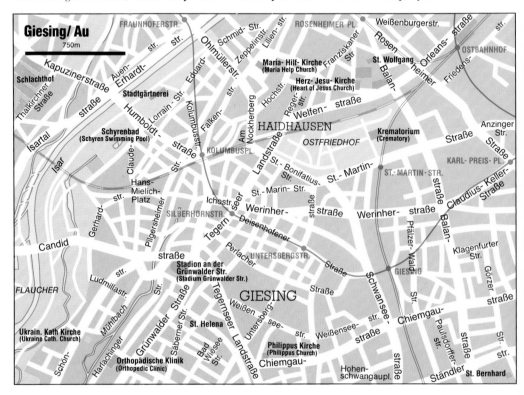

eyes may focus on city streams which are still uncovered. Or perhaps you would prefer to see the prison cells at **Neudeck** and listen to the tales passed down through the years.

If you're the curious onlooker type, you will gain much from an introductory lesson in Munich architecture. Behind the dramatic New Gothic **Heilig-Kreuz-Kirche** (Church of the Holy Cross)—designed by Ludwig II's architect Ludwig Dollmann and standing on the bank of the river—are some narrow streets where the people lived, the **Herbergsgassen** (Obere and Untere Grasstraße).

A few metres further on is the **Tela-Post** (Tegernseer Landstraße) which was built on a functional design by the architects Verhoelzer-Schmidt in 1928 as an example of a "Hypermodern style", and which has caused much controversy. Today that piece of information may come as a surprise, but it

shows just how narrow the distinctions are in Munich and how extremism can develop. That which is mundane elsewhere becomes avant-garde in Munich. Differences in opinion tend to lead to a public outcry.

Of course, it follows that the folk singer and only true Bavarian intellectual Karl Valentin, who could be hailed as a Dadaist anywhere else, came from the Au (Zeppelinstraße 41). In fact he still belongs to this side of the river, not to the people in Maximilianstraße who praise him today. The angry young Bavarian poet Konstantin Wecker, pays tribute to this "genius loci", with his incipient Bavarian anarchism in his **Kaffee Giesing**.

Otherwise, a pleasure seeker in Munich would hardly ever set foot in Au or Giesing. **La Marmite** (Lilienstraße 8) is worth a visit, that is if you want to study its smoke-stained stucco work, and taste the two traditionally

Below, he mends all the bikes in the Au. Right, the movie star Walter Sedlmayr at the *Bleck'n* in the Nockerberg.

French menus (be warned there's no a la carte menu).

The Fifth Season

If they wanted to guard against the threatened decline of the Bavarian lifestyle, the inhabitants of Munich whether housewife, aesthete or beer drinker, all visit this formerly miserable area at least once or twice a year.

The Au was, in fact, only incorporated into the city after much jealous wrangling in 1854. It is in the Au that the real Munich festivals are held, although they have not been adapted to the needs of the tourist market. They are celebrated with undiminished enthusiasm by the people of Munich. In the Au, more than anywhere else in Munich, having fun and getting drunk is enjoyed to the full, whether by those in the *Dult* (Fair) in Mariahilfplatz or by the inveterate beer drinkers who turn up at the *Berg* (Mountain) in the **Salvatorkeller am Nockherberg** to ply their skills at the strong beer festival.

There the national pastime of drinking great quantities of local beer is still genuinely Bavarian, not Prussianised as in the Hofbräuhaus. Once a year, for two weeks from the Saturday before *Josephi* (St. Joseph's Day) on 19 March, the Salvator-Märzen beer is served, which has about 20 percent original wort and 6 percent alcohol. For the people of Munich, this is such an important day of the year that it has been nicknamed as "the fifth season". The boozing is traditionally kicked off with a satirical show in true Bavarian style, where local politicians, dignitaries and bigwigs present themselves and sportingly take the mickey. Then the leader of the state government, always a conservative of course, is presented with the first *Maß* (mug) of beer, which he faithfully downs to the traditional cry

The carousel...

of "*Salve pater patriae! Bibas, princeps optime!*"

After that the atmosphere becomes infused with beer sodden contentment, from which not even the social democrats are excluded. For the next two weeks, the *Berg* belongs to the people. Even if they do wonder sometimes what sense it makes to sit in cramped, smoke-filled halls with the music of several brass bands blasting in their ears at once, they try to make conversation at the tops of their voices. Usually, they give up and limit themselves to the occasional *Prost!* (Cheers!). However, even if they had the most dreadful hangovers the morning after, they'll come back the following year. In the summer, the Nockherberg is turned into a secluded beer garden

Politics, drunkenness and the intellect are said to be catered for in the Au. It is also said that the second institution for which the Au is famous, the *Dult*,

...and the flea market on the Auer Dult.

which is held three times a year in Mariahilfplatz, was established in 1796 by the Prince Elector of the day while he was under the influence of the strong beer. All your dreams can come true here. "Der Billige Jakob" combines cabaret with incredibly cheap silk stockings, which you can as buy the definitive cure for rheumatism. There are items at giveaway prices and no visitor to Munich should miss out on this bargain haunt.

There are "art deco" cradles for sale, and anything from rusty door handles to to irreparable electric gadgets. Second-hand books, some of which are rare finds and which would delight for book lovers, can be bought for a song. But some odds and ends don't stand out so well to the light of day that, albeit decorative, their uselessness becomes obvious. Still, never mind, it is fun all the same even if you merely window-shop at the bazaar.

THE WIES'N - THE CHARM OF ANOTHER WORLD

At the end of September when summer in Munich is at its best, the die-hard Munich grumbler has a heavy decision to make: should he stick to his principles this time, that every so often wild horses couldn't drag him to the *Wies'n*, as the October festival is known locally. Doesn't he get angry each year at the moral degeneration out on the Theresienwiese (Theresa Meadow). Now the beer is being served even from containers—of all things—which are disguised as

radishes they've brought, outside the tents because they just can't help going to the *Wies'n* in the end.

Even if it's only for nostalgia when a Maß of beer cost only DM 2.95 (that was in 1971; today the price is more than DM 6!), or childhood memories of their first visit to the "*Schichtl*", a booth where a volunteer from the audience stands by a guillotine, and the head "replaced" afterwards. This act has been ingrained in the mind of the local chap

wooden barrels. Beer flows into the barrels after passing through the pipes from the aluminium tanks. The popular snacks at the *Wies'n*—grilled chicken, pork sausages and fish—are now served on paper and plastic plates. And as for the foreigners ...there are more and more every year. They attack the festival tent as if they were storming a fortress and then in the ensuing chaos, perform their victory dances on the wooden tables.

Yes, there's plenty for the people of Munich to complain about regarding their *Oktoberfest*. But they do it over a *Maß*, with

that the expression "*Auf geht's beim Schichtl*" (Let's go to the Schichtl) now is part of his daily conversation. The local folks are unlikely to give up on this spectacle. When the booth was threatened with closure due to tax liability, it drew a petition; money was raised to save the Schichtl.

The people of Munich still love their *Wies'n*, though perhaps less today than the time when dubious spectacles and sensational acts were a regular part of the *Wies'n*. The people seemed to enjoy those few hours of performance put up by international shows of the *Gründerjahre* (years of expansion) in the early 1870s.

The real attraction of the *Oktoberfest* has always been the charm of another world, an escape from the mundane to the curious. It's a world found once a year in a small meadow at the foot of the statue of Bavaria. There are Bedouins, Kirghiz and Tartars—for most people of Munich, their only chance to see such people would be at the *Wies'n*. Then there are the world premieres in 1820, the gas

or later as a demonstration of integration of Pan-Germany, under the National Socialists. But the *Wies'n* always managed to remain more of an unbridled, orgiastic intoxication for the masses, rather than a kind of folk euphoria ordered by the authorites. The compulsory breaks due to the two wars had little effect when one tent was used and diluted beer (!) was served. The people of Munich managed to put away 1.5 million Maß of that swill—and there were not many

balloon flight, and the animal shows. It is the desire to break off from daily routine which has kept this festival alive for over 175 years.

In fact the festival was established after the wedding celebrations of the Bavarian Crown Prince Ludwig to Therese von Sachsen-Hildeburghausen. Since its beginning, the rulers wanted to use the spectacle for their own purposes, whether to stress the national characteristics under Crown Prince Ludwig,

Left, they keep coming to the *Weis'n*. Above, family fun in the beer tent.

foreigners to help them then!

It's hard to say what it is really like today. The statistics alone cannot determine how much of the half a million grilled chickens and the 6 million Maß of beer were consumed by locals. The people of Munich probably just want to enjoy their festival discreetly. They cash in on the food and drink vouchers from their employers. Then perhaps a final snack of roasted almonds to wind up their visit to the *Wies'n*. They've caught a glimpse of another world, one which tourists shouldn't miss either.

THE STOMACH OF MUNICH

Behind the Theresienhöhe and almost out of sight from the bright city lights, you are still in Munich. Here a part of the city stays far from the tourist trail but nevertheless comes out its own attractions. In the old days, where sulphur, pitch and rubber factories polluted the air, where beer was brewed and timber processed, and where the social services alleviated the workers' lot, is where you'll still find the neglected city outskirts.

The Glockenbachviertel

A walk through Sendling, Glockenbachviertel and Westend will quickly dispel these notions, since each area has its own character and local group of inhabitants.

In the last century, there was a swing from the classical city planning of the Bavarian kings, Max I. Joseph and Ludwig I, to the communal architecture of the Gründerzeiten (Period of Expansion). In particular, the Max-Vorstadt (Suburb) and the Gärtnerplatzviertel (Gardeners' Square District) were quite innovative in concept. These ideas took hold in the Glockenbachviertel after 1870. For the first time, building projects were not undertaken simply for the owner's use; tenement houses were built also by the wealthy.

Neo-Baroque Courtyards

The **Frauenhoferstraße** marks the end of the Gärtnerplatzviertel and the beginning of Glockenbachviertel. Here stands one of the real alternative cafés of Munich, the legendary **Frauenhofer** (No. 9). There the notorious **Werkstattkino** (workshop cinema) offers

Preceding pages, view over the rooftops of Munich.

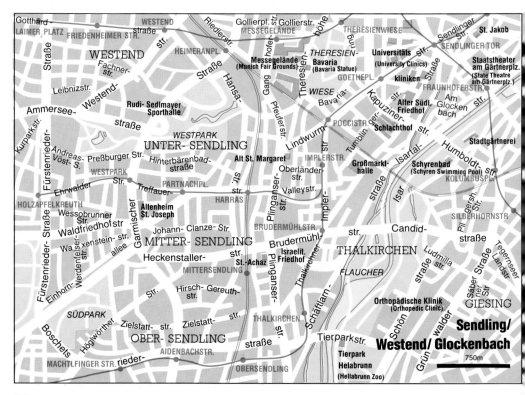

distinctly unbourgeois entertainment patronised by tourists and locals.

As you move on towards Baader-straße, you'll notice the well-preserved, pretty facade of the **Frauenhofer-Apotheke** (Frauenhofer Chemist). Continue your walk along Ickstatt-straße and you pass many courtyards which are still used for manufacturing purposes. Then you reach the **Hans-Sachs-Platz** and the street of the same name. The houses, built in the main from 1897-1900, are in neo-baroque style and are a picturesque piece of architectural history. The Glocken-bachviertel too has its own particular kind of residents. Although the poor and the old, the foreigners and the communes are still the majority, the smart set is gradually moving in. There are still many *Tante Emma* or corner shops, as well as second-hand shops in this district, despite the rising rents. The area around Hans-Sachs-Straße is the

The flea market finds its niche in Glocken-bach.

homosexual district of Munich with bars, pubs and discos.

Nostalgia

The Hurth cogwheel and machine factory, which moved here in 1911, was one of the largest undertakings in Glockenbach with its 1,900 workers. Part of the community rejoiced when the complex was demolished in 1983, but some people mourned the disappearance of this rare example of industrial architecture of the 1930s. There was dissent too over the new "luxury" dwellings which replaced it. In Holz-straße 28-30 is the administrative division of the electro-technic factory of Alois Zettler. The complex and factory in Jahnstraße (built in 1906 on the site of the western mill) clearly show the close juxtaposition of the residential and office premises, which were characteristic of the Glockenbach area at the turn of the century. There is a kind of bitter charm about the place.

After the **Holzplatz** (Timber Square), where landed logs were once stacked, and Pestalozzistraße, you arrive at **Westermühlbach** (Western Mill Stream). Here you can see part of what used to be the extensive canal system of Munich. Today, the only reminders of that era are street names such as Dreimühlen-, Westermühl- or Müllerstraße (Three Mills-, Western Mill- and Miller Street). These waterways were considered a hindrance for a city of cars, and so most of them were concreted over in the 1960s, an action regretted not only by the nostalgic minority but by the group of city ecologists as well.

Along a small footpath from the Pestalozzistraße, you find yourself in the **Alter Südlicher Friedhof** (Old Southern Cemetery), which has great historical significance for the people of Munich. It began as the plague cemetery outside the city in 1563. In 1789, it became the main cemetery for the city of

Munich. In 1855, it was extended with the "Campo santo" along Italian lines in the south.

A walk through the park-like cemetery leads you past the graves of many famous people of Munich, from painter Carl Spitzweg to chemist Justus Liebig, to optician and inventor Joseph von Fraunhofer. The names of the deceased can be looked up on a plaque by the main gate. In the summer nights, it's not just the dead who sleep here. The place is popular among local tramps and impecunious tourists.

While at Dreimühlenstraße and past the Kapuzinerstraße (Capuchin Street), relax at the "Greek Beer Garden", the **Rembetiko**. Opposite this courtyard haven is the high-rise administrative building of the Rodenstock Optical Works. Through Ehrengutstraße, you arrive at the enormous **Schlacht- und Viehhof** (The Cattle and Slaughter Stock Yard). With over 1,500 employees, it has grown to become the most important centre for cattle slaughter in Southern Germany.

Where the butchers meet in the morning for breakfast, rock fans meet in the evening for live concerts. Now well-known through television, the rustic pub **Zum Schlachthof** (The Slaughterhouse) is the venue for the concerts. In fact, the whole area is becoming more interesting with various places to go, from the Greek tavern **To Steki** (Dreimühlenstraße 30), to the smart **Humphrey Bogärtchen** (Isartalstraße 26) and the beer cellar **Zum Thomas-bräu** (Kapuzinerplatz 5).

The Westend

Poor living conditions and low rents have made the traditional working class area of **Westend** a place for foreign workers and retired people to live. As early as 1830, there were only thirty

Second-hand items up for sale in Frauenhoferstraße.

houses on Sendlinger Heide, where day labourers without citizenship found refuge here. As the years passed, the railway began to play a key role and it soon determined the development of the area.

In the 19th century, the Munich "Gallows Hill" was initially a middle class estate; traces of this can still be seen in some of the buildings and their facades, like the west side of Schieß- stättstraße for instance. However, the image was short-lived and since then, the Westend has had a somewhat dubious reputation. It used to be called the "Broken Glass District", but is now more often referred to as "Munich's Little Istanbul". Although not wholly true, the epithet does give an indication of the population, and there are indeed several foreign bars and shops. The **Schwanthalerstraße** area has developed extensive automobile trade with the East. It is precisely this mix of cultures and nationalities which gives the Westend its own particular charm, and which now attracts students and intellectuals as residents.

Between the streets of Holzapfel, Westend and Schwanthalerstraße is the oldest part of Westend. This is an area marked for redevelopment, although a number of the buildings are to be preserved as examples of rare pre-1870 residential apartments.

There is a longstanding tradition of beer brewing in Westend; ceaseless activities which go on within the walls of the local breweries can help vouch for the claim. You can hardly miss the **Hacker-Pschorr A. G.** complex on Bayerstraße. Reflected on the large display windows of the **Sudhaus** (Brewing House) on Grasserstraße is the rustic brick building of the **Augustiner- brauerei**, the second brewery to be established in Westend.

If you stop at Theresienhöhe and look

Below, the market hall in Sendling is the "Stomach of Munich". Right, hanging out at the slaughter- house.

south, you'll see the main entrance to the Trade Fair area, the **Messegalände**, on Messeplatz. Munich is currently one of the largest trade-fair towns in Germany, and the locals of Westend suffer for it. Delivery vans are seen everywhere and most stop at random, even if it's for a while; parked vehicles fill the already busy streets and entrances to the buildings. The chaos contributes to the antagonism of the residents. The proximity of the fair, with its rather extravagant visitors, explains the somewhat incongruous presence of **Le Gourmet** in Ligalstraße.

The "Wies'n"

On the Theresienwiese (Theresa Meadow) is the bronze statue of **Bavaria**. One can climb 121 steps, right to the top of this 18.5-metre figure. She was originally designed by Klenze and Schwanthaler, and eventually cast by Ferdinand Miller. It was the first time in 1844 that anything so enormous had been cast in bronze. During the reign of Ludwig I in 1850, the Bavaria was set up as a memorial to famous Bavarians. Around her is Klenze's **Ruhmeshalle** (Hall of Fame).

At the feet of Bavaria is the **Theresienwiese**, which is known as the "Wies'n" for short. This is where the world-famous annual *Oktoberfest* (October Festival) is held. Unfortunately, the place has not always been a scene for entertainment. On 2 February 1918, workers of the Munich armaments industry went on strike and gathered here to protest at the continuation of the war. Among other things, they demanded the release of Kurt Eisner, who had proclaimed the "Free State of Bavaria" in November 1918. During the Oktoberfest in 1980, a member of the neo-Nazi military sports group, Hoffmann, sparked off a riot which caused the

Turkish women workers add a colourful touch to the thoroughfare.

death of 13 people, and injury to more than 200 people.

If you proceed further into the heart of the Westend, you'll find tenement buildings on Tulbeckstraße and Gollierstraße, which are a reminder of the days when Westend was an industrial district of pitch, sulphuric acid and rubber factories, and one in which the working class resided.

There is little activity here in the evenings, apart from the **Theatre im Westend** (Guldeinstraße 47) and the **Westend Cinema** (Ligalstraße 20). There are also quite a number of pubs, such as the cosy Greek **Entaxi** or the **Realwirt-schaft Stragula** (both located in Bergmannstraße).

Gollierplatz (Gollier Square), lies directly opposite the functionalist Bauhaus style brick building of the **Ledigenheim** (Home for Singles), which was constructed in the 1920s to reduce the number of aimless streetwalkers.

Here, in summer, one of Munich's better known flea markets is held during the weekends.

Sendling

Motorists are familiar with the name Sendling from the occasional radio broadcast, "*Heavy traffic on the Heckenstallerstraße and Brudermühlstraße.*" The wide asphalt band of the Mittlerer Ring (Middle Ring Road) cuts Sendling in half.

Sendling, which stretches from the Isar to Westpark, is traditionally an industrial area. It is also home to the "Stomach of Munich" (the huge market hall between Thalkirchnerstraße and Kochelseestraße) which is one of the largest fruit and vegetable markets in Europe. You'll have to get up early if you want to catch the action; the busiest time comes at around five in the morning. Sendling also offers a great attrac-

Below, the flea market vendor takes five to hug his pet. Right, kebab specialty from the chef himself.

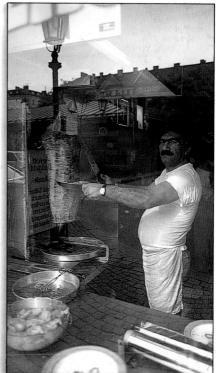

tion in the **Flaucher** with its famous beer garden and the islands in the Isar for sun-worshippers.

Past **Gotzinger Platz**, the St.-Korbinians-Kirche and the Implerstraße, you arrive at busy **Lindwurmstraße**, which was formerly the Sendlinger Landstraße. After a short, steep climb, you reach the **Sendlinger Bergl** (Sendlinger Hill), first recorded as "Sendlinga" in 782 in monastic writings, and is today the historical centre of the old village. The church of **Alt-St.-Margaret** (Old Church of St. Margaret) meets at the junction of the streets of Pfeufer-, Plinganser- and Lindwurmstraße. The "Sendlinger Bauernschlacht" (Sendlinger Peasants' War) took place here in 1705. Alt-St.-Margaret is a typical Upper Bavarian baroque village church which has been well preserved. On the northern outside wall, a fresco by Wilhelm Lindenschmit (1830) is a reminder of the battle, and those who lost their lives are buried in the cemetery. Directly opposite the church is a memorial erected in 1911 to the legendary leader of the uprising, the **Smith of Kochel** .

On the other side of Pfeuferstraße, you can smell cows despite the fact that you are amidst urban dwellings. The smell comes from the **Stemmerwiese**, the last farmyard in Sendling and a relic from the days when Sendling was the fruit and vegetable garden of Munich.

From the Sendling maypole to the left and in the direction of Harras, you can have a good view of the **Dorfschmiede** (The Village Smithy). Until a few years ago, this low building was still a blacksmith's operation. It was said to have been built from the stones of the demolished Münchner Hoftheater (Munich Court Theatre) in 1823. It has since been converted into a pub.

Carry on through Jägerwirtstraße, past an old *Marterl* (crossroads) to the

Memorial
o the Smith
of Kochel in
Sendling.

new **St.-Margaret-Kirche** (Church of St. Margaret). This area has managed to retain some of its village atmosphere, in marked contrast to nearby **Harras**. The once-lovely centre of Sendling, named after Coffee House owner Robert Harras, is now filled with heavy traffic. Along the congested Plinganerstraße and Mittlerer Ring, you come to the **Israelitischen Friedhof** (Israeli Cemetery) on Die-tramszeller Straße, the origin of which goes far back to the 13th century. Most notable is the memorial created by Johann von Klenze for the dramatist Michael Beer. Looking rather modest next to the wide arterial road, the Neuhofer Kirche **St. Achas** was one of the last neo-baroque churches to be built in Munich.

In Mitter- and Ober (Middle and Upper) Sendling, the visitor finds himself deeper within the industrial estates which were built in 1900, and which moulded the character of Sendling: Lin-

A respite from work for some.

des Ice Machine AG, Deckel Machine Factory, Philip Morris Cigarettes and the giant electronics plant of Siemens which moved its headquarters from a divided Berlin to Munich after the war.

You carry on through the extensive residential area built by co-operative building societies, and the Sendlinger allotments, to **Luise-Kiesselbach-Platz**. From here, you have a good view of the towers of the **Altenheim St. Josef** which have been a landmark in Sendling since 1928.

A short walk further on the asphalt and steel strip of the Mittlerer Ring, brings you to **Westpark**, which has been converted into a park since the original barren land was spruced up as the venue for the 1983 International Garden Festival. Park lovers including joggers, cyclists and casual strollers will enjoy the presence of lawns, artificial lakes and the little Chinese and Tibetan temples.

OF PRINCES AND BEER BREWERS

If you arrive in Munich by train from the west, you will go under three bridges which join the beer brewing areas of Westend and Neuhausen. The last bridge is the ancient looking **Hackerbrücke** (Hacker Bridge), an iron structure of 1892 now under a preservation order. This bridge is of particular importance during the Oktoberfest for it's here that the tourists and people of Munich cross the river to the Wies'n or Theresienwiese (Theresa Meadow) for the annual beer festival.

Neuhausen

Neuhausen is one of those areas in Munich which suffered not only during World War II, but also during the so-called second destruction of Munich by town planners in the 1960s. An example of this is the **Donnersbergerbrücke** over which the Mittlerer Ring (Middle Ring Road) cuts Neuhausen around the Rotkreuzplatz in two.

Alfred Andersch, the well-known author born in Olgastraße 50, depicts this period between the wars: "It was a time of harsh suffering. Old trams, silent barracks and anarchy were destined by fate to come together." In his stories, he describes the fascination of how the empty spaces left after bombing raids have been filled during the building boom of the 1960s. The once-lovely Landshuter Allee was sacrificed to the demands of the Olympic Games for a wider Donnersbergerbrücke.

North of the Hackerbrücke, between Arnulfstraße and Blutenburgstraße, is the **Marsfeld** (Field of Mars) where people were executed in the 18th century, and military drills undertaken during the 19th century. Now breweries

Preceding pages, evening silhouette of the Nymphenburg Palace.

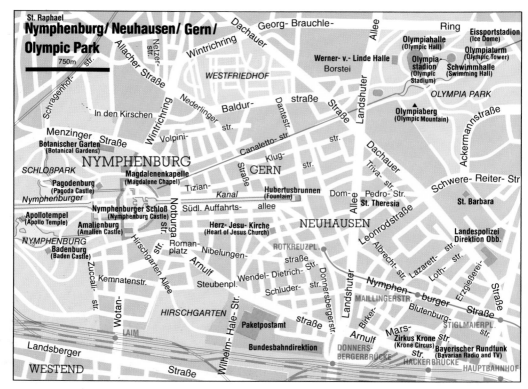

share this area with the post office and the railway. Thus, along the railway lines in Arnulfstraße, you'll find the container station, the railway administration offices and the **Paketpostamt** (Parcel Post Office) in Arnulfstraße 195. In the 1960s, this was the largest prefabricated cantilever hall in Europe.

If you carry on north from the Hakkerbrücke (Hakker Bridge), you reach the breweries of Neuhausen. Not far away are the winter quarters of the **Zirkus Krone** Circus; they have been there since 1919. From Christmas till the end of March, you can visit the circus on Sundays and public holidays. During circus tours, rock concerts are also held in the Krone-Bau (Krone Building). These concerts are very popular because of the intimate atmosphere of the hall.

Where Munich beer is brewed.

On the other side of the road is the **Spatenbrauerei**. If you're thirsty by now, take heart for it's only a short walk to the **Löwenbrauerei** beer garden in **Stiglmaierplatz.** There's the shady **Augustinerkeller** beer garden in Arnulfstraße 52, where you can enjoy a foaming tankard, or *Maß*. You can go inside the **Löwenbraükeller**—burnt down in 1986 and subsequently rebuilt—if the weather is bad. The breweries are in this area because it was outside the city gates of Neuhauser Berg that ice cellars were once constructed to keep the beer cool.

If you continue westwards along **Nymphenburger Straße** you pass the **Justizgebaude** or Law Court (No. 16) and **Erzgießerstraße** where the Bavaria statue was cast. It took three weeks to transport the individual pieces of the stature to the Theresienwiese. The royal casting works no longer exist.

Finally, the Nymphenburger Straße leads to the centre of Neuhausen, the **Rotkreuzplatz.** This is dominated by the dull high-rise **Schwesternschule**

(Sisters' School). However, efforts have been made recently to integrate the square into the area. The old village pond is now a fountain area. Children and teenagers come here for the best ice cream in Munich, at **Sarcletti** (Nymphenburger Straße 155). The structure of the quiet square is reflected in the architecture of Kaufhof department store. Opposite is the **Jagdschlößl** (The Hunting Lodge), an old inn decorated with hunting artifacts and antlers. There's a beer garden here where you can wait for the tram to Schloß Nymphenburg (Nymphenburg Palace) or to Schwabing.

When people talk about the "new" pubs of Neuhausen, they are referring to the area around the **Platz der Freiheit** where in the evenings, one can wander along old streets from the smart **Café Freiheit** (Leonrodstraße 20) to the more relaxed **Frundsberg** (Frundsbergstraße 46). Also well-

known here for its gourmet-breakfast-on-a-summer-terrace is the **Ruffini** (Orfstraße 22). Despite the appalling building signs perpetrated in Neuhausen, the **Maria-Trost-Kirche** church with its small cemetery has been preserved in Winthirstraße 15. There are many memorial tablets on the outside walls of this little church which remind you of the local personalities, such as the caster Stiglmaier and the extensive family of his nephew Ferdinand von Miller.

Nevertheless, the fame of the legendary Winthir outshines all others laid to rest here. The Irish-Scottish name was given to the remains of the "missionary of Neuhausen", estimated to be about 1,000 years old but discovered only in 1933. He thus went down in history as the first inhabitant of Neuhausen.

Hans Döllgast built the **Siedlung Neuhausen** (Neuhausen Estate) for the middle-class between 1928 and 1930.

In the brewery district near the Hacker Bridge.

This exemplary housing development of 1,900 apartments with open fields sandwiches Wendl-Dietrich-Straße between Rotkreuzplatz and Steubenplatz.

Arcadia

By the **Rondell Neuwittelsbach,** traces of the working class and brewery district of Neuhausen have all disappeared. The proximity of Schloß Nymphenburg is the determining factor in the social structure here. However, one last attraction for the ordinary folk is Munich's best loved beer garden, The **Hirschgarten** (The Deer Park). With its playgrounds and football pitches, the park is a paradise for children and adults, and is well frequented by the people from the city. The **Magdalenenfest** in July organises a variety of items for sale, such as fabrics and crockery and of course, beer. The Hirschgarten took its name from the deer which

Kurfürst (Prince Elector) Karl Theodor kept in the park in 1780. The fallow deer enclosure is still there.

Schloß Nymphenburg

Here begins that arcadian part of Munich which seems to have escaped the ravages of time. Geese, ducks, swans and well-fed carp enjoy the canals and lakes of the palace grounds. However, when the water is frozen in winter, ice skaters turn the whole garden into a scene from Brueghel. It is a sight not to be missed.

It was Kurfürst Ferdinand Maria who gave the *Schweige Kemnath* (Royal Ladies' Residence), to his wife Henriette Adelaide on the birth of their son Maximilian Emanuel II in 1663. The foundation stone for the summer residence now known as *Schloß Nymphenburg*, was laid a year later and by 1675, the central pavilion designed by

Playful lass at waterworks on Rotkreuzplatz.

Zuccalli and Barelli was complete. Construction of the palace and the park continued well into the 19th century, with the greatest influence coming from Max Emanuel (1662-1726). While he was regent, the **Schloßrondell** (round flower-bed), the canals and the park with its little summer residences were created. One of his architects was Joseph Effner, who was responsible for the Chinese style **Pagodenburg** (Pagoda Palace), the **Badenburg** (Bathing Palace)—a rare installation of its kind built in the 18th century, and the **Magda-lenenklause** (Magdalen Retreat). The latter, deliberately designed with cracks and fissures, was to aid the ageing Prince in his meditations upon spiritual matters. Unfortunately, Max Emanuel died before it was completed. Under Karl Albrecht, the **Amalienburg**, by François Cuvilliés the Elder, was one of the better examples of German rococo. The park in the palace, originally laid out on formal symmetrical lines in the French baroque style, was drastically altered at the beginning of the 19th century by the landscape architect von Schell, who changed the style to follow the English pattern. Thanks to him, this park resembles the Englischer Garten (English Garden) and is one of the loveliest recreation areas of Munich.

It is well worth visiting the palace, if only to see Ludwig I's Gallery of Beauties, where portraits of women from all walks of life are displayed. You'll get to look at personalities like Munich beauty Helene Sedlmayr, a shoemaker's daughter, and Lola Montez, the king's mistress who was partly responsible for his unwilling abdication in 1848. After a visit to the **Marstallmuseum** (Royal Stables Museum) and its splendid state carriages from the royal past, rest at the beer garden of the **Schloßwirt-schaft zur Schwaige**.

Time out in the Hirschgarten.

Near the **Palmenhaus-Café** (Palm House Café) in the park, a side door leads to the **Botanischer Garten** (Botanical Garden), which shows off open land and beautiful tropical houses.

Gern

If you have time and feel like taking a walk, you can continue along the southern Auffahrtsallee to **Gerner Brücke** (Gern Bridge). Cross the bridge and walk down Gerner Straße and you'll find yourself in an exclusive neighbourhood of villas. This area was developed just before the turn of the century and was known as the **Familienhaus-Colonie** (Family House Colony). It was much loved by the artists of the time. All terraced houses, each unit costs 9,500 Gold Marks and comprises four rooms with kitchen, bathroom and cellar. You can see some of these in Böcklinstraße. There is also a quaint museum of cham-

ber pots, the **Nachttopfmuseum**, with exhibits spanning two thousand years.

At the end of the canal is the **Hubertusbrunnen**. Max Emanuel had wanted to connect the canal at Nymphenburg with Schloß Schleißheim and the city residence. Created by Hildebrand in 1903, the neo-baroque fountain reflects the Arcadia which Neuhausen once was. Behind bars, the bronze Hubertus deer "roars". Further down is the **Taxisgarten** (Taxisstraße 12).

Before returning to the former barracks area of Neuhausen—a major **Flohmarkt** (flea market) is held here on Fridays and Saturdays at Dachauer Straße 128—spend time to look at the **Borstei**.. This was formerly a spacious upper middle class estate completed by the private builder Bernhard Borst, in the area bounded by Dachauer Straße, Pickelstraße and Lampadiusstraße. Borstei was among the first few popular estates which had amenities.

Freeze and fun by the Nymphenburg Canal.

THE OTHER SIDE OF THE MIDDLE RING

In the open countryside of the Isar valley south of Munich lies one of the largest zoos in Europe. Founded in 1910, Hellabruun is the first zoo landscaped on geographical lines, on the principles stipulated by Karl Hagenbeck. Big game is kept in pleasant surroundings, as close as possible to the animals' natural habitat. One of the zoo's most popular attractions is the children's section, where kids can feed, touch and stroke the animals.

Not far from here is the **Asam-Schlößl "Maria Einsiedel"** (Benediktbeurer Straße 19). This small palace was transformed from an ordinary house into a royal country residence with paintings on the facadeby Cosmas Damian Asam in 1729-32. A must for jazz lovers is the **Waldwirtschaft Großhesselohe** where live music is played. It is only a few minutes walk from the bridge of the same name, a big iron structure across the Isar.

On the northern side of the extensive Forstenried Park is the baroque **Schloß Fürstenried** (Fürstenried Palace), the starting point for the magnificent hunting parties of King Max II. The whole complex, arranged rather like Schloß Nymphenburg, is aligned with the eight-kilometre long Frauenkirche (Church of Our Lady). Sadly, the view down the avenue of lime trees is today interrupted by a motorway.

Between the noisy Verdi and Pippinger Streets, and the motorway in the direction of Stuttgart, is the idyllic palace of **Schloß Blutenburg**. The former summer residence and hunting lodge of the Wittelsbachs dates from the 15th century. It served as a love nest for Agnes Bernauer (who was drowned in the Danube at Straubing in 1435 and

Crystal clear country setting in The Blutenburg.

was accused of being a witch) and her suspected secret lover Duke Albrecht III. The **Schloßkirche St. Sigismund** (Palace Church of St. Sigismund) is Late Gothic, with the paintings of the winged altar-piece and glass paintings by Jan Pollack. Also of interest to the visitor is an old Bavarian village inn at the **Alter Wirt** in Obermenzing in Dorfstraße 38.

Among the huge tenement buildings, wide arterial roads and beer gardens stands one of the oldest pilgrimage churches in Bavaria, the **St. Maria in Ramersdorf** at Aribonenstraße 9. The Gothic building of 1400 was renovated in the baroque style in 1675. With the neighbouring sacristan's house and the cemetery, it makes up the centre of the old village.

The centre of **Alt-Perlach** (Old Perlach) has also retained some of its original village atmosphere, and with the baroque parish church of the **St. Michael**, the Hachinger Stream and the restored common village.

Utopia in Grau

There can be no greater contrast to Alt-Perlach, than **Neu-Perlach** (New Perlach), the largest satellite town of Germany with 60,000 inhabitants. There are huge blocks of flats, complex road networks and green roundabouts. On the one hand, there are wide empty spaces. On the other, claustrophobic and cramped conditions. When the foundation stone was laid in 1967, what was seen as an innovative piece of social planning, is now regarded as a prime example of inhuman housing development policies. More successful is the so-called **Bavarian Silicon Valley** complex built by the giant Siemens, at the edge of the dormitory suburb. Here researchers work on the the latest development of microelectronics.

Sticking their necks out at the Hellabrunn Zoo.

You will hear jets taking off and landing at the nearby **Flughafen Riem** (Riem Airport), soon to be replaced in 1991 by the enormous München II (Munich II) Airport in Erding. You now come to the **Trabrennbahn Daglfing** (Trotting Course of Daglfing) with its ultra-modern stands, the almost dilapidated **Olympia Reitstadion** (Olympic Equestrian Hall) and the **Riemer Galopprennbahn** (Riem Gallop Race Course). On racing days, there's much exciting betting (Tel: 930 0010). You don't have to react quite as violently as one Munich newspaper publisher, who died of a heart attack while watching a trotting race.

But it is not just the Porsche and Jaguar owners who take their opulent picnics to the traditional beer garden of **Zur Emmeramsmühle** in the Englischer Garten at Oberführing. One should however have good provisions. Then, in Ismaninger Straße, there's the excellent but rather expensive Japanese restaurant **Mifune**, named after the famous film star.

The Other Side

In the north of Munich, it literally stinks to high heaven. Near the former **Freimann** residential suburb is the largest sewage works in the Federal Republic is to be found. Next to this are various refuse depots and even a hill of rubbish, which is the highest elevation in the gravel plain of Munich.

Within walking distance in Wallnerstraße are the modern oriental **Moschee der Islamischen Gesellschaft** (Islamic Community Mosque) and the 14th century **Fröttmaninger Heiligkreuzkirche** (Fröttmaninger Church of the Holy Cross), which is literally sinking in the mire. If you plan to visit the church, it is advisable to approach the caretaker of the compound.

Left, exotica in the Westpark. Below, the mosque on Schuttberg. Right, this maypole appears to be on the alert for the next festival.

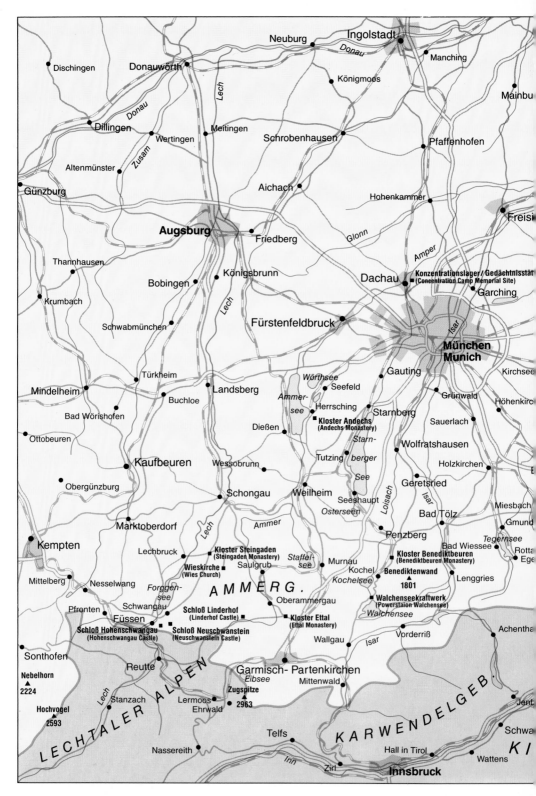

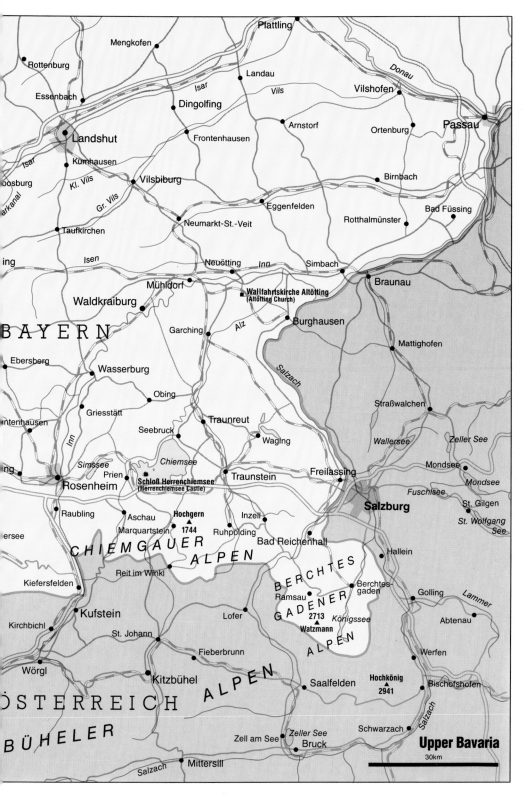

UNDER THE BAVARIAN SKY

"Lord, those whom you love, let them live in this land!"
—Ludwig Ganghofer

This is a fervent prayer, sent up to the pale blue Bavarian sky by the local poet long ago. If God had answered his prayer, then the Bavarians would all be pious indeed.

What is undeniably true, however, is that Upper Bavaria boasts of such glorious scenery and is considered one of the most beautiful parts of Germany. Here you will find alpine lakes of all sizes, formed by the action of glaciers in the Ice Age. They are surrounded either by soft green meadows and forests or steep, magnificent mountains. At almost every corner is a little village so neat and pretty that the scene appears to be unreal. Collectively, they look like an enormous outdoor museum instead of a living landscape. Streaming down from the mountains, winding round the hills and past the villages, are brooks and rivers flowing into the Danube, then to the Black Sea.

Progress has obviously left its mark on the idyllic Upper Bavarian landscape. The forests, particularly those in the mountains, are dying. The rivers and lakes are cleaned up with much difficulty, although the process has been quite successful in Starnberger-see and Ammersee. In the alpine foothills, the roads leading out south are overcrowded and the queues on the motorways used by European north-south traffic grow longer each year. Each weekend, more people try to escape into one of the last outposts of nature.

Preceding pages, technology and pastoral scene in Raisting; fountain figures in the Linderhof Palace. Left, out into the countryside.

EXCURSIONS INTO THE BAVARIAN COUNTRYSIDE

The nearest lake to Munich is the Starnberger See (Starnberger Lake), which is also known as Würmsee (Worm Lake). The Würm, a tributary of the Amper River, flows from its northern tip. However, there is a local explanation for its rather curious name. Apparently, there is an enormous worm—or reptile of some kind—which lives on the bed of the lake and stirs up the currents, sweeping the water even when there isn't a breath of wind. The story goes

Starnberg on the northern tip of the lake has lost some of its former beauty. However, it can still boast of the lovely old **Pfarrkirche St. Joseph** (Parish Church of St. Joseph) with the altar by Ignaz Günther, apart from a glorious palace.

Empress Sissy

On the western shore, 5 km south of Starnberg, is **Possenhofen** with its palace

that if the creature should ever surface, the world would come to an end. So each time the water heaves, folks bow down and pray that they may be spared the bitter cup.

There is another curious feature of this lake. You will find it quite impossible to look at the southern bank from the northern shore, even if you stand on tip-toe. But rather than worry about the earth's curvature, just look upwards to the scenic mountain ranges, the Benediktenwand, Karwendel, Estergebirge, Wetterstein and Ammergauer Bergen. The best view is from the lake itself so it could be worth taking a boat trip.

built in 1536. It was there that Kaiserin (Empress) Elisabeth of Austria, known as Sissy, spent the years of her youth. In later years, when the empress returned to Possenhofen, she often received a visitor from **Schloß Berg**, which lies directly opposite. That was where King Ludwig II stayed, but he would dress up in Austrian uniform and make his way over to Sissy, and then stay until late into the night. The situation became even more delicate when the king insisted on seeing the empress alone, contrary to convention and protocol. However, the reader should not jump to conclusions, as many of

Ludwig's contemporaries did, for these visits were in fact rather strenuous and even boring for Sissy. The empress' admirer had merely wanted to worship his soul-mate in silence, and had sat before her for hours without uttering a word.

In **Feldafing**, only a stone's throw from the shore of the lake, there is a small wooded island where Ludwig's father King Max II had a villa built. He planted 15,000 rose stalks, hence the name **Roseninsel** (Rose

over the Alps and the lake itself. The Ilka-Höhe is just south west of Tutzing near Oberzeismering. You can wander across to Unterzeismering and on to **Bernried** which takes about 1 1/2 hours. In Bernried is a wonderful park with gnarling oak trees and birches. You can cool your swollen feet in the water at **Seeshaupt**.

When you can get your boots back on, try to make a brief detour to see the nature reserve of **Osterseen** with its 21 bog-lakes

Island). In Ludwig's day, it too was a place for him and Empress Sissy to meet, or a place where they could leave letters for each other. "Seagull" Sissy would send greetings to her "Eagle" Ludwig, from the foaming waves up to the eternal snow. The "Eagle" would then thank the "Seagull" for the greetings that landed at the eyrie of a distant shore.

If you put on your walking boots, and climb up the 738-metre high **Ilka-Höhe**, you will be rewarded with a spectacular view

among forests and meadows. This beautiful area is great for enjoyable walks.

The eastern shore of the Starnberger Lake is more rural and less built up. After **Ammerland** and **Leoni** you come to **Berg**, where a signpost points the way to the votive chapel, the memorial church of Ludwig II. There is an annual pilgrimage in his honour on the anniversary of his death, 13th June. In the lake, a memorial cross marks the place where he was drowned (or shot?). In Berg is the start of a footpath, the **König-Ludwig-Weg**, which leads to Neuschwanstein, the fairy-tale castle Ludwig had built in Füssen.

Left, boating on the Starnberger Lake. Above, where land, sky and sea meet at the Osterseen.

A "Rocking" Lake

Instead of a mythical creature, **Ammersee** has only ordinary fish to offer. There is a physical-geological curiosity, in that the lake exhibits a strange "rocking wave". Every day the water rises and falls about 10 centimetres every 24 minutes. Why this should happen, no one really knows. The strange thing is that no legendary monsters have surrounded this fact. Perhaps the fisher-

main road. The best way is to combine a boat trip and a walk. Take the boat which leaves **Kochel** regularly, to as far as **Altjoch**. From here there is a lovely rocky path to **Schlehdorf**, where you can board another boat to return to Kochel. To the north of the Kochelsee is the nature reserve area of **Rohrsee**, where ornithologists can see many species of rare birds. There is a path through here to **Brunnenbach** where you will find refreshment in the local inn.

men on Ammersee are a more rational breed than those on Starnberger See? At any rate, a boat trip here would possibly be less dangerous. It takes about 3-5 hours and starts out from **Stegen** on the northern tip of the lake.

The **Kochelsee** is another "Pearl of Upper Bavaria". It has been called this because of its wonderful location. One end of the lake lies in the plain, and the other is surrounded by high mountains. The **Herzogstand** is one of these, and its 1731-metre summit towers over the water. A walk around the lake, which is 6 square kilometres in area, is not recommended, as you would have to take the

Another Lake Monster?

The larger sister lake of the Kochelsee is **Walchensee**. This lake is the deepest lake in Bavaria, with a depth of 192 metres. It seems the deeper the lake, the more stories and legends grow around it. It's therefore not surprising to find that Walchensee is said to be inhabited by a giant sheathfish, which is so enormous that it has to take its tail in its mouth in order to fit into the lake! And woe to the Bavarians who lead sinful lives, for then the monster will rise up, knock down the **Kesselberg** with its tail, and cause a tidal wave to submerge the land, including the city of Munich. As a precautionary measure, the Prince Electors of Bavaria used to throw a golden ring into the lake each year, to ensure the goodwill of the great fish. Walchensee is one of the most beautiful lakes of Bavaria. There is a wonderful 6-km walk along the eastern shore, from Urfeld to **Niedernach**, which is highly recommended. You can bathe almost anywhere.

People of modest means live on Starn-

Mahler moved to Tegernsee. On the southern tip of the lake is **Rottach-Egern** where in **Café Jaedicke**, you can taste the world famous pyramid cake. For a panoramic view of Tegernsee, you should "climb" the **Wallberg** mountain. To "conquer" the mountain, all you have to do is take a cable-car ride up, and then walk on for half an hour. The exclusive bathing resort of **Bad Wiessee** is on the western shore. There the world famous iodine and sulphur spas can be found,

berger See, but those who can afford it live on **Tegernsee**. Even in the Third Reich, Tegernsee had the reputation of being suited for the big-wigs, as many top Nazis had houses there. The lake has never lost its exclusivity, and Flick, Thyssen, Underberg, among others, have residences on the lake, as did the late Bavarian politician Franz Joseph Strauß. As early as the beginning of the century, writers such as Ludwig Ganghofer, Ludwig Thoma and Hedwig Courths-

Left, morning calmness at Ammersee. Above, the towering Bavarian mountains.

although they were discovered in a rather curious manner. People were drilling for oil, and instead struck on mineral water, so the proposed oil producing area became a spa.

If you still have a few pennies left, you can try your luck at the casino. From behind the Wiesseer school house a path leads through the Zeiselbachtal valley to the Sonnenbichl on **Aueralm**. There you can enjoy a mountain snack of milk, cheese, pea soup or the delicious *Schmarrn* (hot sliced pancake).

Ten kilometres east of Tegernsee, lies **Schliersee**, a tiny lake which makes up in quality for what it lacks in quantity. It is set in lush hilly country, surrounded by mountains not too high or steep, and is one of the most romantic lakes in Bavaria. The main landmark is the pointed peak of the 900-metre high **Brecherspitze**. The lake presumably got its name from the town of **Schliersee** which traces its history back to a monastery named Slyrse—the name slowly changing to Schliers—which was founded in 779. The attractive little church there is an early work of Johann Baptist Zimmermann.

It takes a little longer to walk around **Chiemsee**. This lake, over 80 square metres in area, is the largest lake in Bavaria. However, that is not the reason it came to be known as the "Bavarian Sea". The name comes from the violent storms, and it has earned the respect of fishermen throughout the ages. A few thousand years ago, the lake was three times the size it is today. It is filled up by sedimentation and in 7,000 years from now, the lake will be no more than a puddle!

An Old Custom

Every year on 6th November, at St. Leonards-Kapelle (The Chapel of St.Leonard) in **Fischhausen**, the farmers of the area meet to form a colourful procession. The traditional **Leonhardi-Ritt** (Leonhardi's Ride) is celebrated with horses and wagons in the small town on the northern tip of the lake. There is a wonderful one-hour walk to **Schliersbergalm** but if you prefer, it takes only a few minutes on the chair lift. Within two hours, you can walk around the lake on the path which is signposted "K1".

The wonderful scenery on the west side of the lake in particular is much favoured by artists and painters.

If you want to get to know this region, you must not miss the islands of Herren- and Frauenchiemsee (Men's and Women's Chiemsee). Both names originated from cloisters founded by the Benedictines there. On **Frauenchiemsee** was the convent, and on Herrenchiemsee, the monastery. Both were destroyed by the Hungarians in the 10th century. The less-frequented and smaller Frauenchiemsee island should be worth a trip, especially if you want to see the old lime trees, pictures-que fishermen's houses, and the convent where the nuns make their world famous liquor.

In about 1130, the Augustinians erected buildings on **Herrenchiemsee**, of which all that remains now is the "Old Palace". Although the buildings of the former Augustinian canons' church can be seen from the landing stage, most people walk straight past them. For *the* attraction of the island is the "New Palace" which Ludwig II had built in

Along the Isar

For those who don't want to go far outside Munich, but don't want to miss a walk in the Bavarian countryside, a walk along the River Isar is recommended. You can take the left bank from **Höllriegelskreuth** to **Kloster Schäftlarn** (Schäftlarn Cloister). Or if you prefer the right bank, then start from **Grünwald**. Along the lovely path on the high bank of the river, you will pass through

1878, and which was modelled on the Palace of Versailles. Unfortunately it was never completed. The glorious hall of mirrors was, until a short time ago, the venue for candlelight concerts. Sadly, these have been discontinued because of the damage from the soot. Another attraction is the *Tischlein-deck-dich* (a table where your every need is met), a table which lowers to the kitchen, and rises up into the king's dining room.

Left, she's been triming the grass for decades. Above, afternoon get-together on the raft between Wolfratshausen and Munich.

Römerschanze into **Mühltal** (The Valley of Mills) and past the Brückenwirt (Bridge Inn) to the Schäftlarn Cloister, with its idyllic beer garden. From here, well-marked paths lead through the Isar river valley, with its many channels, to **Wolfratshausen.** On sunny weekends, rafts made up of a few logs leave here for Munich from the end of May to the beginning of September. Two hundred years ago, it was dangerous to raft logs to Munich down the fast flowing river. Today, it is a pleasurable experience to enjoy the sunshine, beer and brass bands as you drift towards the city.

BEER AND BAROQUE

In His infinite goodness, the Creator has kindly provided the Upper Bavarians with an abundance of lakes. The natives expressed their gratitude by building innumerable cloisters and churches, so that the visitor to this part of the country is constantly discovering lakes, or stumbling upon cloisters. But these cloisters have their own attraction for the sybaritic and less culturally-minded tourist too. The Bavarian monks were known to ease their fastings—when meat was forbidden—with brown fluids, which they brewed behind the silent monastery walls. Over the years, they became expert beer brewers.

The Monastic Brewing Tradition

The Benedictine monastery of **Andechs** on "Heiligen Berg" (Holy Mountain) is worthy of mention. Pilgrims do come here, usually to taste the famous dark *Bockbier* or to try the excellent light ale. As a result, this particular place of pilgrimage which falls on the month of May has retained its popularity. If you can pull yourself away from the beer, you can find a peaceful place for meditation and reflection in the baroque church at the grave of Carl Orff. The Pilgrim's Church was originally built in the Late Gothic style around 1400, but it is now a splendid baroque, with stucco, ceiling and wall paintings by Johann Baptist Zimmermann.

Opposite the Domberg (Cathedral Mountain) at Freising, is "The Oldest Brewery in the World", in the former Benedictine monastery of **Weihenstephan** (Dedicated to Stephan). This is perhaps a rather dubious boast, as the Ancient Egyptians were known to drink beer. However, the monastery was known to have brewing rights as early as 1146, and in the 17th century the Bavarian State Brewery was set up here. Nowadays, Weihenstephan is also dedicated to academic research, with the Faculties of Agri-

culture and Brewing of the Technical University of Munich being set up there.

Rococo Dreams and Music

Also near to Munich in the Isar valley is the monastery of **Schäftlarn**. This famous Benedictine monastery was founded in 760. The buildings you see these days, are from the 18th century, and are a wonderful example of the Bavarian rococo. The most

famous Bavarian baroque and rococo artists, such as F. Cuvilliés the Elder, J.B. Gunezrainer, J.B. Zimmermann and J.B. Straub, all contributed. If you attend any of the concerts in Schäftlarn (try to obtain a copy of the monthly events calendar from the Tourist Information Office in Munich), you will learn to appreciate the ambience of the glorious monastery church while you listen to spiritual hymns.

If you drive on along the B11 in the direction of Mittenwald, through the Tölzer Land, 57 kilometres from Munich you will come to the oldest Benedictine monastery north of

Left, "When will we meet again?" Right, the monastery church of Andechs.

257

the Alps. **Benediktbeuren** was founded in mid-8th century. The present monastery church, a basilica, was built in the 17th century from a design by Kaspar Fichtmayr. The frescoes are by Hans Georg Asam. (Visiting hours for the monastery during summer are from 2.30 p.m.; in winter, it opens only on Wednesdays and Sundays. The Basilica's visiting hours in summer are 9 a.m. to 6 p.m.; in winter, it closes an hour earlier. Tel: 08857/881). From June to Sep-

Plays to Counteract the Plague

Only a stone's throw from Ettal is **Oberammergau**, which is known worldwide for its passion plays held once every ten years. The plays have their origin in a vow made by the inhabitants in the year of the plague of 1633. The vow was fulfilled for the first time in the following year. The next passion plays are to be performed in 1990. Oberammergau is also the centre for crucifix carving, and

tember, the Benediktbeurer concerts are held in the Baroque Hall and in the Basilica (Contact Bayerischer Volksbildungsverband e.V. Munich, Widenmayerstraße 42, 8000 Munich 22. Tel: 089/292625).

Towards Garmisch on the B2 and 85 km away from Munich, is the Benedictine cloister of **Ettal**. It houses a Pilgrim's Church and was built for the Bavarians in 1330 by Ludwig IV to fulfil a vow. The twelve-sided Gothic building with a two-storey covered walk is a historical landmark. Baroque-style alterations were undertaken in the 18th century, but they did not affect the basic layout.

there is a museum showing the origins of the craft, (Dorfstraße 6, Easter, Whit and Christmas: daily 10 a.m. to 12 p.m., and 2 p.m. to 5 p.m. Summer: 2 p.m. to 5 p.m. Information from the Verkehrsbüro [Tourist Office], Postfach 60, 8103 Oberammergau. Tel: 08822/4921).

For the finest view over a wide area of Upper Bavaria, drive on south about 25 km from Ammersee. There the road will lead up to the 998-metre high **Hohenpeißenberg**, from which the view over the chain of the Alps and eleven lakes, is quite breathtaking. Up there is the former Pilgrim's Church of

Mariae Himmelfahrt (Assumption of the Virgin Mary). It was built in 1619 and in its simple Renaissance interior is a magnificent high altar on pillars. In 1772 the first mountain weather observatory was installed on the roof of the church.

Bavarian-Swabian Baroque

A visit to the **Wieskirche** (Meadow Church) 20 km south of Hohenpießenberg is

roof of an inn, until the farmer Maria Lory found it and took it home. On 14 June 1738, tears flowed from the figure's eyes, a miracle which from then on drew many pilgrims to a small wooden chapel, then erected for the figure. The stream of pilgrims increased steadily and by 1746, there was a demand for a large Pilgrim's Church. Dominikus Zimmermann undertook the building, which was completed in 1757. The stucco and paintings inside the church are mostly contributed by

a must. The Pilgrim Church, dedicated to the *Scourged Redeemer*, is affectionately known as *die Wies* or "the Meadow". It is a major work of the Bavarian-Swabian Baroque, the most mature ecclesiastical building of that epoch. The history of *die Wies* begins in 1730, when two monks from Steingaden carved a wooden figure of the *Scourged Redeemer* for a Good Friday procession. They covered the figure with linen and painted it. Later, from 1734, it was said that the figure of Christ was placed on the

Left, Ettal Monastery. Above, the Wieskirche.

his brother, Johann Baptist Zimmermann, who executed his best work here. The master builder Dominikus did not want to be parted from his work, and so built himself a small house nearby and stayed until his passing in 1766. From the outside, the church looks rather rustic and is amply surrounded by meadows and trees. Inside, you find yourself "in a radiant hall, so shining with light and colour, that it does not seem built of solid material, but out of the wild flowers outside, and the clouds over the Trauchbergen." (Schtzkammer Deutsch-land, *The Treasury of Germany*, 1978).

BISHOPS, PRINCES AND IMPERIAL CITIES

Long before the founding of Munich, Bavaria was a land of culture and settlements. The Romans founded cities such as Regensburg (Castra Regina) and Augsburg (Augusta Vindelicorum). The lines ran along the Danube and ever since Charlemagne deposed the Bavarian Duke Tassilo and banished him to a monastery in 788, the development of Bavaria has been very much an integral part of the history of Germany. If you walk through Munich and miss out on a museum, you will not be able to notice any trace of the medieval city, apart from the Alter Hof (Old Court). Munich was founded relatively late, and many historical landmarks disappeared during World War II. Nevertheless, each city has its own heritage from the Middle Ages. If you have time, do visit and get to know more about Freising, Landshut, Wasserburg, Regensburg and Augsburg.

"Modus Doctus"

Until the late Middle Ages, Freising was actually the cultural centre of the Land and for many years the bitter foe of Munich. Originally a Palatinate, it became a bishopric in the 8th century. In 724, Pope Gregory II sent the frank missionary bishop Korbinian to Bavaria for missionary work. As the bishop was crossing the Alps, his mule was attacked and killed by a bear. Unperturbed, the bishop made the bear carry his luggage for him instead of the mule. For his innovation, Korbinian became the saint of Freising, His remains lie in the crypt of the cathedral which is named **St. Maria und Korbinian**. The white twin towers of the basilica, built in 1160-1205, are visible from afar. The outside of the cathedral still reflects the original Romanesque style of its founding period. However, the inside was decorated in baroque style in 1723 by the Asam brothers, with stucco and paintings depicting scenes

Left, inside the Freisinger Cathedral. Right, past and present.

about the life of St. Korbinian. The crypt, which has been kept to its stark Romanesque style, is quite remarkable. There you will find, apart from the sarcophagus of St. Korbinian and of Bishop Hitto who died in 835, the famous beasts column, around the base of which are dragons and demons whose symbolism is still unclear to this day.

Whether you drive from Munich, or came on the S-Bahn (city train) you really should climb the **Domberg** (Cathedral Mountain)

on foot. On a clear day, you can see right up to Munich and in the *Föhn* weather, as far as the Alps. This "learned" mountain was where Bishop Otto of Freising, probably the most notable historian of the Middle Ages, used to carry out his work.

If you go to Freising, you should not miss the **Weihenstephan Brauerei** (Weihenstephan Brewery), reputedly the oldest brewery in the world. There is a lovely beer garden here too, mostly populated by the students of the **Fachhochschule** (Professional School) where the finer points of brewing are taught.

Prince's Wedding

If you are interested in culture, then go on to visit one of Germany's loveliest towns, **Landshut**, 40 kilometres away. Founded in 1204 by Duke Ludwig of Kehlheim, it has to a great extent kept its medieval character. The town is dominated by the magnificent Late Gothic St.-Martins-Kirche (Church) which has the highest brick tower in the world (133 metres). Inside the church is a

hochzeit (Prince's Wedding Pageant) which is held every four years, with the next due in 1989. On this occasion, the people commemorate the wedding anniversary of Duke Georg to the daughter of the Polish King, Jadwiga; it took place in 1475. Unfortunately, the royal marriage ended sadly. The Duke banished his wife to the castle of **Burghausen am Inn**, because she could not provide him with an heir. At the festival are tournaments, court games and music, all in

radiant **Madonna** by Hans Leinberger. Construction of the church commenced in 1380 and the building became a political symbol, as the tower reaches to the height of the Wittelsbach Princes' castle of **Burg Trausnitz** on the high bank of the Isar. From the castle—it has a wonderful courtyard—you can easily capture a glorious view of the town. Landshut has a Southern European charm, with its **Stadtresidenz** (Town Palace) in the old part of the town, and its *Palazzo* in the Italian Renaissance style. Perhaps you will be lucky enough to visit the town at the time of the Landshuter **Fürsten-**

medieval style, so that you can really experience camp life in the Middle Ages. The reputation of the festival has spread far and wide; there is always plenty of food and drink to enjoy as well. On the four festival Sundays, there is a procession of bridal couples through the town.

The castle is the largest complex of its kind in Europe—in area at least— and if it isn't too far for you, it should be worth a visit. The town of Burghausen is also worth seeing, but nearby **Wasserburg** (Water Castle) is particularly interesting. This lovely old town is set in a loop of the Inn River and its wonderful medieval centre reflects the proximity of Bavaria to Italy.

Two Imperial Cities

At least one day should be reserved for a trip to **Regensburg**, which lies about 150 km east of Munich. This former Imperial City is now a modern industrial and university city, but the centre is still medieval in character. There is much to see here. Take a

chronicles in 730, and thus the oldest of Bavarian cloisters. On the way there, you will pass renovated courtyards, and walk over the **Steinerne Brücke** (Stone Bridge) which was built in 1135. From there you can see the supposedly dangerous waters of the Danube. Stop at the centre of the bridge to take in the wonderful view of the city. Next to the bridge, on the banks of the Danube, is the time-honoured *Wurstkuchl* where sausages have been manufactured for a very

look at the Gothic **Dom** (Cathedral) which was begun in 1250, then walk on to the **Herzogshof** (Duke's Court), the old **Königspfalz** (King's Palatinate). Wander through the narrow streets and alleys of the medieval city to the **Rathaus** (Town Hall), which was the seat of the "Eternal Imperial Diet" of the Holy Roman Empire of the German Nation from 1663 to 1806. You shouldn't miss the cloister of **St. Emmeram**, first mentioned in

Left, merry procession commemorating the Landshut Prince's Wedding Pageant. Above, the Town Hall and the Perlach Tower in Augsburg.

long time.

About 70 km away west of Munich is **Augsburg**, the second city of Bavaria after Regensburg which traces its history to a Roman settlement. This city too is worth visiting. There is the Gothic **Dom** (Cathedral) and the **Rathaus** (Town Hall) built by Elias Holl in 1618, in the Renaissance style. There is also the **Fuggerei**. Jakob Fugger, one of the richest men in the late Middle Ages, designed this settlement for needy citizens. The 53 houses are still occupied and their tenants pay the same rent fixed by Fugger—one Rheinisch guilder, or DM1.90.

SPLENDOUR AND MISERY IN THE PAST

In the north of Munich, the Princely splendour of the past is captured in the palace of Schloß Schleißheim. But the horrors of the Nazi era are also commemorated in the concentration camp memorial of **Dachau**, on the eastern edge of the city. About 500 exhibits document the terrible fate suffered by the prisoners here and in the other Nazi concentration camps. As early as 1933, Dachau was a camp, but it was not until 1938 that it became an actual concentration camp.

ing. In some of the palace rooms are exhibits of the folk museum, and in Dachau itself stand houses dating as far back as the 17th and 18th centuries.

Demonstrations of Power

On the eastern side of the Dachau moor are the three palaces of **Schleißheim**. The name Schleißheim comes from the word *Schwaige*, a farm where cheese is made. Duke

It was to be the model for further camps, and all future concentration camp supervisors were to be trained here. In the 600-metre by 250-metre enclosure fenced with barbed wire, more than 206,000 prisoners were held and of whom about 32,000 died.

There is another side to Dachau, the side which draws the attention of the inhabitants. It is the **Renaissance Schloß** (Renaissance Palace) built between 1546 and 1573, and renovated in 1715 by Dachau-born Joseph Effner. Of the four Renaissance wings of the palace, only one has remained and it has a large banquet hall with a richly-carved ceil-

Wilhelm V bought it in 1597. There, he built five chapels with cells for retreats, as well as the Wilhelmsbau, his retirement residence. His son, Prince Elector Maximilian I, transformed this into a royal palace modelled on Italian lines, in 1617-1623. This became the Alte Schloß (Old Palace).

The **Neue Schloß** (New Palace) is a building 330 metres long. Its lower middle portion is connected by passages with arcades, joined by two corner pavilions. This "Versailles of Munich" was commissioned by Prince Elector Maximilian II, and as the largest palace complexes of its day, was to express the growing power coveted by the Wittelsbachs.

Baroque Splendour

The basic construction, begun by Enrico Zuccalli in 1701-1704, was not continued due to the defeat of Maximilian II in the decisive battle of the Spanish War of Succession. It was not until 1719 that Joseph Effner was given the order to continue the construc-

successful Turkish wars. The exquisite gallery in the New Palace displays one of the most remarkable collections of baroque painting in Europe, as well as of Italian, Dutch and Flemish paintings from the 17th and 18th centuries.

The park, 1,250 metres long by 350 metres wide, is one of the few remaining passed down from the Republic's absolutist past.

The central canal flows through the whole park and opens up to encircle **Schloß Lus-**

tion, but on more modest lines. Leo von Klenze, the master builder for Ludwig I, changed the facade to a classical design. However, when the palace was rebuilt during 1959-1962, the original baroque facade of Joseph Effner was incorporated in the design. The interior, by Effner and a host of Bavarian rococo artists, remained intact for the most part, and there are stucco works and murals depicting Maximilian II Emanuel's

Left, frontal view of the Schleißheim Palace. Above, a peek at the Concentration Camp Memorial of Dachau.

theim. This palace, which could only be reached by boat then, was planned as an island of happiness or *île de cythère*. It was constructed by Enrico Zucalli and modelled aftern a plush Italian garden casino in 1684-1688. Maximilian II Emanuel gave the palace as a present to his bride Maria Antonia, who was the daughter of the Hapsburg Emperor. The murals inside are of Maria Antonia portayed as the hunting goddess Diana. There is a museum **Meißner Porzellan** (Meissen Porcelain) inside the palace, with exhibits of the first fifty years of manufacture since 1710.

THE FAIRY-TALE KING

No true Bavarian wants to hear a word said against King Ludwig II. The Bavarians not only honour him in their hearts, but on T-shirts, beer mugs, towels and plates. For true-blue loyalists, there is no surface where they cannot put the likeness of their beloved *kini* (King).

Such prosaic popularisation of his life would have deeply distressed the king. During his lifetime, he took great pains to protect his dreams and works from the people. The only public he ever wanted for his fantasies—which others were able to realise for him—was himself. This absolutism probably explains his own veneration for the absolute monarch of France, his namesake Louis XIV. But while the Sun King's motto was *L'Etat c'est moi* (I am the State), the motto of the king of Bavaria was *Le Goût c'est moi* (I am Taste).

In order to realise this motto in the form of nonsensical fairy-tale castles, he dug deep into the state coffers. He did not inherit this extravagance from his father, Max II, for he saw the position of king as one of duty, and was concerned to impart a sense of responsibility to his children from an early age. Thus meals were frugal, and the royal children were often so hungry that they were given extra food by Liesl, the chambermaid. Pocket money was extremely modest too. But the paternal upbringing was not successful. As soon as Ludwig was declared king, he announced an end to all excessive thrift and penny pinching. This attitude, coupled with Ludwig's lack of understanding of the value of money, explains his mania for building castles. At a time when the world was moving towards democracy and industrialisation, Ludwig glorified the monarchy upon which the sun was setting. His grandfather fought bitterly against any intimidation of democracy, and thus—but not only for that reason, as a certain Lola Montez had a role to play too—was forced to abdicate the throne

Above, Ludwig II, the "Fairy-Tale King", in coronation robes.

in 1848. Ludwig, by contrast, was determined to express his neo-absolutist ideals in aesthetic form.

The King and the Composer

So it was only understandable that once he had ascended to the throne on 10 March 1864, he sent for Richard Wagner. The composer offered the king his whole life and every word and note he had written. He did

well, for Ludwig showed his love for *Lohengrin* in cash, then the most important form of appreciation for an artist. For the erstwhile court orchestra director, the adulation of the king of Bavaria came just at the right time. After a dramatic life, punctuated by great highs and lows, the 51-year old composer at that time found himself fleeing from his admirers. Provided with the best working environment—first he composed, courtesy of Ludwig, in the country estate of Tribschen near Luzern, then later in Villa Wahnfried in Bayreuth—the "genius was able to show others" that he was indeed a genius. He completed the *Ring der Niebelungen*, one of the many operas which had their first performance in Munich. Wagner had, as he himself admitted, struck a note with the king. It was to Wagner's music and themes, that Ludwig drifted further and further away from reality as his reign continued, and he built a world of his own.

The King's Castles

The three castles built by the Fairy-Tale King—Neuschwanstein, Linderhof and Herrenchiemsee—are exciting tourist attractions of Upper Bavaria, almost like a kind of home-grown Disneyland. The difference between the two personalities Ludwig and Disney is analogical to that between democracy and the monarchy. Ludwig created his world for himself alone. Disney had the masses in mind from the beginning. And while Disney became a millionaire, Ludwig turned debtor, albeit one who didn't have to pay his own debts. So it was a good thing that Ludwig's behest—that on his death, the castles should be blown up, to preserve them from the uncultured outside world—was ignored. Just one month after his death, Neuschwanstein was open to the public, at DM3 per entry. Today, with hordes of tourists streaming through the castles, one can say that there is no longer any difference between Ludwig and Disney. The King's castles have proved to be the biggest tourist draw in Bavaria.

In 1868 the fourth year of his reign, Ludwig II wrote to Wagner that he intended to rebuild the ruined castle of Hohen Schwangau on the Pöllatschlucht (Pöllat Gorge), and to go and live there in three years time. However, the impatient king had to wait a little longer and it was not until 1884 that he moved into his neo-romantic knight's castle of **Neuschwanstein**. When he died on 13 June 1886, it was still incomplete. The royal chambers and banquet halls were almost finished then. The *pièces de résistance* are the Byzantine style throne room—with-

out a throne—and the *Sängersaal* (Singers' Hall), which is the heart of the castle, and which is decorated on the theme of the Parzival saga.

Below Neuschwanstein lies the castle of **Hohenschwangau** (not to be confused with the ruined castle mentioned above), which King Max II had built between 1833 and 1855 as a summer residence. Ludwig spent much of his youth there in the "Fairy-Tale Castle" as his grandfather called it. In the Hall of the Knight of the Swan, the story of *Lohengrin*—it was to have a strong influence on Ludwig's thinking—was told in vivid pictures.

Not far from Hohenschwangau, on Alpsee (Alp Lake), was where the king enjoyed his happiest moments. Here, on his 20th birthday on 25 August 1865, a scene from *Lohengrin* was produced. A big, elaborate swan pulled Lohengrin over the Alpsee in a boat. The Knight of the Swan, represented by aide-de-camp Prince Paul von Thurn und Taxis, and the swan were beautifully lit by electric lamps. From the bushes, where Johann Wilhelm Siebenkäs the master of music hid together with the orchestra of the 1st Infantry Regiment, came strains of Wagner's *Lohengrin*, while the aide-de-camp faithfully sang the arias at the top of his voice. Later in the evening , there was a spectacular fireworks display. Unfortunately, a rocket exploded in the bushes and seriously injured 16 musicians. King Ludwig probably thought this extraordinary disturbance of the opera as nothing more than a short accoustic discord. Such profane happenings had to be kept at a distance from the king, naturally.

The workmen climbed up the hill and began work on the building of Neuschwanstein in the spring of 1869. King Ludwig would sit in the Tassilozimmer (Tassilo Room) of Hohenschwangau and watch their dogged progress through a telescope. The craftsmen and artists literally worked until they dropped. In a bid to finish his work on time, poor Professor Wilhelm Hauschild painted St. George on the eastern gable wall until he fell off from the scaffold.

Two years after his longing to move into Neuschwanstein, the king was arrested on 11th June 1886. For a long time, his building projects had led him into financial difficulties. His modest annual income of 4,029,580 guilders was by no means enough for him. The king not only had to finance his projects from this sum, he also had to maintain the whole royal household with it. He fell into

11 June. Ludwig, who had earlier asked his footmen to measure the depth of the Pöllatschlucht, left the dining room with the tower key. Was he going to avoid the dishonour of arrest by leaping into the Pöllat Gorge? Dr. Bernhard von Gudden, the senior medical officer, eventually approached the king and certified him insane. His majesty was taken to Schloß Berg (Berg Castle) on Starnberger Lake. A day later, on 12 June, King Ludwig and the doctor went for a walk

debt, and on 22 May 1886, a Munich newspaper posed the question "Can His Majesty the King be brought before the courts on a charge of private liability?" Shortly afterwards, on 9 June, the *Fangkommission* (Commission for Arrest) was set up and a hunt for the king was called. But they were not in luck! King Ludwig's servants, a dozen gendarmes, firemen and a host of true Allgäuer held off the bailiffs with loaded guns and drew swords. The commissioners had to return to Munich without accomplishing their mission. However, the captors were once again at the king's door on the night of

along the lakeside. At 10.30 p.m., the body of the king was found, and that of Dr. Gudden too, in the lake, about 6.5 metres from the shore. Everything else—whether the king wanted to flee, or whether he killed Gudden, then himself—is pure speculation. To this day, no one knows what really happened that fateful night.

Like a Fairy-Tale Come True

The only castle which Ludwig did manage to complete building was the Palace of **Linderhof**. This rococo palace lies surrounded by beautifully laid out gardens in the unspoiled forest and mountain scenery of the Graswangtal valley. The commission was given to Ludwig's architect, Georg Dollmann, with a budget of 31,312 guilders and 45 creuzers. By the time it was finished, in 1789, the total amount spent was 8,460,937 Guilders. Outside the entrance hall with its marble pillars and bronze equestrian statue of the Sun King (much admired by Ludwig) is the impressive 30-metre high fountain,

on for one and a half years. But that is not all. In the park is the **Maurische Kiosk** (Moorish Pavilion) with its Peacock Throne. It was originally exhibited at the Paris Fair of 1867 and was brought to Linderhof, with great difficulty. The second curiosity in the park is the **Venusgrotte** (Venus Grotto), made of gypsum and cement, exactly as described by Richard Wagner in his opera *Tannhäuser*. The king would often be rowed in his golden, ornately-carved boat across the lake of the

which links palace and garden. Inside the palace, treasures and curiosities vie for attention. First, there is the bedroom with an enormous purple bed, then a *Tischlein-deckdich* (table which fulfils your every need) which lowers from the dining room down into the kitchen, and the mirror room which gives the illusion of an infinite number of rooms. The king made all his wishes come true, just like in a real fairy-tale. There is a rosewood table, which 15 carpenters worked

grotto and enjoy the wonderful scene. Meanwhile, in the background, an electrician would be feverishly occupied with the 24 Siemens dynamo machines, which provided the power for the 24 arc lamps, the wave machine and the rainbow apparatus. A team of servants were kept busy warming the stalactite cave at the required temperature of 20 degrees Celsius.

The Bavarian Versailles

The third jewel, the Palace of **Herrenchiemsee**, is on the *Herreninsel* (Men's

Far left, Hohenschwangau Palace. Left, Neuschwanstein Palace. Above, Linderhof Palace.

Island) of Lake Chiemsee and was to be a Bavarian version of the Sun King's Palace of Versailles. Only the location of the palace displeased the king; he missed the mountain peaks and valleys. But the king had complete faith in his craftsmen and proclaimed that "Art alone shall make the unpleasant pleasant, and it shall make one forget the scenery and the lake." Unfortunately, the construction had to be discontinued in 1885 due to the appalling state of Bavarian finances. Never-

for seven years. Strangely enough, the king never for once slept on it; the bed was exclusively dedicated to the long since dead Sun King. The second marvel in the palace is the magnificent Hall of Mirrors, copied from the *Galerie des Glaces* in Versailles. With a length of 98 metres, it is longer than the original. The hall is well lit by 1,848 candles on 44 stands and 33 glass chandeliers. It is believed that the king had the candles lit 52 times, and that it took 15 minutes to light

theless, the main complex of the palace is open to visitors.

The Hall of Mirrors

In the palace stands the 103-metre long building which faces the garden. But most interesting of all in this building is the tale-carrying gala bedroom with its 3-metre by 2.6-metre bed, on which thirty girls worked

Above, the funeral procession for Ludwig II in 1886 (passing through the Karls Gate). Right, the Hall of Mirrors in Herrenchiemsee.

them all. Ludwig's beloved French king is honoured once more in the palace. In the conference room of Schloß Herrenchiemsee is a clock and a figure emerges on the hour. It is none other than that of the Sun King Louis IV himself.

Herrenchiemsee too has a *Tischlein-deck-dich*, and in the park is a **Latonabrunnen** (Latona Fountain) where stone frogs squat around the Greek goddess Latona and spit water. According to the legend, the goddess was infuriated by some of the village peasants who had mocked her and so turned them into frogs.

TRAVEL TIPS

GETTING THERE

BY AIR

The international airport of **München-Riem** is in the east of the city. Due to increasing air traffic congestion, there are frequent delays. In the early 1990's München-Riem will be replaced by a new airport in the north of the city.

From Riem, there is a bus to the city centre, to the main railway station, which operates as a shuttle service between 6.40 a.m. and 6.30 p.m., departing every 20 minutes. The tariff is DM 5 for adults, DM 3 for children between 4 and 14 years old. The trip takes about 25 minutes. A taxi to the centre of the city costs about DM 25 to DM 30.

In the airport itself, there are restaurants, snack bars, shops, (open until 8.00 p.m.), banks and money changers, car rental agencies, shower rooms, a post office, hairdresser, a children's waiting room, clinic, travel agency and an accommodation service run by the Tourist Information Office of Munich, in the main concourse (Mon-Sun 8.30 a.m. -10 p.m., Sun 1.00 - 10 p.m. Tel. 907256). For **flight information** you can dial Tel. 92112127.

BY ROAD

When you visit Munich by car, you arrive from the Nürnberg/Würzburg direction or from Stuttgart/Augsburg, Salzburg/Kufstein or Garmisch-Partenkirchen. Those unfamiliar with the area, can avail themselves of the following **Lotsendienst-Stationen** (Driver-Guide Services) at the motorway exits. The Nürnberg motorway : Exit Station Freimann, Tel. 325417; Salzburg motorway: Exit Station Ramersdorf, Tel. 672755; Stuttgart motorway: Exit Station Obermenzing, Tel. 8112412. Central Office of the Driver-Guide Service: Valpichlerstr. 9, Tel. 571016. Tariff: DM 26 per hour. Other information bureaus to provide motorists with invalauable tips are:

ADAC-Information, Tel. 505061

ADAC-Pannenhilfe,(Break down service), Tel. 19211

ACE Auto Club Europa e.V., Emergency Service, Tel. 536502

DTC-Deutscher Touring Automobilclub Break down service, Tel. 8111212

The Service-Welle (wave length) of the Bayerischegrn Rundfunk radio, on **Bayern 3** also furnishes motorists with information on traffic congestion and alternative routes. Frequency: 98 MHz.

BY RAIL

The main railway station of Munich, the **Hauptbahnhof** is a terminal station (Gleis or platforms 11-26) with two neighbouring stations, the Holzkirchner Bahnhof (Gleis 1-10) and the Starnberger Bahnhof (Gleise 27-36).

From the **Holzkirchner Bahnhof** in Bayerstraße, trains depart in the direction of Wolfratshausen, Lenggries, Tegernsee, Bayrischzell and Mühldorf; from the **Starnberger Bahnhof** in Arnulfstraße, trains leave for Garmisch Partenkirchen.

The **Ostbahnhof** (East Station) on Orleansplatz is the point of departure for trains and S-Bahnen (fast trains) for Ismaning, Markt Schwaben, Erding, Mühldorf, Grafing, Rosenheim, Daisenhofen, Holzkirchen and Kreuzstraße. At the same time the Ostbahnhof is the loading point for the "Auto im Reisezug" (Motor rail service).

München-Pasing is the station in the west of the city and the first stop in the city area for long distance trains from the west.

All stations also serve the S-Bahn lines, check with the rail authorities.

Initial information may be obtained from The Tourist Information Office at the south exit of the station (daily, 8 a.m-11 p.m. Sun 1-11.30 p.m. Summer season 8-11 p.m). For emergencies the main railway station has a Travellers Aid Society bureau.

Information Offices for the Bundesbahn (Federal Railways), provide valuable information to those visiting Munich by train. The following is but a list of what you may wish to know:

Telephone Train Information
Tel. 592991 and 593321

Ticket Reservations
Tel. 1285994

Special Trains and Special Trips
Tel. 1285846

Door to door Baggage Collection
Tel. 1285855

Auto im Reisezug (Motor Rail Service)
Tel. 12884405

Tariff Information
Tel. 1286397

Lost Property Office
Tel. 1285859

Bundesbahn-Hotel, Bahnhofsplatz 2
Tel. 558571.

There are some **important train connections** which those travelling by train should take note of the following train lines:
Hannover - Hamburg andBremen 1153
Austria and Southern Europe 11532
Tyrol, Italy, Switzerland 11533
Bonn, Cologne, Dortmund, Paris, Holland, Belgium 11534
Frankfurt am M. 11535.

TRAVEL ESSENTIALS

MONEY MATTERS

Money changers in the main hall of the main railway station or Hauptbahnhof, daily 6 a.m.-11 p.m. and in the Arrival Hall of the Riem Airport, open daily 7 a.m.- 8.30 p.m.. The counters of the Deutschen Verkehrs-Kredit-Bank are open daily (including Sundays) in the main railway station from 6 a.m.-11.30 p.m. and in the airport of Riem from 7 a.m - 10 p.m. You may obtain cash there against a Eurocheque or credit card.

CUSTOMS

The following goods are duty-free when entering The Federal Republic of Germany subject to certain regulations:

TOBACCO

This applies to those 17 years and above:
a) from countries in the European Community, (Belgium, Denmark, France, Greece, Great Britain and Northern Ireland, The Republic of Ireland, Italy, Luxemburg, The Netherlands, Portugal, Spain not inclusive of the Canary Islands 300 Cigarettes or 150 Cigarillos or 75 Cigars or 400 grams of Tobacco.
b) from other countries, from tax-free-shops, from The Canary Islands, from the island of Helgoland and on entry by ship from the high seas: 200 Cigarettes or 100 Cigarillos or 50 Cigars or 250 grams of Tobacco.

ALCOHOLIC BEVERAGES

For this item, the following apply to those 17 years and above:

a) from countries of the European Community : 1.5 litres of distilled alcohol or spirits, with an alcoholic content of more than 22 % of volume, or 3 litres distilled beverages or spirits or aperitifs made from wine or alcohol, with an alcohol content of 22 % volume or less, or 3 litres of sparkling wine or liqueur wine and 5 litres of other wine.

b) from other countries, from tax-free-shops, from The Canary Islands, from the island of Helgoland and on entry by ship from the high seas : 1 litre distilled beverage or spirits, with an alcohol content of more than 22 % volume, or 2 litres distilled beverages or spirits or aperitifs made from wine or alcohol with an alcohol content of 22 % volume or less, or 2 litres of sparkling wine or liqueur wine **and** 2 litres of other wine.

COFFEE

This applies to those 15 years and above:

a) from countries of the European Community: 1000 grams coffee or 400 grams of coffee extract or essences.

b) from other countries, from tax-free-shops, from the Canary Islands, from the island of Helgoland and on entry by ship from the high seas: 500 grams of coffee or 200 grams of coffee extracts or essences.

TEA

Duty-free regulations for this items are:

a) from countries of the European Community: 200 grams of tea or 80 grams of tea extracts or essences.

b) from other countries, from tax-free-shops, from The Canary Islands, from the island of Helgoland and on entry by ship from the high seas: 100 grams of tea or 40 grams of tea extracts or essences.

COSMETICS

For these products, the concessions are:

a) from countries of the European Community: 75 grams perfume and 0.375 litres of toilet water.

b) from other countries, from tax-free-shops, from the Canary Islands and from the island of Helgoland and on entry by ship from the high seas: 50 grams perfumes and 0.25 litres toilet water.

OTHER GOODS

With the exception of gold, gold alloys and gold plating, unfinished or semi-finished (e.g. bars), the following apply:

a) from countries of the European Community: up to a total value of DM 780.

b) from other countries, from tax-free-shops, from the Canary Islands, from the island of Helgoland and on entry by ship from the high seas: up to a total value of goods of DM 115.

GETTING ACQUAINTED

ECONOMY

As capital city of the Free State of Bavaria, and of the administrative district of Upper Bavaria, central administration was dominant, along with manufacture and trade. The industrial development of Munich began relatively late, shortly before the turn of the century. Meanwhile, Munich has surpassed important industrial cities such as Berlin and Hamburg, according to the Sonderheft der Mnchner Statistik (Special Publication of Munich Statistics), by the turnover figures on the one hand, and the number of those employed in industry in Munich, on the other. In particular in the field of new technology, Munich and the surrounding area is now one of the most important centres of electronics in Europe.

In addition to micro chips and other electronic building components, factory plant and equipment for industrial metrology and automatic control technology, entertainment electronics as well as military and civil information and news technology are manufactured and marketed here. Munich has also become one of the leading centres for air and space technology, information and communications technology, machinebuilding, industrial engineering, energy and environmental and medical technology as well as biotechnology.

This development began shortly after 1945 with the transfer of the Siemens corporation from Berlin to Munich. Apart from the old-established firms such as BMW, Krauss-Maffei, MAN, MTU and Rodenstock, and others such as IBM, Intel, Digital Equipment, Motorola, Wang, Nixdorf and MBB have substantial investments in the Bavarian capital.

In addition to the large scale industries, Munich is the most important publishing city in the Federal Republic. There are more publishing houses here, more bookshops and sales outlets for newspapers and magazines than in any other city in Germany (Sonderheft der Münchner Statistik). The same is true of the audio-visual media, which has made the capital of Bavaria, the capital of the German film industry.

Numerous trade fairs throughout the year ensure that Munich is an important international trade centre. Not to be forgotten are the six large breweries which contribute greatly to the economic life of the city.

GEOGRAPHY

The centre of Munich, the tower of the Frauenkirche, is 48°8′23′ latitude north, and 11°34′28′ longitude east. Within Europe, that is the same latitude as Orleans and Vienna, and the same longitude as Oslo and Innsbruck. As regards communications geography, Munich is the centre of the two axes of Hamburg - Rome and Paris - Vienna.

Topographically, Munich lies in the centre of the Swabian Bavarian Plateau with an average height of 530 m. The total city area of Munich is 310,39 sq km (compare to Berlin: 888 sq km), of which 53.1% is urban, or built-up area.

With 1.28 million inhabitants in the actual city area, and 2.31 million in the city region, Munich is, after Berlin (West) and Hamburg the third largest city of the Federal Republic.

CLIMATE

The climate of Munich is determined by its position in the path of the westerly winds and by its location in the Alpine foothills. Because of the moving high and low pressure areas, and the changing flow of air masses from north and south, from the sea or the inland continental land mass, the weather is changeable.

There are stark contrasts even within the seasons. There are low pressure areas from the Mediterranean Sea which cross the Alps and are the cause of a high amount of precipitation. Stable weather conditions, which can set in for several weeks, are the result of air masses from the east, which have passed over wide expanses of land, and which in summer cause dry, hot periods, and in winter long spells of cold weather.

Climatic Chart (Average readings in Centigrade)

	Min.	Max.
Jan	-5.6	1.4
Feb	-5.1	3.4
Mar	-1.5	8.7
April	2.81	3.5
May	6.6	18
June	10	21.3
July	12.1	23.2
Aug	11.4	22.7
Sep	8.4	19.6
Oct	3.7	13.3
Nov	0.1	6.6
Dec	-3.8	2.3

One of the climatic anomalies in Munich is the "Föhn", a warm down wind from the south, caused by a simultaneous high in the Alpine southern edge and a low in the Alpine north edge. The Föhn is responsible for many headaches in Munich, and much lethargy. But on the other hand it makes the air so clear that it seems to bring the Alps within touching distance.

It is basically advisable to take some very warm clothes with you between October and April. Even in summer, you should always pack a warm pullover as well a mackintosh.

BUSINESS HOURS

Retail stores and **department stores** of all kinds are subject to the German retail legislation, which means that they are closed after 6.30 p.m.But at the main railway station you can buy groceries at two delicatessen shops until 10 p.m. (including Sundays). On Saturdays, from 1 p.m., and all day Sunday, the shops are closed. As a rule, banks are open from 8.30 a.m. - 12.30 p.m. and from 1.30 - 3.30 p.m.. **Offices** and **Consulates** and other such establishments should be open between 8. a.m. and 12 p.m.,

as they are normally closed to the general public during the afternoons.

FESTIVALS

The start of the **Munich year** is marked by **Twelfth Night** (6th January) on the Viktualienmarkt (Victuals Market), the ball season begins, with about 3,000 balls before **Shrove Tuesday**. These are held in the following carnival centres: Bayerischer Hof, Deutsches Theater, Hofbrauhaus, Löwenbräukeller, Mathäser, Max-Emanuel-Brauerei and Schwabinger Bräu. The streets (Marienplatz, Odeonsplatz, Max-Josephs-Platz and the Pedestrian Precinct) are full of action on **Shrove Sunday**. There are jazz, pop and brass bands as well as street theatre and all kinds of revellers holding private parties. On Shrove Tuesday, this first season in the Munich year ends where it began, on the Viktualienmarkt, where the market women invite you to dance.

The **Schäffler Tanze**, (Coopers' Dances), a tradition dating back to the time of the plague in the 16th Century, are held every seven years. The next dances are scheduled for 1991, when the coopers will dance once again at balls and in the public squares.

On **Aschermittwoch** (Ash Wednesday), at the Fischbrunnen (Fish Fountain) in Marienplatz, the traditional ceremony of washing the money bags is held. Afterwards the people retire to the numerous hotels and pubs, where a special fish dish is served to mark the beginning of the fasting period of Lent.

The **Starkbierzeit** (Strong Beer Time): In the old days the monks would alleviate the deprivations of the fasting time with their own home brewed strong beer (higher original wort of up to 20%, approx. 6% alcohol). Although in predominantly Catholic Munich hardly anyone fasts these days, the Strong Beer Time has remained and has come to be known as the fifth season of the year in the city. It begins about two weeks after Ash Wednesday when Munich's celebrities attend the official opening on the Nockherberg. Then only beer ending in "ator" is consumed.

Salvator, Triumphator, Maximator and

Optimator can also be drunk on May 1st, when the traditional **Maibock-Anstich** (Hofbräuhaus) ceremony marks the beginning of the Beer Garden Season.

On the last Saturday in September, the season in Munich begins, when the brewers, complete with teams and waggons, proceed to the "Wies'n" (Theresienwiese) for the **Oktoberfest** (October Beer Festival). The next day, that is the first Sunday of the festival, there is a procession by the military as well as by people donning traditional costume through the inner city to the Wies'n, where the festival continues until the first Sunday of October.

The **Auer Dult** (flea market and recreational park) held three times a year on the church square of the Maria-Hilf-Kirche in Au, should not be missed when visiting Munich. (May Dult: last week in April to beginning of May, 9 days; Jakobi Dult: end July, 9 days; Kirchweih Dult: from mid October, 9 days).

The Munich year ends with the **Christkindlmarkt** (Christmas Fair) on Marienplatz and in Münchner Freiheit in Schwabing (1st Advent to Christmas Eve).

COMMUNICATIONS

MEDIA

The daily papers are not only sold in the many kiosks in the city, but are also available fresh from the presses in the evenings over the counter in many establishments. You can also buy them at every street corner, from the newspaper boxes, which have become as much part of the Munich scene as the towers of the Frauenkirche. But don't think you can get away without paying, for the boxes are sometimes watched by unobtrusive pedestrians, and the newspaper thief will be apprenhended and fined.

NEWSPAPERS

The most widely read daily in Munich is the Abendzeitung (AZ) or Evening Paper. This paper is above all infamous for its no holds barred supplement, where the star journalist "Ponkie" doesn't mince words. The AZ is the left or liberal tabloid of the Süddeutsche Zeitung, which is an equally liberal daily, reporting comprehensively on events world wide, in Bavaria and in Munich. Catholic, somewhat tedious and close to the CDU and CSU political parties of the right, is the daily Münchner Merkur. There is a tabloid edition of this too, with gossip about the upper classes or nobility. The mouthpiece of the CSU is the weekly "Bayernkurier", in which Wilfried Scharnagl once wrote, what the Bavarian premier Franz-Josef Strauß thought, and vice versa. For homosexuals, drop-outs, punks and other original thinkers, there is the bi-weekly Münchner Stadtzeitung. Apart from small ads for used fridges and particular sexual wishes, it contains an extensive calendar of events with tips and information on the underground music and social scene.

RADIO & TELEVISION

The four channels of the Bayerischer Rundfunk (BR) radio are facing competition from the many small private stations, such as Radio Charivari, Radio 89, Radio Gong 2000 or München 92.4. The television station of the Bayerische Fernsehen is not alone, as the other legal public stations of ARD and ZDF have been set up. A wider range of programmes is available through TV weiß-blau, Tele 5 and Eureka, and the cable TV on RTL Plus and SAT 1, which offer mainly old films, the shortest possible news bulletins, cheaply produced game shows and a lot of advertising.

POSTAL SERVICES

The Hauptbahnhof Postamt at 32, Bahnhofplatz 1, Tel. 53880 is always open; Public Telex Office 7 a.m.-11 p.m. Mail sent to the main poste restante is to be found here. Post office savings, cheques and money changers, as well as an overnight postal service are also available.

At the airport, postal services are available at: Postamt 87, Flughafen München-Riem (Departure Hall), Tel. 908013, Mon-Fri 8 a.m.-9 p.m., Sat 8 a.m-8 p.m. Sun 10.a.m.- 1 p.m. and 2-7.30 p.m. Public Holidays 10 a.m -1 p.m. and 2-4 p.m.

TELEPHONES

In modern Munich, pay telephones are easily accessible. The traveller may wish to take note of some of the key telephone numbers which might prove to be useful during his stay in the city:

ACE- Breakdown Service	536502
ADAC- City Breakdown Service	19211
Apotheken-Notdienst	594475
Babysitter-Service	229291/394507
Bavaria-Management-Service	3071024
Bundesbahn, Railway Information	592991

Child Care Telephone	555356
Cinema Programme:	
City Centre A-K	11511
City Centre L-Z	11512
Church Information	1157
City Lost Prperty Office	233-1
DTC- Breakdown Service	8111212
Emergency Service	222666
Federal Postal Administration	1262/552
Fire Service	112
Flight Information	9211-2127
Interpreter, Federal Association	283330
Lady Interpr./Escort-Service	309968
Locksmith	342552
Lost Property Office	
at the Ostbahnhof	12884/409
MMG-Munich Trade Fair and	
Exhibition Company	5107-0
Municipal Authorities	2331
MVV-Munich Traffic and	
Tariff Association	238030
Police/patrol car	110
Railway Lost Property	
Office (Hb)	1286664/1285859
Special events/exhibitions, fairs	11516
Student Service	5234011/5234012
Suicide Prevention Centre	334041
Taxi Central Office	1611
Telephone Information:	
(national)	1188
(international)	01188
Telegramme receipt	1131
Telephone-Emergency	
number for addicts	282822
Telephone Ministry:	
(protestant)	11101
(catholic)	11102
Theatre and Concert	
Central Office	11517
Time Annoucement Service	1191
Wake-up Call	1141
Weather Forecast	1164
Weather Forecast for travel	11600
Where to go tonight	11518
Youth Information Centre	531655

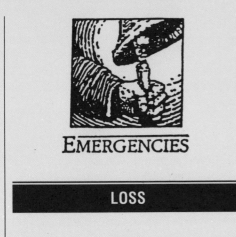

EMERGENCIES

LOSS

Should you lose anything, you can enquire at the Municipal Lost Property Office (for objects found on the streets and on public transport): Ruppertstr. 19, Tel. 233-1, Mon-Fri. 8.30 a.m.-12 a.m., Tues from 2 -5.30 p.m. Or else, check with the Railway Lost Property Office, Hauptbahnhof, Bahn-hof-platz 2, opposite Gleis 26, Tel. 128/5859, Mon-Thurs 8 a.m.-4.p.m., Fri until 5.15 p.m. and on Sat 8-12 a.m. There is also the Lost and Found in the Ostbahnhof (for property found on the S-Bahn), Tel. 12884/409, Mon-Fri 8 a.m.-5 p.m., Sat 8 a.m.-12 p.m. and as a final resort, contact the Bundespost Lost Property Office (for objects lost in the post or in telephone kiosks), Arnulfstr.195, Zi. 106, Tel. 1262552, Mon-Fri 8.00-11.30 a.m. and from 1 p.m-1 a.m.

LEFT LUGGUAGE

There are Left Luggage Offices located in the main train station and at the airport to help the hapless traveller locate any misplaced luggage. Be sure to check them out when you run into anything difficulties.

GETTING AROUND

PUBLIC TRANSPORT

Munich has more than 3,500 taxis, many of which operate into the early hours, and some right around the clock.

TAXI

There are over 100 taxi stands in the city area, or you can call the **Zentrale**, (Central Office) Tel. 2161-1. The minimum charge is DM 2.90 (for collection from home, DM 3.90), a kilometer within the city limits costs DM 1.70, and outside the city, DM 2.00.

PRIVATE TRANSPORT

Visitors to Munich can rent a car from any of several car rental agencies and explore the many sights of the city by car in a conveni.ent fashion.

CAR RENTAL

Autohansa
Schießstättstr. 12
Tel. 504064
Flughafen Riem
Tel. 908090

Autoverleih Neuhausen
Arnulfstr. 300
Tel. 177577/177578

Avis
Nymphenburger Str. 61
Tel. 126000-20
Arabellastr. 6

Tel. 918004
Balanstr. 74
Tel. 497301
Flughafen Riem (Riem Airport)
Tel. 9211-8250
Moosacher Str. 45
Tel. 3514084

AVM
Nymphenburger Str. 26
Tel. 184030

Bayern-Garage
Karlstr. 72
Tel. 591443.
R Blank Small Bus-Service/Limousine with chauffeur,
Tel. 718888

Europacar
Schwanthalerstr. 10a
Tel. 594723
Flughafen Riem
Tel. 908108/908236

Hertz
Nymphenburger Str. 81
Tel. 1295001
Leopoldstr. 194
Tel. 36993
Klisterhof 142
Tel. 786335
Flughafen Riem
Tel. 908744/ 907674/ 907323
Rosenheimer Landstr. 91
Tel. 6095991
Reservierungszentrale
Tel. 01302121

Inter Rent
Leopoldstr. 234
Tel. 366021
Ingolstädter Str. 64 c
Tel. 3161033
Hirtenstr. 14
Tel. 557145
Flughafen Riem
Tel. 908734/ 907155
Berg-am-Laim-Str. 127
Tel. 435003
Regional Verk. Ltg.
Tel. 631231
Bayernwald 631282
Distrikt Ltg.
433069

Mages
Verdistr. 112
Tel. 8119999/8119995

Motorent
beim Kulturzentrum Gasteig
Tel. 4150-313/317

Royal Rent
This agency   also provides a chauffeur-driven service at Auto-König
Eggenfeldener Str. 100
Tel. 9300040

WHERE TO STAY

HOTELS

Munich has almost 30,000 beds ready for its guests. But even this enormous number is not always enough. Beds are scarce, not only in the warm summer months, but also during the Oktoberfest (in the second half of September). Then there are the huge trade fairs (mostly in spring and autumn) and cultural events of international standing such as the Opera festival are held. It is thus advisable to book ahead, particularly during these times, either by writing directly to the hotel or to the Fremdenverkehrsamt München, Postfach, 8000 München1. For information on accomodation contact: Fremdenverkehrsamt München, Tel. 089/2391256 or 2391266. If you want a better hotel room in Munich it will cost about DM 100 per night.

The following list of hotels is but only a selection of the numerous ones in Munich. The prices are inclusive of breakfast and VAT, but may be subject to change,

Adria (garni)
Liebigstr. 8a, M 22, Tel. 293081,
DM 75 - 165
Alfa
Hirtenstr. 22, M 2, Tel. 598461,
DM 70 - 145
Ambassador
Mozartstr. 4, M 2, Tel. 530840,
DM 90 - 160
Am Maxmonument-Dollmann
Thierschstr. 49, M 22, Tel. 238080,
DM 90 - 125
Am Ring
Heimeranstr. 65, M 2, Tel. 503562,
DM 48 - 95
Am Sendlinger Tor
Blumenstr. 40, M 2, Tel. 231880,
DM 78 - 135

An der Oper
Falkenturmstr. 10, M 2, Tel. 228711,
DM 105 - 120
Apollo
Mittererstr. 7, M 2, Tel. 539531,
DM 105 - 160
Arabella
Arabellastr. 5, M 81, Tel. 92320,
DM 185 - 240
Arabella Olympiapark
Helene-Meyer-Ring 12, M40, Tel. 3516071,
DM 155 - 175
Arabella Westpark
Garmischer Str. 2, M 2, Tel. 5196-0,
DM 180 - 250
Arosa
Hotterstr. 2, M 2, Tel. 267087,
DM 60 - 110
Astor
Schillerstr. 24, M 2, Tel. 558031,
DM 98 - 128
Austrotel Deutscher Kaiser
Arnulfstr. 2, M 2, Tel. 53860, DM 170 - 180
Bayerischer Hof and Palais Montgelas
Promenadeplatz 2-6, M 2, Tel.21200,
reservation, Tel. 2120900, DM 186 - 256
Biederstein
Keferstr. 18, M 40, Tel. 395072,
DM 102 - 115
Bosch
Amalienstr. 25, M 2, Tel. 281061,
DM 75 - 110
Bristol
Pettenkoferstr. 2, M 2, Tel. 595151,
DM 110 - 195
Carlton
Fürstenstr. 12, M 2, Tel. 282061,
DM 70 - 150
Central garni
Schwanthalerstr. 111, M 2, Tel. 510830,
DM 165 - 180
City
Schillerstr. 3a, M 2, Tel. 558091,
DM 98 - 138
Continental Royal Classic Hotel
Max-Joseph-Str. 5, M 2, Tel. 551570,
DM 222 - 317
Crest Hotel Munich
Effnerstr. 99, M 81, Tel. 982541,
DM 164 - 194
Europäischer Hof
Bayerstr. 31, M 2, Tel. 551519,
DM 55 - 140
Excelsior
Schützenstr. 11, M 2, By the station.

Tel. 551370,
DM 178 - 228
Germania
Schwanthalerstr. 28, M 2, Tel. 51680,
DM 168 - 218
Hilton
Am Tucherpark 7, M 22, Tel. 3845-0,
DM 198 - 300
King's Hotel
Am Hbf, Dachauer Str. 13, M 2, Tel. 551870,
DM 140
Kraft
Schillerstr. 49, M 2, Tel. 594823,
DM 95 - 140
Krone (garni)
Theresienhöhe 8, M 2, Tel. 504052,
DM 130 - 165
Lord
Herzogstr. 3, M 40, Tel. 348094,
DM 80 - 110
Mercure
Am Deutschen Theater
Senefelderstr. 7-13, M 2, Tel. 551320,
DM 115-184
Metropol
Bayerstr. 43, M 2, Tel. 530764,
DM 71 - 115
Nicolai
Maria-Josefa-Str. 4, M 40, Tel. 397056,
DM 95
Olympiapark
Helene-Mayer-Ring 12, M 40,
Tel. 3516071,
DM 87 - 115
Platzl
Platzl 1, M 2, Tel. 237030,
DM 120 - 160
Residence
Artur-Kutscher-Platz 4, M 40,
Tel. 38178-0
DM 168 - 193
Sheraton-Hotel
Arabellastr. 6, M 81, Tel. 92640,
DM 180 - 360
Stachus
Bayerstr. 7, M 2, Tel. 592881,
DM 65 - 120
Trustee Park Hotel
Parkstr. 31, M 2, Tel. 519950,
DM 146 - 226
Verdi
Verdistr. 123, M 60, Tel. 8111484,
DM 46 - 55
Vier Jahreszeiten Kempinski Munich
Maximilianstr. 17, M 22, Tel. 230390,

DM 215 - 275.

AIRPORT HOTELS

Gästehaus-Pension Ampletzer
8011 Putzbrunn, Glonner Str. 20, Tel. 089/
46 92 74
Ideal situation: 500 m from the motorway
Munich-Salzburg, Exit Putzbrunn, 3 km
from the edge of Munich.
Crest Hotel
8000 Munich 81, Effnerstr. 99, Tel. 98 25
41, Telex 5 24 757
Hotel Friedenspromenade
8000 Munich 82, Friedenspromenade 13,
Tel. 089/430 90 44
Motorway Salzburg-Munich, 5 minutes to
Exit Haar.
Penta Hotel
8000 Munich 80, Hochstr. 3, Tel. 448 55 55
Hotel Winhart
8000 Munich 90, Balanstr. 238,
Tel. 089/68 31 17, 68 22 26
Alter Hof
8011 Vaterstetten, Fasanenstr. 4,
Tel. 08106/20 11
Hotel Cosima
8011 Vaterstetten, Bahnhofstr. 23, Tel.
08106/3 10 50, 3 10, 59
Hotel Eisenreich
8000 Munich 80, Baumkirchner Str. 17
Tel. 089/43 40 21-23

INNS

These inns are called hotel-pensionen
(guest houses) which offer a room for DM
40 to 50. Here is a selection of guest houses
in this range:
Agnes
Agnesstr. 58, M 40, Tel. 1293061
Amalien
Amalienstr. 71, M 40, Tel. 283971
Amsel
Gräfstr. 91, M 60, Tel. 882932
Am Kaiserplatz
Kaiserplatz 12, M 40, Tel. 349190 (DM 35)
Am Markt
Heiliggeiststr. 6, M 2, Tel. 225014

Am Siegestor
Akademiestr. 5, M 40, Tel. 399550/51
Armin
Augustenstr. 5, M 2, Tel. 593197
Beck
Thierschstr. 36, M 22, Tel. 220708
Erika
Landwehrstr. 8, M 2, Tel. 554327
Frank
Schellingstr. 24, M 40, Tel. 281451
Fraunhofer
Fraunhoferstr.10, M 5, Tel. 2607238
(rooms with several beds)
Geiger
Steinheilstr. 1, M 2, Tel. 521556
(from DM 30)
Harras
Albert-Roßhaupter-Str. 64, M 70,
Tel. 7605565
Herzog Heinrich
Herzog-Heinrich-Str. 3, M 2, Tel. 532575
Hungaria
Brienner Str. 42/II, M 2, Tel. 521558
Luna
Landwehrstr. 5, M 2, Tel. 597833
Marion
Luisenstr. 25, M 2, Tel. 592554
(about DM 35)
Theresia
Luisenstr. 51, M 2, Tel. 521250
(about DM 37)
Toskana (garni)
Schwanthalerstr. 42, M 2, Tel. 531970
Weigand
Lucile-Grahn-Str. 39, M 80, Tel. 473752
Zöllner
Sonnenstr. 10, M 2, Tel. 554035
(from DM 35)

GUEST HOUSES

AGAH
Hohenzollernstr. 97, M 40, Tel. 2717844,
DM 60 - 65
Am Karlstor
Neuhauser Str. 34/IV, M 2, Tel. 593596,
DM 52 - 70
Am Nordbad
Schleißheimer Str. 91, M 40, Tel. 180857,
DM 60 - 85
Braunauer Hof
Frauenstr. 40, M 2, Tel. 223613,

DM 59 - 69
Englischer Garten
Liebergesellstr. 8, M 40, Tel. 392034-36,
DM 68 - 96
Häuser an der Universität
Schellingstr. 11, M 40, Tel. 281006,
DM 50 - 80
Lämmle Gästehaus
Friedenheimer Str. 137, M 21, Tel. 571529,
DM 50 - 60
Mariandl
Goethestr. 51, M 2, Tel. 534108, DM 48 - 65
Monopteros
Oettingenstr. 35, M 22, Tel. 292348,
DM 43 - 73
Occam
Occamstr. 7, M 40, Tel. 393934, DM 60 - 90
Victoria
Oskar-von-Miller-Ring 34-36, M 2
Tel. 281048, DM 50 - 75

YOUTH HOSTELS

Christlicher Verein Junger Männer (YMCA)
Landwehrstr. 13, M 2, Tel. 555941.
Simple but cosy. Three single rooms (DM 30-34), 22 double rooms (DM 55-63), 11 three -bed rooms (DM 73.50-85.50). Reductions for groups. Additional accommodation for 30-70 persons. It has a restaurant.
DJH-Gästehaus
Miesingstr. 4, M 70, Tel. 7236500.
Open from 7 a.m.-1 a.m. for those with a valid Jugendherbergs-Ausweis (Youth Hostel Card). DM 15-22 per night. Not far from the zoo. Has a restaurant, disco, table tennis and conference rooms.
Jugendherberge München
Wendl-Dietrich-Str. 20, M 19, Tel. 131156.
Overnight with breakfast DM 10.30 (to 24 years) DM 12.30 (to 27 years). Only with valid Youth Hostel Card.
Jugendherberge Burg Schwaneck
Burgweg 4-6, 8023 Pullach, Tel. 7930643.
Has bed rooms from 4, 6 to 8 persons per room with prices ranging from DM 10-11.20. At the edge of Munich, with sauna and bowling alley.
Haus International
Elisabethstr. 87, M 40, Tel. 185081-83.
Young People's Hotel

For those between 14 and 33 yrs. Rooms with one to five beds. Single room: DM 39-56, Double room: DM 74-96. With bar, disco, restaurant and table tennis room. It also takes those who don't have a Youth Hostel Card.

Jugendhotel Marienherberge
Goethestr. 9, M 2, Tel. 555891.
Only for girls up to 25 years old, with reservation. DM 25-27. In central position, with tea kitchen and table tennis room.

Jugendlager Kapuzinerhälzl
Franz-Schrank-Straße, M 60.
Youth camp. Has a 300-person tent with wooden floor. Open from the last day of June to the first week of September. Overnight DM 4 with sleeping bag and air bed.

CAMPGROUNDS

Campingplatz Thalkirchen
Zentralländstr. 49, M 70, Tel. 7231707.
Open from mid March to the end of October. Near the zoo at Hellabrunn. Has a supermarket and swimming pool.

Campingplatz Obermenzing
Lochhausener Str. 59, Tel. 8112235.
At the beginning of the Stuttgart motorway. Open to 5th November. With a self service shop, playground and tavern.

Campingplatz Langwieder See
Eschenrieder Str. 119, M 60, Tel. 8141566.
Open from 1st April to 15th October; on the lake, bathing opportunities, restaurant, grocer's shop, mini-golf, boat and caravan hire. Warm water, showers and a communal kitchen.

Campingplatz Nord-West
Dachauer Str. 571, M 50, Tel. 1506936.
Open all the year round. With restaurant and shop, swimming pool and solarium.

FOOD DIGEST

WHAT TO EAT

Simple and solid is the reputation of **Bavarian cuisine,** and that is just what it is. You really can't slim in Bavaria, if you try **"Beuscherln"**, **"Semmelknödel"** or "Reiberdatschis", to name but a few local dishes which sound Chinese even to the Germans. The Bavarian calls them **"Schmankerln"** (delicacies or titbits) and by that he means something he likes.

That it's made from at least 51% veal, is all we are giving away about the legendary **"Weißwurst"** (White Sausage) which is not supposed to hear the chimes of midday. **"Leberkäs"** (liver cheese), another Bavarian delicacy, has neither cheese nor liver in its list of ingredients, and is thus an example of the same Bavarian logic as that of the comedian Karl Valentin, who noted that there was no beer in beer sausage, and no wool in wool sausage either. Leberkäs is in fact made of a mixture of roast pork and beef into a kind of paté, and like the Weißwurst is eaten with mustard and pretzel. But back to the secretive Beuscherln: they are part of Bavarian cooking which was born of necessity. Those unable to afford meat in the old days, used the offal. Today these poor man's dishes such as preserved calves' lungs, chitterlings, sour calves' liver and kidneys are to be found on many menus of gourmet restaurants. They are served with the obligatory **"Semmelknödel"** (white bread dumplings), a mixture based on old rolls, eggs, onion and parsley. The variations on the Knödel theme are endless, you can have them with semolina, ham and bacon as well as sweetened for a main course of potato pastry and plums with brown butter, sugar and cinnamon.

What pasta is to Italy, and rice to China,

flour and potato dishes are to Bavaria. There are potatoes in the "**Pichelsteiner Eintopf**" (a thick soup of meat and vegetables) as well as combined with flour in soufflés and noodles. But the absolute acme of the potato and flour combination is in the celebrated "Reiberdatschi", a flat pancake which can be served with meat dishes, or with sweet apple purée. Radishes, cabbage, celery and black salsify provide the vegetable balance of Bavarian cuisine. Whether they can compensate for the fat content of crisp piece of roast pork, a veal shank or a golden grilled chicken, is another matter.

WHERE TO EAT

The following are some of the restaurants where Bavarian cuisine and atmosphere can be enjoyed.

BAVARIAN RESTAURANTS

Alter Wirt
8022 Grünwald, Marktplatz 1
Tel. 641855, daily 7 a.m.-12 a.m. Reservation preferred. Rustic elegance, not cheap.

Am Glockenbach
M 5, Kapuzinerstr. 29
Tel. 534043, daily 12 a.m.-2p.m. and 7 p.m.-1 a.m. Reservation advisable for evenings. A good tip for gourmets in the Schlachthofviertel (slaughter house area). French and Bavarian cuisine in intimate drawing room atmosphere.

Atzinger
M 40, Schellingstr. 9,
Tel. 282880. Typical Schwabing students' "in" place.

Augustiner Großgaststätte
M 2, Neuhauser Str. 16
Tel. 2604106, daily 9 a.m.-12 a.m. Traditional Bavarian fare in real Munich atmosphere (1,000 seats, and is a "small" Beer Garden seating 200).

Boettner
M 2, Theatinerstr. 8
Tel. 221210, Mon-Fri 11 a.m.-12 a.m., Sun 11 a.m.-3 p.m. Reservation advisable. Tiny gourmet paradise in old English style, hidden behind a delicatessen. French and regional cuisine, only the best ingredients, and

corresponding prices.

Donisl
M 2, Weinstr. 1
Tel. 220184, daily 9-1 a.m. Reservation preferred. Bavarian specialities consumed in the old Munich atmosphere.

Franziskaner Fuchs' Stub'n
M 2, Perusastr. 5
Tel. 2318120, daily 8 a.m.-2 a.m. Reservation advisable. It's always full here, where suckling pig, calf and pork shank and of course (apparently the best in Munich) Weißwürste are devoured by the hundredweight. Finer cuisine is available too, at corresponding prices.

Hackerkeller
M 2, Theresienhöhe 4
Tel. 507004, daily 5 p.m.-1 a.m. Ox on the spit is the speciality of the house, served to Bavarian traditional music and the prices are quite reasonable.

Haxnbauer
M 2, Münzstr. 5
Tel. 221922, daily 11 p.m.-1 a.m. Reservation preferred. Old Bavarian inn where the shanks are turned over open beech wood fires. The prices will vary according to shank size.

Hofbräuhaus am Platzl
M 2, Am Platzl
Tel. 221676, daily 9 a.m.- 12 a.m. This must be the most famous pub in the world. traditional Munich snacks at good prices. Brass band music. The question is - do any locals ever go there?

Hundskugel
M 2, Hotterstr. 18
Tel. 264272, daily 10 a.m.-1 a.m. Reservation advisable. Munich's oldest inn, first mentioned in 1440.

Löwenbräu-Keller
M 2, Nymphenburgerstr. 2
Tel. 526021, daily 9 a.m.-12 a.m. Traditional Munich beer cellar with one peculiarity: In the beer garden , there is a self service for food but for the beer, it is served in half litre measures!

Mathäser Bierstadt
M 2, Bayerstr. 5
Tel. 592896, daily Bar 8 a.m.-12 a.m. Restaurant from 10.30 a.m. This typical Munich beer cellar has over 450 seats, and thus is by far the largest pub in the world. Apart from the bar and banqueting hall, there is a restaurant where one can eat cheaply and well.

Nürnberger Bratwurstglöckl
M 2, Frauenplatz 9
Tel. 220385, daily 9 a.m.-12 a.m. Reservation definitely advisable. The best Nürnberger Schweinswürste (pork sausages) of Munich are grilled over a beech wood fire and served with horse radish on pewter plates.

Ratskeller
M 2, Marienplatz 8
Tel. 220313, daily 9 a.m.-12 a.m. Elegant and one of the biggest of Munich's cellar restaurants in the catacombs of the Town Hall, with delicacies at reasonable prices.

Schlachthof
M 2, Zenettistr. 9
Tel. 765448. Former slaughter house inn, here Bavarian cuisine is combined with cultural events.

s'Wirtshaus
M 2, Am Platzl 4
Tel. 294686, daily 9 a.m.-4 pm. For night owls who are hungriest at 3 in the morning.

Straubinger Hof
M2, Blumenstr. 5
Tel. 2608444, daily, except weekends and Public Holidays 9 a.m-11 p.m. Good value for money, traditional Bavarian home cooking, two dining rooms.

Weinhaus Neuner
M 2, Herzogspitalstr. 8
Tel. 2603954, daily except Sun 5 p.m.- 1 a.m. Reservation advisable. Regional cuisine, combined with French Cuisine Nouvelle, an excellent venue for wine lovers.

Weinstadl
M 2, Burgstr. 6
Tel. 221047, Mon-Sat 10 a.m.-11.30 p.m., Sun and Public Holidays 4-12 a.m. Palatinate cuisine is served in this, the oldest house in Munich, where the Late Gothic pillars have been preserved as has the facade which dates from the 16th Century. In one of the loveliest courtyards in the city, one can relax and enjoy a glass of wine.

Weißes Bräuhaus
M 2, Tal 10
Tel. 299875. Large restaurant in the centre of the town, with an enormous selection of Bavarian dishes. Just renovated, but still wonderfully cosy.

Wurstkuchl
M 40, Amalienstr. 87
Tel. 281577, daily 10 a.m.-12.30 a.m. Simple dishes and home made sausages cooked over a charcoal fire at reasonable prices in the atmosphere of a Bavarian living room.

Zum Pschorr-Bräu
M 2, Neuhauser Str. 11
Tel . 2603001, daily 8 a.m.-12 a.m. One of the traditional, rustic beer cellars of Munich with typical Munich fare.

Zum Spöckmeier am Roseneck
M 2, Rosenstr. 9
Tel. 268088, daily 9 a.m.-12 a.m., Sun closed after 5 p.m. Reservation advisable. Traditional old Munich inn, where one meets to eat Weißwurst in the morning.

Munich also has a good variety of gourmet restaurants which serve some of the exquisite cuisine in the country. To be sure that you will have the opportunity to sample them, reservations are always advisable.

CHINESE

Asian
Einsteinstr. 133, M 80
Tel. 472124
Cheap, average cuisine.

Jasmin
Franziskanerstr. 16, M 80
Tel. 4486913
Average cuisine, corresponding prices.

Canton
Therersienstr. 49, M 2
Tel. 522185

China Bauer
Nymphenburger Str. 193, M 19
Tel. 164263

Bamboo Garden
Hochbrückenstr. 3 M 2
Tel. 293520

Mandarin
Ledererstr. 21, M 2
Tel. 226888

Man Fat
Barer Str. 53, M 40
Tel. 2720962

Tai Tung
Prinzregentenstr. 60, M 80
Tel. 471100

FRENCH

Le Gaulois
Hörwarthstr. 4, M 40
Tel. 367435
Fish and game specialities.

La Marmite
Lilienstr. 8, M 80
Tel. 482242
Pleasant brasserie, and the prices can be said to be reasonable.

Rue des Halles
Steinstr. 28, M 80
Tel. 485675
Smart interieur, not cheap, but with real Parisian atmosphere.

Le Zig Zag
Andréestr. 10, M 19
Tel. 1679104
Brasserie for people with a hearty appetite. Local and fair prices.

Le Cezanne
Konradstr. 1, M 40
Tel. 391805
The master chef Joel Noguier conjures delicacies for the palate at prices within one's means.

Tantris
M 40, Johann-Fichte-Str. 7
Tel. 362061, Tues-Fri 12 a.m.-3 p.m. and 6.30-10.30 p.m., Mon and Sat only evenings. The second top restaurant in Munich, managed by Heinz Winkler. The cuisine: French.

GERMAN

Aubergine
M 2, Maximiliansplatz 5
Tel. 598171, daily except Mon, Sun and Public Holidays. Reservations definitely advisable for lunch and dinner. One of the most famous chefs in the world cooks here: Eckart Witzigmann.

Dallmayr
M 2, Dienerstr. 14-15
Tel. 2135100, Mon-Fri 9 a.m.-12 a.m. closed Sat evenings and on Sun. Food from the Delicatessen can either be taken home, or eaten immediately.

Das kleine Restaurant im Gasthof Böswirth
M 60, Waidachanger 9
Tel. 8119763, Wed-Fri 5 -11 p.m., Sat, Sun closed Mon and Tue. Cuisine nouvelle in the restaurant and Bavarian regional dishes in the public bar next door.

Grüne Gans
M 5, Am Einla ß5
Tel. 266228, daily except Sat evenings. Intimate Munich gourmets meeting place, with seating for just 30 in a cosy and homely atmosphere.

Halali
M 22, Schönfeldstr. 22
Tel. 285909, closed for Sat lunch, Sun and Public Holidays. Old traditional Munich venue, owned by the Witzigmann pupil, Hans Mair. Good bourgeois fare, (relatively) good prices.

Käfer-Schänke
M 80, Schumannstr. 1
Tel. 41681, closed on Sun and Public Holidays. Hidden behind the gourmet shop, are several elegant rooms where one may dine undisturbed.

GREEK

Dionysos
Leopoldstr. 42, M 40
Tel. 333302
For those hungry after 1 a.m. (open until 3 a.m.)

Entaxi
Bergmannstr. 46, M 2
Tel. 506950
Cosy atmosphere in one of the smallest Greek taverns. Typical food.

Olympia
Kellerstr. 29, M 80
Tel. 488082
Cheap and good, so always full

Rembetiko
Dreimühlenstr. 2, M 5
Tel. 773312
Good and cheap, with live music.

To Steki
Dreimühlenstr. 38, M 5
Tel. 771610
Live music at the weekends.

Kytaro
Innere Wiener Str. 36, M 80
Tel. 4801176
The "in" Greek restaurant (reservations definitely advisable) and the prices here are very reasonable.

Lyra
Bazeillestr. 5, M 80
Tel. 486661

Kyklos
Wilderich-Lang-Str. 10, M 19
Tel. 162633

Omikron
Einsteinstr. 143, M 90
Tel. 471951

INDIAN

Taj Palace
Kurfürstenstr. 47, M 40
Tel. 2724454
Bombay
Kurfürstenstr. 47, M 40
Tel. 2724454
Maharadscha
Hohenzollernstr. 12, M 40
Tel. 338736
Maharani
Rottmannstr. 24, M 2
Tel. 527912
Shalimar
Fasanenstr. 4, M 19
Tel. 180710
Shi Raj
Leonrodstr. 56, M 19
Tel. 1293974
Sultana
Sternstr. 20, M 22
Tel. 226917
Tandoori
Baumstr. 6, M 5
Tel. 2012208

ITALIAN

Bei Mario
Adalbertstr. 15, M 40
Tel. 2800460
Luisenstr. 47, M 2
Tel. 521519
Bella Italia
Weißenburgerstr. 12, M 80
Zweibrückenstr. 8, M 2
Sendlingerstr. 66, M 2
Hohenzollernplatz 8, M 40
Leopoldstr. 44, M 40
Canale Grande
Ferdinand-Maria-Str. 51, M 19
Tel. 174565
Prices, a little stiff, otherwise it offers good cuisine.
Il Gattopardo
Georgenstr. 67, M 40
Tel. 2716525
Rustic decor, but fine cuisine.
Il Mulino
Görresstr. 1, M 40
Tel. 523335
Average cuisine, but in the summer the beer garden is interesting as it will be crowded with a festive air about it.

Da Pippo
M 80, Mühlbauerstr. 36
Tel. 4704848,
Daily except Sun and Public Holidays, lunch and dinner. Italian cuisine. Specialities of the house : Tatar di salmone, Ossobuco diagnello. Loupfilet in nettle sauce.
El Toula
Sparkassenstr. 5, M 2
Tel. 292869
La Casera
Hohenzollernstr. 11, M 40
Tel. 345152
La Cucina
Leopoldstr. 194, M 40
Tel. 340971
Tre Colonne
Hiltenspergerstr. 43, M 40
Tel. 2717246
Vini e Panini
Nordendstr. 45, M 40
Tel. 2721743
This a stand-up snack bar that serves a wide variety of Italian fast food.
La Mer
M 40, Schraudolphstr. 24
Tel. 2722439. Only open in the evenings except Mon. Fish and crustaceans are served in splendidly decorated surroundings.
La Piazzetta
M 2, Oskar-von-Miller-Ring 3
Tel. 282990, Sat from 6.30 p.m. One of Munich's best Italian restaurants. A large Jugendstil restaurant, with a simpler Rosticceria next door, where night owls can eat (open until 6 a.m., live music).
Le Gourmet
M 2, Ligsalzstr. 46
Tel. 503597, open only evenings except Sun. Special regional cuisine offered by Otto Koch. Specialities: Semmelkn del-Souffle with flat mushrooms. Seafood Weißwurst in mustard butter. Lamb saddle Krautwickel, Calf filet served in cream. A mouth-watering experience.

JAPANESE

Daitokai
Kurfürstenstr.59, M 40
Tel. 2711421
Mifune
M 80; Ismaninger Str. 136
lTel. 987572

The S-Bahn and U-Bahn in Munich

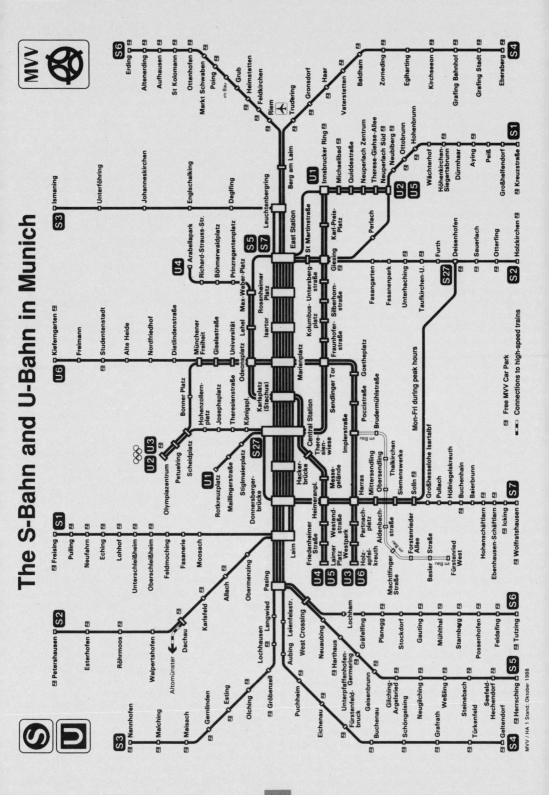

MVV / HA 1 Stand: Oktober 1988

LATIN AMERICAN

El Chaco
Kirchenstr. 79, M 80
Tel. 476699
A good recommendation for lovers of Argentinian steaks.
Tango Uno
Hiltenspergerstr. 32, M 40
Tel. 2718591
Modern setting, good Argentinian and Uruguayan cuisine.
Pancho & Petro
Humboldstr. 5, M 90
Tel. 6564722
Churrasco
Tal 74, M 2
Tel. 294661
Nikolaistr. 9, M 20
Tel. 344712
Asado
Belgradstr. 10, M 40
Tel. 367677

OTHER ASIAN

Arabesk
Kaulbachstr. 86, M 40
Tel. 333738
Lebanese specialities in this restaurant.
Waikiki
Neureutherstr. 39, M 40
Tel. 2711146
Thai and Indonesian specialities.

SPANISH

Casa Pepe
Klopstockstr. 4, M 40
Tel. 366900
Eat to fiery live music.
Centro Espagnol
Daiserstr. 20, M 70
Tel. 763653
Pub with cultural ambitions, always full.
Bodega Dali (Wine Bar)
Augustenstr. 42, M 2
Tel. 5234280
Don Quijote
Biedersteinerstr. 6, M 40
Tel. 342318
La Paella
Rotwandstr. 1, M 80
Tel. 6972153

El Cid
Belgradstr. 45, M 40
Tel. 3003268

VEGETARIAN

Café Gollier
Gollierstr. 87, M 2
Tel. 501673
A different restaurant, captivating, and not only because of the great variety of the menu.
Jahreszeiten
Sebastiansplatz 9, M 2
Tel. 2609578
Excellent, highly nutritious food, good value for money and pleasant surroundings.
Vitamin-Buffet
Herzog-Wilhelm-Str. 25, M 2
Tel. 2607418
Good nutritious vegetarian food for a wide range of customers.
Keyno
Steinstr. 42, M 80
Tel. 4487356
Must be the finest vegetarian restaurant in Munich.
Kornkammer
Haimhauserstr. 8, M 40
Tel. 341135
Café Wildwuchs
Leonrodstr. 19 (im Werkhaus), M 19
Tel. 160474
Yello
Baaderstr. 74, M 5
Tel. 0214787
Cantina
Weißenburger Str. 39, M 80
Tel. 4470922
Café des Frauenkulturhauses
Richard-Strauß-Str. 21, M 90
Tel. 4705212

VIETNAMESE

Viêt-Nam
Corneliusstr. 1, M 50
Tel. 265749
A little patience is needed, but it's worth the wait. Unpretentious with reasonable prices.
Mekong
Lachnerstr. 1, M 19
Tel. 169092
Although it is expensive, it serves excellent Vietnamese cuisine.

CAFÉS

Altschwabing
Schellingstr. 56, M 40
Viennese style, and stucco, very romantic.
Baader Café
Baaderstr. 47, M 5
Social meeting place, in the Gärtnerplatzviertel.
Café Ça Va
Kazmairstr. 44, M 2
Relaxed Westend pub, nearly always full.
Café Extrablatt
Leopoldstr. 7, M 40
Pseudo celebrities meeting place, with the former gossip columnist of the Bild-Zeitung newspaper.
Café Münchner Freiheit
Münchner Freiheit 20, M 40
Well frequented café with fantastic ice cream concoctions, which one can enjoy in the summer.
Café Wiener Platz
Innere Wiener Str. 48, M 80
Cool, stylish, with artistic flair.

BRUNCH SHOPS

Drugstore
Feilitzschstr. 12, M 40
Slightly antiquated pop atmosphere.
Café Größenwahn
Lothringerstr. 11, M 80
Portions not that big, and it's not that cheap either.
Mövenpick
Lenbachplatz, M 2
Good, well served food, plenty of space.
Reitschule
Königinstr. 34, M 40
The atmosphere is a mixture of the '60's and post modern, interesting, particularly for horse lovers.
Ruffini
Orffstr. 22, M 19
Excellent breakfast is served on the terrace in summer.

DRINKING NOTES

Although one is allowed to bring one's own snack along (only the beer has to be bought, and in one-litre mugs), Bavarian delicacies and titbits are served in all.

BISTROS

Café d'Accord
Nordendstr. 62, M 40
For dynamic youth.
Kay's Bistro
Utzsehneiderstr. 1 a, M 5
Worth a visit just for the continually changing decor, and the handsome and charming waiters. Meeting place of celebrities.
Kuczynski
Preysingstr. 20, M 80
Since Haidhausen has become part of the social scene, a meeting place for the "in" crowd, particularly for Super-Brunch on Sunday.
Oase
Amalienpassage, M 40
A pleasant and restful place in an inner courtyard. Outside in summer.
Tommi's Bistro
Clemensstr. 7, M 40
Exactly what one imagines a Bistro to be.
Zest
Adalbertstr. 23, M 40
Modern style, but romantic nevertheless.

BEER GARDENS

The visitor is advised that before venturing into a beer garden he should be sensitive to Bavarian singularities and customs to avoid any misunderstanding.
Augustinerkeller
M 2, Arnulfstr. 52
Tel. 594393, daily 10 -1 a.m. Apart from the restaurant (reservation requested) there is a beer garden seating 5,000 with self service, snack stalls and sometimes a brass band.
Bräustüberl der Forschungsbrauerei
M 83, Unterhachinger Str. 76
Tues-Sat 11a.m.-11 p.m. Sun 10 a.m.-11 p.m., Tel. 6701169. Bavarian sausage specialities in the original brewery with a large garden. Families are welcomed to these

places which are easily affordable.

Chinesischer Turm
M 40, Englischer Garten
Tel. 395028, in good weather 11-1 a.m. Every visitor to Munich must come here. It has 7,000 seats and all on self service.

Flaucher
M 70, Isarauen 1
Tel. 7232677, daily 10 a.m.-11 p.m. A place to make a trip to, and a good tip. One of Munich's best beer gardens at reasonable prices. Specialities, game (in the hunting season). A must for visitors.

Hofbräukeller
M 80, Innere Wiener Str. 19
Tel. 489489, daily 8.30 a.m.-12 a.m. A secret known to beer garden fans. Bavarian cuisine at reasonable prices.

Hirschgarten
M 19 , Hirschgartenalle 1
Tel. 172591, daily 11.30 a.m. - 10 p.m., Nov-Feb., closed Tues. Munich's largest beer garden, seating 8,000 with adjoining game enclosure and everything your heart desires.

Hirschau
M 40, Gyßlingstr. 7
Tel. 369942, Always open in good weather, Restaurant closed on Mon. Excellent Steckerl fish. Children's playground, which can be conveniently supervised from the beer table.

Im Grüntal
M 81, Im Grüntal 15
Tel. 980984, daily except Mon 11 a.m.-1 a.m. Reservation advisable in the evening. Smart set beer garden with corresponding food and prices.

Max-Emanuel-Brauerei
M 40, Adalbertstr. 33
Tel 2715158, daily 10-1 a.m. Reservation requested (in the Restaurant) Famous not only for the folk music performances, but also for the "White Festivals" at carnival, and for its jazz concerts.

Menterschweige
M 90, Harthauser Str. 70
Tel. 640732, daily 11 am.-12 a.m. Reservation requested (in the Restaurant). This lovely restaurant caters to excursions on the bank of the Isar that has been going on for 300 years, but the Provençal cuisine and Boules are relatively new.

Osterwaldgarten
M 40, Keferstr. 12
Tel. 346370, daily 11 - 1 a.m. Old Schwab-ing beer garden with very old chestnut trees. Sundays early beer from 11 a.m.

Pschorr-Keller
M 2, Theresienhühe 7
Tel. 501088, daily 8 a.m.-12 a.m. A typical Munich cellar inn (total 3,500 seats, beer garden 600) with music by a quartet and suckling pig grilled. It's not cheap to eat here, apart from the Reiberdatschi with apple purée.

Salvator-Keller
M 90, Hochstraße
Tel. 483274, daily 9-11 p.m. One of the beer centres of Munich, (Seating 2,000 inside and 3,000 in the beer garden). Good bourgeois cuisine, good value for money.

Sankt Emmeram's Mühle
München-Oberföhring, St. Emmeram 41
Tel. 953971, daily except Tues 11-1 a.m. The local elite meets there, and those who would like to be among their number.

Waldwirtschaft Großhesselohe
8023 Großhesselohe, Georg-Kalb-Str. 3
Tel. 795088, Beer garden daily in good weather, Restaurant except Mon and Tues, 10.30 a.m.-11.30 p.m. Well known particularly by jazz fans. In the summer known and unknown bands play here. Specialities: suckling pig with dark beer crackling. Game in the hunting season (prices are slightly more expensive).

Wirtshaus am Hart
M 45, Sudetendeutsche Str. 40
Tel. 3116039, daily 11-1 a.m., Sat from 5 p.m. This beer garden with its yellow walls is different, welcoming all including children. The portions are large, the prices small.

Zum Aumeister
M 45, Sondermeierstr. 9
Tel. 325224, daily except Mon 8 a.m.- 11 p.m. Favourite excursion destination, on the northern edge of the Englischer Garten (beer garden: 2,500 seats).

Zur Schwaige
M 19, Schloß Nymphenburg
Tel. 174421, daily 11.30 - 1 a.m. This castle inn offers a cosy beer garden with excellent food at reasonable prices. A recommendation not only for asparagus lovers.

THINGS TO DO

CITY

TOURS

Daily city tours in buses are offered by the Münchener Fremdenrundfahrten OHG, Arnulfstr. 8, Tel. 1204-248.

Point of departure is the Bahnhofsplatz opposite the main entrance of the station.

Short Tours (approx. 1 hour) begin at 10 a.m. and 2.30 p.m. and cost DM 13 (with visit to the Site of the Olympic Games and ascent of the Olympiaturm DM 20).

Long Tours (approx. 21/2 hours) take place twice a day (apart from Mondays). The morning tour (starts 10 a.m.)includes a visit to the alten Pinakothek gallery and the Frauenkirche. The afternoon tour (starts at 2.30 p.m.) includes a tour of Schloß Nymphenburg (Price DM 23). On Fridays and Saturdays you can see Munich by night, starting at 7.30 p.m., the tour lasts about five hours. It costs DM 100, inclusive of dinner, and you get to go to three "typical" Munich establishments.

For people interested in the "other" side of Munich, the Deutsche Gewerkschaftsbund (German Federation of Trades Unions) offers a tour every first Saturday in the month, which gives an alternative insight into the city, with visits to the site of the November-revolution of 1918, the Socialist Republic of 1919, the rise of the NSDAP and the anti-facist resistance. Bus departure: Gewerkschaftshaus Schwanthalerstr. 64, at 10 a.m. Reservation is advisable, Tel. 5141675 (for groups from 8 Persons).

TOWER ACENTS

Olympiaturm (290 m): Daily 8 a.m.-12 p.m. cost: DM 4/2.50, Children under 6 years old, free.

Peterskirche (92 m) Rindermarkt: Mon-Sat 9 a.m.-5 p.m., Sun 10 a.m.-7 p.m. Public Holidays until 6 p.m. The cost ranges from DM 2.00/1.00/0.50.

Rathaus (85 m) on Marienplatz: Mon-Fri 9 a.m.-4 p.m. Sat, Sun 10 a.m.-6 p.m. Closed on Public Holidays. DM 2.00/1.00.

COUNTRY

TOWNS AROUND MUNICH

Andechs
By train: take the S5 just to Herrsching, from there walk through the Kiental valley to the monastery, Kloster Andechs 3 km. By road: it is the Autobahn (Motorway) E 61 in the direction of Lindau to exit at Oberpfaffenhofen, through Weßling and Herrsching.

Augsburg
Take the A8 train heading in the direction of Stuttgart.

Baierbrunn
The S7 heading for Wolfratshausen will get you there. Or by road take the B11.

Benediktbeuren
The B11 train heading for direction of Mittenwald will take you there.

Chiemsee
Take the A8 also going towards the town of Mittenwald.

Dachau
By train, it is the S2 in the direction of Petershausen and by road take the B304.

Ettal
Take the ride on the E6 to Starnberg then switch to the B2 heading for Garmisch-Partenkirchen.

Freising
By rail it is the train destined for Freising while by car head for the Motorway or the E 11 in the direction of Landshut.

Großhesselohe
By train take the S7 in the direction of Wolfratshausen or take the road B11 that

leads to Wolfratshausen.

Herrenchiemsee
This tourist spot is open from April to September, daily 9 a.m.-5 p.m.; in winter the Schloß (Palace) is opened from 10 a.m. to 4 p.m. but the Museum is closed. To get there: take the A8 heading for Salzburg to Bernau, then exit in the direction of Prien.

Ilkahöhe
By train it is the S6 for Tutzing. By car take the road E6 to Starnberg, then the B2 going to Murnau.

Kochelsee
B11 Direction Mittenwald or motorway direction Garmisch-Partenkirchen to Großweil.

Landshut
Take the B11 or A92.

Linderhof
Open: April-September, daily. 9 a.m.- 12.15 p.m. and 12.45 p.m.- 5 p.m.; June - August: afternoons to 5 p.m.; in winter the Grotte and Kiosk are closed; Schloß: daily 9 a.m.-12 p.m. and 12.45 p.m.-5 p.m. Fountains between 9 a.m. and 5 p.m. on the hour. To get there take the B2 to Ettal and then change direction towards Füssen.

Neuschwanstein
Open: daily. 9 a.m.-5 p.m. To get there, get on the B2 to Ettal, then to Füssen.

Oberammergau
Hop on the A95 heading for Garmisch-Partenkirchen to Oberau.

Regensburg
It is by way of the A9 to Ingolstadt to the motorway triangle at Holledau and then take the A 93.

Schäftlarn
Hop on the train S7 heading for Wolfratshausen or by road on the B11 to Richtung Wolfratshausen.

Schleißheim
Take the E6 in the direction of Ingolstadt.

Starnberger See
Either take the train S 6 going to Tutzing or by road to Mittlerer Ring West, Autobahn Garmisch-Partenkirchen to Starnberg. By boat is also possible; for boat information: Tel. 08143/299 or for general information call Starnberger See and Ammersee: Fremdenverkehrsverband Starnberger Fünfseenland, 8130 Starnberg, Wittelsbacherstr. 9a, Tel. 08151/5911.

Schliersee
Take the A8 to Salzburg and Weyarn, then exit in the direction of Miesbach.

Tegernsee
Again take the A8 this time heading for Salzburg to Holzkirchen, then switch to the B318 towards Rottach-Egern. For more information, contact Staatliche Seenverwaltung Tegernsee, Seestr. 70, 8180 Tegernsee, Tel. 08022/4760.

Walchensee
The B11 heading towards Mittenwald or take the Autobahn by way of Garmisch-Partenkirchen to Grosweil to get there.

Wallfahrtskirche Wies
Ask for the E6 to Starnberg or the B2 to Welheim, B472 to Peiting as well as the B17 to Steingaden/Wies.

Wasserburg
Take the B304 to reach there.

Weihenstephan
The train S2 to Freising or by road B 11 in the direction of Landshut will get you there,

CULTURE PLUS

MUSEUMS

Munich, both the city and the surrounding area boast of many fine museums to enthrall the culturally inclined.

WITHIN MUNICH

Alte Pinakothek
Barerstr. 27
European painting of the 14th to the 19th Century in 19 halls and 36 small rooms. Extensive collection of world famous old German and Flemish masters, as well as paintings from the Italian, Dutch, French and Spanish schools.
Daily except Mon 9 a.m.- 4.30 p.m. Tues and Thurs evening opening 7 p.m.- 9 p.m. Tel. 233805-215/216.

Bayerisches Hauptstaatsarchiv
Schönfeldstr. 5
Collection of approximately 400,000 original certificates, the oldest of which dates from Charlemagne in 777. Also a collection of coats of arms and seals, Tel. 2198596.

Bayerisches Nationalmuseum
Prinzregentenstr. 3
Historical collection of sculpture, paintings and craft from the Middle Ages to the 19th Century. Art historical collections of : porcelain, fayence, majolica and pottery. Folkloric collections, peasants'rooms, crafts, traditional costumes, religious traditions and ceramics. Daily except Mon 9.30 a.m.- 5 p.m. Tel. 21681.

Bayerische Staatssammlung für allgemeine und angewandte Geologie
(Bavarian State Collection of General and Applied Geology)
Luisenstr. 37
The earth's crust and mineral resourses.

Mon-Fri 8 a.m.-6 p.m. Tel. 52031.

BMW-Museum
Petuelring 130
Collection of cars, motor bikes, motors and engines in a setting designed by artists. Films, videos and slide shows in one of Munich's best cinemas. Also featuring are exhibitions of contemporary art.
Daily 9 a.m.- 5 p.m. Tel. 38953306.

Deutsches Jagd- und Fischereimuseum
(German Museum of Hunting and Fishing)
Neuhauser Str. 53
Hunting trophies, weapons and implements, paintings, graphics and tapestries; state hunting sleighs in Baroque, Rococo and Empire styles. Fishing tackle from the Stone Age to the present day. Special tactile section for the blind and children. Permanent changing exhibition. Daily 9.30 a.m.-4 p.m. Mon also from 7-10 p.m. Tel. 220522.

Deutsches Museum
Museumsinsel 1
By the Ludwigsbrücke, is the most important museum of the historical development of the natural sciences technology and industry. If you walk the 16 km concourse, you will see approximately 1,700 objects on display. Most interesting are the "hands on" exhibits which you can work yourself, and the Zeiss-Planetarium. Permanent special exhibitions, events and conferences. Daily 9 a.m.-5 p.m. Tel. 21791.

Deutsches Theatermuseum
Galeriestr. 4a
Collection, archives and library on the world history of the theatre. Special exhibitions. daily except Mon 10 a.m.-4p.m. Library Tues and Thurs 10 a.m.-12 p.m. and 1.30 p.m.-4.30 p.m. Tel. 222449.

Feuerwehrmuseum
Hauptfeuerwache Blumensraße 34
The profession of the fireman from 1899 until the present. Sat 9 a.m.-4 p.m.

Glyptothek
Königsplatz 3
Collection of Greek and Roman sculpture. Tues, Wed, Fri, Sun 10 a.m-4.30 p.m.,Thurs 12.30 p.m.-9.30 p.m. Tel. 286100.

Haus der Kunst
Prinzregentenstr. 1
This National Socialist building house the "Staatsgalerie moderner Kunst" (State Gallery of Modern Art) (see below) in the West Wing. In the centre and East Wing, the main Munich Art Exhibition is held in the sum-

ALTE PINAKOTHEK

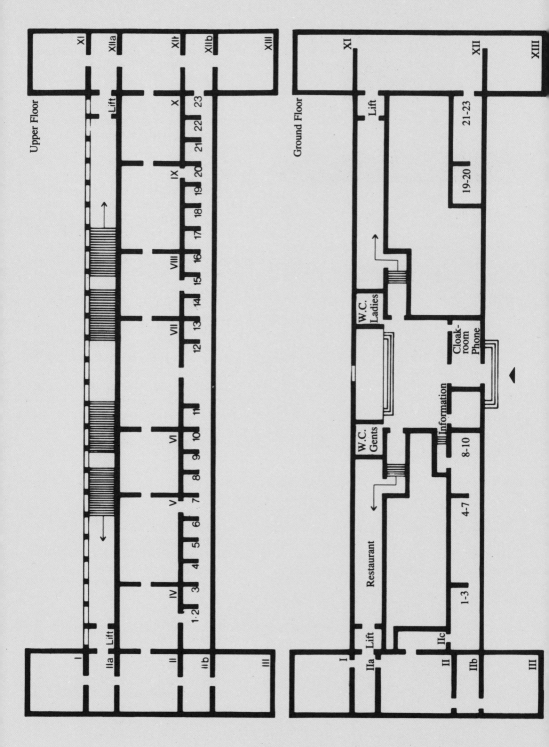

Upper Floor

XI
XIIa
XIIr
XIIb
XIII

Lift
X
23
22
21
IX
20
19
18
17
VIII
16
15
VII
14
13
12
VI
11
10
9
V
8
7
6
5
IV
4
3
1-2

I
IIa
Lift
II
IIb
III

Ground Floor

XI
XII
XIII

Lift
21-23
19-20

W.C. Ladies
Cloak-room
Phone
W.C. Gents
Information
8-10
4-7
Restaurant
1-3

I
IIa Lift
IIc
II
IIb
III

mer, and in autumn, the German Art and Antiques Fair. Daily except Mon 9 a.m.-1.30 p.m. Also Thur 7- 9 p.m. Tel. 222651.

Historisches Nähmaschinen- und Bügeleisenmuseum
(Historical Sewing Machine and Ironworks Museum)
Heimeranstr. 68-70
Collection of sewing machines of Oskar Strobel. Mon-Fri 10 a.m.-4 p.m. Tel. 510880.

Künstlerwerkstätten
Lothringerstr. 13
Permanent collection of contemporary and experimental art.
Daily 2-6 p.m. Tel. 4486961.

Kunsthalle der Hypo-Kulturstiftung
Theatinerstr. 5
Successful exhibition activities, which should not be missed when on a visit to Munich. Mon-Sun 10 a.m.-6 p.m.
Tel. 224412.

Kunstverein München e.V.
Galeriestr. 4
Workshop (Tues-Fri 10 a.m.- 4 p.m.) with original contemporary art. Special exhibitions. Tues-Sun 10 a.m.-6 p.m. Tel. 221152.

Kunstraum München e.V.
Nikolaistr. 15
Non-profitmaking institution for the presentation and documentation of contemporary works of art in special exhibitions. Tues-Fri 2-6 p.m., Sat 11 a.m.-1 p.m. Tel. 348920.

Mineralogische Staatssammlung
Theresienstr. 41
Exhibition on the formation and properties of minerals and crystals. Tue-Fri 1-5 p.m., Sat, Sun 1-6 p.m. Tel. 23941.

Münchner Puppenmuseum
(Munich Museum of Dolls)
Gondershauser Str. 37
Collection from 6.30-7.30 p. m. Mon, Thurs 11 a.m.-5 p.m., Sun 10 a.m.-1 p.m. Tel. 328950.

Münchner Stadtmuseum
St.-Jakobs-Platz 1
Exhibition of historical Munich. Brewery museum, morisk dancers, model of the city in 1570 and hall of weapons. Museums of puppets, film, photography, musical instruments and Munich home decor. Changing special exhibitions. Programme information Tel. 233-5586.

Erstes Nachttopf-Museum der Welt
(First Chamber Pot Museum in the World)

Böcklinstr. 30
600 exhibits from a period of 2,000 years. Sun 10 a.m.-1 p.m. Thurs 2-6 p.m., Tel. 1575989.

Neue Pinakothek
Bayerische Staatsgemäldesammlungen
Barer Str. 29
Permanent exhibition of European painting and sculpture of the 19th Century. Daily except Mon 9 a.m.-4.30 pm., evening opens on Tues 7-9 p.m. Tel. 23805-19.

Die Neue Sammlung
State Museum of Applied Art. Prinzregentenstr. 3
Collection of designed utensils from the 18th Century to the present. Changing exhibitions on the environment in the 20th Century. Daily except Mon 10 a.m.-5 p.m. Tel. 227844.

Paläontologisches Museum
Bavarian State collection of Palaeontology and Historical geology. Richard-Wagner-Str. 18
Animal and plant fossils from prehistorical times. Slide show with synchronised commentary. (every 1st Sun in the month, 11 and 2 p.m.). Mon-Thurs 9 a.m.-4 p.m. Fri 8 a.m.-7 p.m. Tel. 5203-361.

Präistorische Staatssammlung
Lerchenfeldstr. 2
Early history of Bavaria, Roman Empire Times, Early Middle Ages through archaeological finds in art, craft, trade and customs. Daily except Mon 9 a.m.-4 p.m., Thurs 9 a.m.-8 p.m. Tel. 293911.

Residenzmuseum
Max-Joseph-Platz 3
The former seat of the Wittelsbachs, built over six building periods from 1560. May be visited during a morning and an afternoon tour. There are Renaissance, Rococo and Classical rooms to be seen, and the treasury with jewels and precious gems from 10 centuries. There is the Antiquarium, Ancestral Gallery, miniatures and porcelain cabinets. Tues-Sat 10 a.m.-4.30 p.m., Sun and Public Holidays 10 a.m.-1 p.m. Tel. 224641.

Schackgalerie
Prinzregentenstr. 9
Collection of the Counts Schack, comprising paintings from the 19th Century, including works by Böcklin, Lenbach, Feuerbach, Schwind and Spitzweg. Daily except Tues 9 a.m.-4.30 p.m. Tel. 23805224.

Siemens-Museum

Prannerstr. 10

Study rooms tracing the historical development of electrotechnology from the beginning to the present day. Mon-Fri 9 a.m.-4 p.m. Sat, Sun 10 a.m.-2 p.m. Tel. 2342660.

Silbersalon
Sendlinger Str. 75/I (Entrance Hackenstr.)
Permanent exhibition of the Stadtmuseum (City Museum): "Historical rooms in the old Hacker house". Sat 1-4.30 p.m. Sun 10 a.m.-6 p.m.

Skulpturenmesse für Blinde (Sculpture Fair for the Blind)
In the school at Wintrichring 84
Casts of Greek and late antique sculptures, all may be touched. Tel. 1781081.

Spielzeugmuseum im Alten Rathausturm (Museum of Toys in the Old Town Hall Tower)
Marienplatz
Collection of Ivan Steiger. Mon-Sat 10 a.m.-5.30 p.m. Tel. 294001.

Staatliche Antikensammlungen
Königsplatz 1
Collection of Greek vases, Greek, Etruscan and Roman small sculpture, as well as gold jewellery and glass. Tues and Thurs-Sun 10 a.m.- 4.30 p.m., Wed 12 a.m.-8.30 p.m. Tel. 598359.

Staatliche Graphische Sammlung
Studiensaal, Meiserstr. 10
Printing graphics and freehand drawings of Late Gothic times to the present. Mon-Fri 10 a.m.-1 p.m. and 2-4.30 p.m. Tel. 5591490.

Staatsgalerie Moderner Kunst
Bavarian State Gallery of Modern Art
Prinzregentenstr. 1
Collection of international painting and sculpture of the 20th Century, including works by Klee, Beckmann, Nolde, Kirchner, Picasso. Changing exhibition of modern artists. Daily except Mon 9 a.m.-4.30 p.m., Thurs also up to 7-9 p.m. Tel. 292710.

Staatliche Münzsammlung
Residenz-Eingang, Residenzstr. 1
Coins, medals and money through a period of several thousand years. Daily except Mon 10 a.m.-5 p.m. Tel. 227221.

Staatliches Museum für Völkerkunde
Maximilianstr. 42
Special as well as permanent exhibitions on non-European art and cultural artefacts. Tues-Sun 9.30 a.m.-4.30 p.m. Tel. 2285506.

Staatliche Sammlung Ägyptischer Kunst
Residenz, Eingang Hofgartenstr. 1

Relics of Egyptian culture from early history through the classical period to the Hellenic influence as well as early Christian art from the Nile Valley and Nubian, Meroitic and Assyrian art. Daily except Mon 9.30 a.m.-4 p.m. evening opening Tues 7-9 p.m. Tel. 298546.

Städtische Galerie im Lenbachhaus
Luisenstr. 33
Collection of works of the Munich school of the 19th and early 20th Century, including works by Kandinsky, Klee, Macke, Marc, Münter and Jawlensky, but also works of important contemporary artists (such as Joseph Beuys). Daily except Mon 10 a.m.-6 p.m. Tel. 521041.

Üblacker-Häusl
Preysingstr. 58
Museum of inns, affiliated to of the Münchner Stadtmuseum. Tues, Thurs, Sun, 10 a.m.-12 p.m. Wed, Fri 5-7 p.m.

Valentin-Musäum
A museum in honour of Karl Valentin and Liesl Karlstadt, which should not be missed by lovers of comedy.
Mon, Tues, Sun 11.01 a.m.-5.29 p.m., Entry Adult:199, Child: 99 Pfennigs, Tel. 223266.

Villa Stuck
Prinzregentenstr. 60
Jugendstil-Villa (Villa in the Jugend style) of the Prince of Art Franz von Stuck, to be viewed with changing exhibitions of art of the classical, modern and present periods. Daily except Mon 10 a.m.-5 p.m. Tel. 4707086.

Zählermuseum Stadtwerk
Elektrizitätswerke, Franzstr. 9
The development of the electricity meter. Wed 9 a.m.-4 pm.

OUTSIDE MUNICH

Burgmuseum Grünwald
Zeillerstr. 3
Branch of the State Prehistorical Collection. Collection of Roman grave and holy stones, reconstruction of a Roman kitchen, history of the castle ascent of the tower and panorama of the Alps. Wed-Sun 10 a.m.-4.30 p.m. Tel. 6413218.

Diözesanmuseum Freising
Domberg 21
Christian art from Bavaria, Salzburg and Tyrol, changing exhibitions. Tues-Sun 10 a.m.-5 p.m. Tel. 08161-2432.

Das Evangelium in den Wohnungen der Völker
Old palace of Schloß Schleißheim
Religious folk art from all over the world.
Daily except Mon 10 a.m.-5 p.m. Tel. 3155272.

KZ-Gedenkstätte Dachau mit Museum
(Dachau Memorial and Museum)
Alte Römerstr. 75
Documentation in five languages of the early history of The Third Reich, the history of the founding of the camp, the living conditions of the prisoners and the SS organisation in Dachau. A walk through the camp with its barracks, roll call square, bunker and crematorium brings home the atrocity of the "Final Solution: " for the Jews envisaged by the Nazis.
Tues-Sun 9 a.m.-5 pm. Tel. 08131/174142.

Meißner Porzellan-Sammlung
Schloß Lustheim, Park of Schloß Schleißheim Daily except Mon 10 a.m.-12.30 p.m. and 1.30-4 p.m. Tel. 3150212.

ART GALLERIES

ASB Gallery
Maximilianstr. 38-40, Tel. 227425
Munich branch of the London parent gallery of art and design.

Galerie von Abercron
Maximilianstr. 22, Tel. 226420
Classical Modern, New Realism.

Galerie Maeder
Maximilianstr. 36, Tel. 299153

Internationale Moderne Galerie Ruf
Maximilianstr. 40 and Oberanger 35, Tel. 227673, 265272
Pictures and sculptures by classical modern artists and contemporary artists.

Architekturgalerie
St.-Anna-Platz 1 a, Tel. 220088
Exhibitions relating to architecture such as proposed city planning projects and stage design.

Produzentengalerie
Adelgundenstr. 6, Tel. 174659
Autonomous gallery, "artist to artist".

Galerie Bernd Kluser
Georgenstr. 15, Tel. 332179
Trendsetting with international avant-garde artists (Joseph Beuys, Andy Warhol etc.).

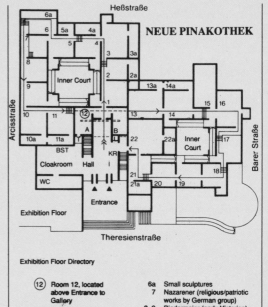

NEUE PINAKOTHEK

Heßstraße

Theresienstraße

Exhibition Floor Directory

⑫	Room 12, located above Entrance to Gallery	6a	Small sculptures
—»—	Path for wheelchair users	7	Nazarener (religious/patriotic works by German group)
L	Lift	8, 9	Biedermeier (early Victorian)
T	Telephone	10, 10a	French collection of late Romantic-Realist period
I	Information/Ticketing Office	11, 11a	German collection of late Romantic-Realist period
BST	Bookstand	12	Projects by Kaulbach
A, B	Alternating Exhibitions of Graphic Arts	13, 13a	Historical and Social paintings
KR	Karl Rottmann	14, 14a	Paintings from the Foundation Period
1, 2, 2a	International art from the 1800s	15	Hans von Marrés
3, 3a	Early Romanticism	16	Böcklin, Feuerbach, Thoma
4, 4a	Court art during the reign of King Ludwig I of Bavaria	17	Leibl and his circle
5, 5a	German Classicists of Rome	18	French Impressionists
6	Georg Schäfer Collection	19	Cézanne, Gaugin, van Gogh
		20	Social Realism
		21	Gérman Impressionists
		21a	Secessionists
		22, 22a	Symbolism and Art Nouveau

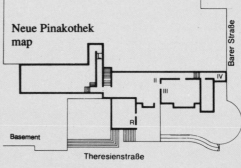

Neue Pinakothek map

Theresienstraße

I   Alternating Exhibitions
II, III   Pedagogical Centre of the Museum
IV   Video Room
R   Restaurant, Café

Galerie Alvensleben
Arcisstr. 58, Tel. 2715656
Principally artists from the 20th century, and photographic exhibitions.
Galerie Neuhausen (Artists' Cellar)
Elvirastr. 17 a, Tel. 1297803
Exhibitions of unknown young artists.
Edition Schellmann
Maximilianstr. 12, Tel. 2222895
International Avant-garde.
Galerie Klewan
Maximilianstr. 29, Tel. 295029
Austrian avant-garde artists of the 1960's, New Realism.
Galerie Michael Hasenclever
Baaderstr. 56 c, Tel. 2015900
Painting, graphics and drawings of the 20th Century, and contemporary art.
Galerie Karl & Faber
Amiraplatz 3, Tel. 221865

Paintings, drawings and graphics of the classical modern.
Galerie Pabst
Stollbergstr. 11, Tel. 292939
20th Century Vienna Jugendstil and Austrian classical modern art.

CLASSICAL CONCERTS

Munich Philharmonic
Kellerstr. 4/III, 8000 Munich 80
Tel. 4184-500/501
Concert Season: Mid Sept. - End July
Advance booking is available from the Kulturzentrum in Gasteig.
Herkulessaal in der Residenz
Kongressaal in the Deutsches Museum

RESIDENZ

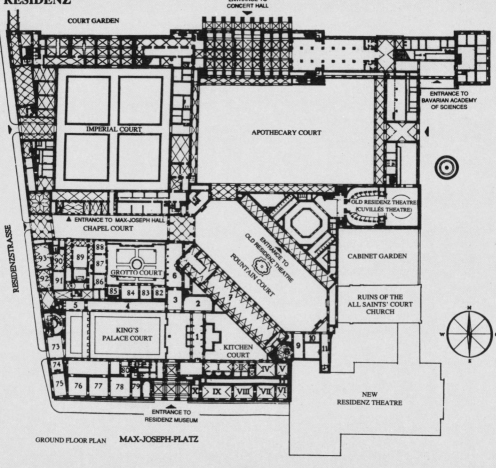

GROUND FLOOR PLAN   **MAX-JOSEPH-PLATZ**

Rundfunkhaus.

In the summer there are concerts in Schloß Schleißheim, in Schloß Nymphenburg and in the church of Schloßkirche Blutenburg. The events are published in the Offizielles Monatsprogramm of the Fremdenverkehrsamtes München (The monthly programme issued by the Tourist Information Bureau).

THEATRES

Munich is a wonderful place for theatre fans. There are more than 50 theatres, cabarets and revues in a spectrum which includes everything from opera to farce. Then there are the annual international cultural events such as the Opera Festival, the Musical Theatre Days and Cabaret Performances as well as experimental theatre, all of which draw audiences to the Bavarian capital. People who live in Munich don't want to miss the action either, so it is advisable to book early for any special performance.

The **"Offizielle Monatsprogramm des Fremdenverkehrsamtes München"** (**Official Monthly Programme of the Tourist Information Bureau of Munich**), which is available for DM 1.30 at any newspaper kiosk or bookstore, gives details of forthcoming events.

ADVANCE BOOKING

For concerts, theater and performances in the Olympiapark:
Abendzeitung-Schalterhalle
Sendlinger Str. 79, 8000 Munich 2,
Tel. 267024.
abr-Theaterkasse
Neuhauser Str. 9, 8000 Munich 2,
Tel. 1204-4.
Bauer Otto
Landschaftstr. im Rathaus, 8000 Munich 2,
Tel. 221757.
Buchhandlung Lehmkuhl
For concerts booking only:
Leopoldstr. 45, 8000 Munich 40,
Tel. 398045.
Hallo Reisebüro im PEP
Thomas-Dehler-Str. 12, 8000 Munich 83,
Tel. 6371044.

Hieber Max
Theater and Konzertkarten, Liebfrauenstr. 1 am Dom, 8000 Munich 2, Tel. 226571.
Inter Trafic
Leopoldstr. 104, 8000 Munich 40, Tel. 338622, 4482640.
Deutsches Theater (German Theare)
Concerts, sport. Radio-RIM. Theater and Concert Booking Office, Theatinerstr. 17,8000 Munich 2, Tel. 551702-53.
Residenz-Bücherstube
Residenzstr. 1, 8000 Munich 2; only for concert tickets, Tel. 220868.
Studiosus-Reisen
For only **student tickets**, these are available at Amalienstr. 73, 8000 Munich 40, Tel. 280768; Theater and Concert Booking Office from 10 a.m.- to 2 p.m.
Olympiapark
This is the permanent advance booking for events in the Olympiahalle and for football matches and the Eissportstadion (Ice Rink) in the Olympiapark, Mon-Thurs 8 a.m-5 p.m . Fri 8 a.m.- 2 pm. Closed on Sat, Sun as well as Public Holidays, Tel. 30613-577.

Other booking offices are:
Kartenverkauf der Bayer. Staatstheater
Staatsoper, Maximilianstr. 11,8000 Munich 22, Tel. 221316.
Staatsschauspiel
Max-Joseph-Platz 1, 8000 Munich 22, Tel. 2185/413 and 225754.
Staatstheater am Gärtnerplatz,
8000 Munich 5, Tel. 2016767.
Kartenverkauf der Kammerspiele (Little Theatre)
Maximilianstr. 26, 8000 Munich 22, Tel. 23721328.

The ticket office for **Herkulessaal** in the Residenz , the evening box office one hour before the performance, is at Herkulessaal, Tel. 224641. Kartenverkauf Kongreßsaal, Tel. 221790. Kartenverkauf Gasteig Rosenheimer Str. 5 (Glashalle), 8000 Munich 80, Tel. 4181-614, Mon-Fri 10.30 a.m.-2 p.m. and 3-6 p.m., Sat 10.30 a.m.- 2 p.m.

The programme of individual theatres is published in the daily press, and in the official monthly publication of the Fremdenverkehrsamt München.

MAIN THEATRES

Nationaltheater
(Bavarian State Opera)
Max-Joseph-Platz, 8000 Munich 22
Advance Booking: Maximilianstr. 11, Tel. 221316.
For Opera Fans; get up early to buy tickets (closed for renovation until 8 April 1989).

Staatstheater Am Gärtnerplatz
Gärtnerplatz 3, 8000 Munich 5, Tel. 2016767. Operettas and Ballet, Musicals and Comic Opera - lighter entertainment.

Prinzregenten-Theater
Prinzregentenplatz 12, 8000 Munich 80
Advance Booking: Maximilianstr. 13 ,Tel. 225754
"Classics" from Shakespeare to Peter Weiss.

Theater Im Marstall
Marstallplatz, 8000 Munich 22
Advance Booking: Maximilianstr. 11, Tel. 221316
Experimental theatre in erstwhile stables of the Residenz.

Münchner Kammerspiele - Schauspielhaus
(Munich Little Theatre)
Maximilianstr. 26, 8000 Munich 22, Advance Booking: Tel. 23721328
Tickets: Tel. 23721326
One of the best German theatres, with well-known directors (Dieter Dorn, George Tabori, Herbert Achternbusch).

Münchner Kammerspiele - Werkraum
(Little Theatre Workshop)
Hildegardstr. 1, 8000 Munich 22
Advance booking, see Kammerspiele, Schau-spielhaus Tel. 23721328
Experimental theatre of the Kammerspiele.

Deutsches Theater
Schwanthaler Str. 13, 8000 Munich 2, Tel. 593427
According to Loriot the most beautiful house in Schwanthaler Straße; for very light entertainment, mainly shows, revues and operettas.

Münchner Volkstheater
Am Stiglmaierplatz (Eingang Brienner Str. 50), 8000 Munich 2,Tel. 5234655
Folk theatre with class (here Achternbusch is performed).

Altes Residenztheater (Cuvilliéstheater)
Residenz, Residenzstr. 1, 8000 Munich 22, Tel. 221316

A pearl of the Rococo theatres, built by F. Cuvilliés the Elder and was rebuilt after World War II.

Residenztheater
Max-Joseph-Platz, 8000 Munich 22, Tel. 2185413
One of the greatest drama theatres in the Bavarian art scene.

Theater der Jugend
in Schauburg, Franz-Joseph-Str. 47, 8000 Munich 40,Tel. 23721365
One of the first (and best) German children's and young people's theatres.

COMEDY AND FOLK THEATRES

Theater "Kleine Freiheit"
Maximilianstr. 31 (Maximilianpassage) 8000 Munich 22, Tel. 221123

Blutenburg-Theater
Munich's "Who done it" Theatre
Blutenburgstr. 35, 8000 Munich 19
Tel. 1233071, 1234300

Kleine Komödie im Bayerischen Hof
Passage Promenadeplatz and Prannerstraße, 8000 Munich 2, Tel. 292810

Kleine Komödie am Max-II-Denkmal
Maximilianstr. 47, 8000 Munich 22. Tel. 221859

Münchner Ludwig-Thoma-Theater
Ledererstr. 10 - Atelier - 8000 Munich 22, Tel. 292239, 2285286

Spieldose
Lenbachplatz 8/II, im Künstlerhaus, 8000 Munich 2
Free entry.

Münchner Volkssängerbühne
Gaststätte Max-Emanuel-Brauerei
Adalbertstr. 33, 8000 Munich 40, Tel. 396743

Millionendorf-Theater
Zielstattstr. 6, Tel. 706880

Volkstheater in der Au
Im Kolpinghaus Entenbachstr. 37, 8000 Munich 90. Tel. 7606468

THEATRE PUBS

These operate on a small budget and a lot of imagination in courtyards and cellars.

Teamtheater
Am Einlaß 4-5, 8000 Munich 5, Tel. 2604333

Theater über dem Landtag

Maria-Theresia-Str. 2 a, 8000 Munich 80
Advance booking from 6 pm. Tel. 479118
Theater rechts der Isar
Wörthstr. 7-9, 8000 Munich 80
Tel. 4483657, 4802111 (from 4 pm.)
Theater 44
Hohenzollernstr. 20, 8000 Munich 40,
Tel. 328748
Theater Scaramouche
Hesseloherstr. 3, 8000 Munich 40
Booking by telephone,
Tel. 334555 from (3 p.m).
Studiotheater München
Ungererstr. 19, 8000 Munich 40
Advance booking, daily from 11 a.m.
Tel. 343827 or 347215
Studiotheater im "PEP"
Thomas-Dehler-Str. 12 in the "PEP"
(Neuperlach), 8000 Munich 83
Tel. 6706080
Modernes Theater
Hans-Sachs-Str. 12, 8000 Munich 5
Tel. 266821, 225473
Booking, daily (except Mon) 4-6.30 p.m.
Theater k
Theater in der Kurfürstenstraße
Kurfürstenstr. 8, 8000 Munich 40,
Tel. 333933
Advance booking from 5 p.m. onwards.
Bel Étage
Theatre in a Drugstore, Munich's Show-
Revuetheatre
Feilitschstr. 12, 8000 Munich 40,
Tel. 339013
TamS
Theater am Sozialamt (Theatre at the Social
Security Office)
Haimhauserstr. 13 a, 8000 Munich 40,
Tel. 345890
Advance booking by telephone Tues and
Sun from 4 p.m.
Theater in der Westermühle
Westermühlstr. 28, 8000 Munich 5,
Tel. 2013538
Box Office from 5 p.m.
pathos-transport 80er Jahre Theater
Dachauer Str. 110 d, 8000 Munich 19,
Tel. 184243 from 5 p.m.
Theater in den alten Ritterwerken
München-Pasing, August-Exter-Str. 1
Advance booking, 1 hour before the per-
formance, Tel. 8341841.
Forum 2 im Olympiadorf
Nadistr. 3, 8000 Munich 40
Tel. 3513780

Tickets at evening Box Office
Off-Off-Theater
Potsdamer Str. 13, Tel. 393729
Theaterhalle
Dachauer Str. 128, 8000 Munich 19, Tel.
1571986
Theater im Westend
Guldeinstr. 47, Tel. 507970

CHILDREN THEATRES

Münchner Theater für Kinder
Dachauer Str. 46, 8000 Munich 2, Tel.
595454, 593858
Münchner Marionettentheater(Puppet
Theatre)
Blumenstr. 29 a, 8000 Munich 2, Tel.
265712
Zaubergarten
Puppet theatre
Nikolaistr. 17, 8000 Munich 40, Tel. 348298

CABARETS

Münchner Lach- und Schießgesellschaft
Haimhauser/Ecke Ursulastraße
8000 Munich 40, Tel. 391997
Booking daily from 2 p.m.
Das Münchner Rationaltheater
Political Cabaret
Hesseloher Str. 18, 8000 Munich 40
Tel. 335040, 334050
Advance booking at booking offices, eve-
ning box office from 5.30 p.m.
Theater Im Fraunhofer
Fraunhoferstr. 9/Rgb., 8000 Munich 5
Tel. 267850 (5-7 pm.)
Hinterhof-Theater
Wirtshaus am Hart, Sudentendeutsche Str.
40, 8000 Munich 45, Tel. 3116039
Kunstkeller Neuhausen
Elvirastr. 17 a, 8000 Munich 19, Tel. 182694
Novak's Schwabinger Brettl
(over 20 years of age)
Occamstr. 11, 8000 Munich 40, Tel. 347289
Drehleier
Balanstr. 23, 8000 Munich 80, Tel. 484337
Schwabinger Kleinkunstbühne
in Theater "Heppel & Ettlich", Kaiserstr. 67,
8000 Munich 40, Tel. 349359
Theaterfabrik Unterführung
Föhringer Allee, Tel. 9504949/9505666

CINEMAS

The schedule of films in Munich's cinemas is published daily in the Süddeutsche Zeitung newspaper. The following are a list of the more popular ones:

ABC
Herzogstr. 1a, Tel. 332300
Premières of high brow, art and entertainment films, mainly in the original versions.

ARRI
Türkenstr. 91, Tel. 393333

AKI
Most modern and comfortable cinema in town. Unfortunately the programme is not of the same quality.
Am Hauptbahnhof, Tel. 592511

Atlantik-Palast
Schwanthalerstr. 2-6, Tel. 555670
Only foreign language cinema in Munich. "Europa im Atlantik"

Autokino Aschheim
Münchner Str., Aschheim, Tel. 907008
Only drive-in cinema in Munich.

Cadillac + Veranda
Rosenkavalierplatz 12, Tel. 912000 or 919999

Cinema
Nymphenburger Str. 31, Tel. 555255
Regular double features, sometimes in the original version.

City Kino Center
Sonnenstr. 12, Tel. 591983

Eldorado
Sonnenstr. 7, Tel. 557174

Elisenhof Kinocenter
Prielmayerstr. 3, Tel. 557540

Fantasia
Schwanthalerstr. 3, Tel. 555754
Premières of high-brow films.

Filmcasino
Odeonsplatz 8, Tel. 220818

Filmmuseum
St. Jakobsplatz 1, Tel. 233-2348
Various series on the history of film. Excellent projects in conjunction with other cultural institutions.

Forum 2
Nadistr. 3, Tel. 983778, 3518137
Fridays and Saturdays, children's cinema, Thursdays: "The Special Film".

Gloria Palast
Karlsplatz 5, Tel. 593721

Munich's largest cinema with over 600 seats. Premières of entertainment films.

Haidhauser Museum
Kirchenstr. 24, Tel. 4485292

Isabella
Neureutherstr. 29, Tel. 2718844
Premières of art and author's films.

Kiko Schwabing
Kaiserstr. 67, Tel. 349359
Schwabing's children's cinema at Heppel & Ettlich.

Leopold 1 + 2
Leopoldstr. 80, Tel. 331050

Lupe 2
Ungererstr. 19, Tel. 347651
An excellent cinema programme with art author's films, new as well as classics.

Marmorhaus
Leopoldstr. 35, Tel. 344046

Mathäser-Filmpalast
Bayerstr. 5, Tel. 595361, 595362

Maxim
Landshuter Allee 33, Tel. 168721

Museum Lichtspiele
Lilienstr. 2, Tel. 482403

Neues Arena
Hans-Sachs-Str. 7, Tel. 2603265
Premières of art and genre films. Regular double features in the original version.

Neues Atelier
Sonnenstr. 12, Tel. 591918

Neues Rottmann
Rottmannstr. 15, Tel. 521683
Premières of high-brow authors' films as well as entertainment films.

Odysee
Schwanthalerstr. 3, Tel. 555754

Neues Rex
Agricolastr. 16, Tel. 562500

Rio Palast
Rosenheimer Str. 15, Tel. 486979

Royal-Filmpalast
Goetheplatz 2, Tel. 533956/7

Sendlinger Kulturschmiede
Daiserstr. 22, Tel. 761435

Sonnen-Filmtheater
Sonnenstr. 9, Tel. 595670

Stachus-Kino-Center
Sonnenstr. 6, Tel. 594275

Studio Solln
Sollner Str. 43, Tel. 796521
Good films featured here followed by some discussions with directors and actors.

Theatiner

Theatinerstr. 32, Tel. 223183
Tivoli
Neuhauserstr. 3, Tel. 264326
Türkendolch
Türkenstr. 74, Tel. 2718844
Classic "Off Cinema".
Werkstattkino
Fraunhoferstr. 9, Tel. 2607250
Small courtyard cinema showing political
and genre films.

NIGHTLIFE

PUBS

Bunter Vogel
Herzogstr. 44, M 40
7 p.m.-1 a.m. For romantic evenings by
candle light.
Flieger
Balanstr. 16, M 80
12 p.m.-1 a.m. It has a cool ambience.
Frundsberg
Frundsbergstr. 46, M 19
Mixed clientele in carousel decor.
Grünes Eck
St.-Martin-Str. 7, M 90
6 p.m.-1 a.m. Alternative, cheap snacks, live
music on Saturday.
Mutti Bräu
Ursula-Str. 10, M 40
3 p.m.-1 a.m. Good atomosphere, and so,
always full.
Mutti Bräu
Thierschstr. 14, M 22
7 p.m.-1 a.m. Meeting place for gays.
Notabene
Klugstr. 158, M 19
Student pub, large ice cream servings.
Stragula
Bergmannstr. 66, M 2
6 p.m.-1 a.m. A real pub.
Studiotheater Café
Ungererstr. 19, M 40
8 p.m.-1 a.m. Relaxed meeting place for
theatre people.
Vollmond (Full Moon)
Schleißheimerstr. 82, M 40
7 p.m.- 1 a.m. When the moon is full, you
may get a free gift.
Wirtshaus im Schlachthof
Zenettistr. 9, M 2
6 p.m.-1 a.m. Sat and Sun 10 p.m.-1 a.m.
Still a haunt of locals. In the mornings the

butchers meet here, in the evenings it's just a place for those with time on their hands. Simple Bavarian food.

JAZZ PUBS

Allotria
Türkenstr. 33, M 40
Traditional Bavarian beer pub with jazz music. Open for early drinks on Sundays.
Kaffee Giesing
Bergstr. 5, M 90
Proprietor: Konstantin Wecker.
La Cumbia
Taubenstr. 2, M 90
For Latin American fans.
Liederbühne Robinson
Dreimühlenstr. 33, M 5
Unabashedly arty. Entrance free.
La Peseta Loca
Oberländerstr. 3 b, M 70
Another one for Latin American fans.
Schwabinger Brettl
Occamstr. 11, M 40
Old Schwabing, with cabaret.
Schwabinger Podium
Wagnerstr. 1, M 40
Dixie jazz played after 9 p.m.
Max Emanuel
Adalbertstr. 33, M 40
For Salsa fans, interesting on Wednesdays and Fridays.
Unterfahrt
Kirchenstr. 96, M 80
Good modern jazz and place where lesser known but good musicians play.
Waldwirtschaft
Großhesselohe, Georg-Kalb-Str. 3
Dixie music and beer, outside in summer. Early drinks and beer on Sundays.

STUDENT PUBS

Atzinger
Schellingstr. 9, M 40
The first port of call after lectures.
Baal
Kreitmayrstr. 26, M 2
The interior is lined with books.
Fraunhofer
Fraunhoferstr. 9, M 5
Always full, always something going on.
Schelling Salon
Schellingstr. 54, M 40
For players (chess, billiards etc.), tramps and students.
Zum Kloster
Preysingstr. 77, M 80
A pub that is a hide-out for sociologists.

BARS

Bodega Bar
Hans-Sachs-Str. 9, M 5
7 p.m.-3 a.m., Beer joint for a real binge.
Gratzer's Lobby
Beethovenplatz 2, M 2
5 p.m.-1 a.m. closed Sat and Sun. Most exclusive, with exclusive prices to match.
Harry's New York Bar
Falkenturmstr. 9, M 2
4 p.m.-3 a.m. closed Sun. Serious and distinguished, with piano music.
Iwan
Josephspitalstr. 18, M 2
11 p.m.-3 a.m. For stylish, liberal city slickers, who have no financial worries.
Nachtcafé
Maximiliansplatz 5, M 2
7 p.m.- 5 a.m. Really only after midnight. Unobtrusive live jazz music, mixed clientele, so quite cosmopolitan.
Schumann's
Maximilianstr. 36, M 2
5 p.m.-3 a.m. Elite and exclusive reputation, more for VIP's than vamps.
Wunderbar
Hackenstr. 3, M 2
6 p.m.- 3 a.m. A bar for everyone.

DISCOS

Aquarius
Leopoldstr. 194, M 40
9 p.m.-4 a.m. Distinguished, with aquarium.
Blue Box
Trautenwolfstr. 6, M 40
10 p.m.-1 a.m. For 60's and 70's fans.
Cadillac
Theklastr. 1, M 2
9 p.m.-4 a.m. For the stylish.
Charly M
Maximiliansplatz 5, M 2
10 p.m.-4 a.m. A luxurious disco with posh-

looking interiors.

Crash
Lindwurmstr. 88, M 2
8 p.m.1 a.m. For hard rock fans.

Far Out
Am Kosttor 2, M 2
9 p.m.- 4 a.m. The" lightest" disco in town

New York
Sonnenstr. 25, M 2
11 p.m.- 4 a.m. For gays and heteros, known for its good music.

Park Café
Sophienstr. 7, M 2
10 p.m.- 3 a.m. Munich's No. 1 night spot.

P 1
Prinzregentenstr. 1, M 2
10 p.m.-4 a.m. In the firm hand of the delicatessen heir Michael Käfe. Reasonable prices.

Philoma Bar
Stiglmaierplatz, M 2
2 p.m.-2 a.m., with longer hours on Fri and Sat . Not only legendary, but really good.

LATE NIGHT RESTAURANTS

Adams City
Pacellistr. 2, M 2
8 p.m.-6 a.m. Sat from 10 a.m. Sun from 3 p.m. Beer cellar for those who still aren't tired at 3 a.m.

La Piazetta
Oskar-von-Miller-Ring 3, M 2
11-6 a.m. A little on the expensive side, but well frequented because of the long hours.

Mathäser Weißbierkeller
Bayerstr. 1, M 2
3 a.m.-7 a.m., 8 a.m.-12 a.m. Plain Bavarian, but Weißwürste and fresh pretzel at rather reasonable prices.

Mc Donalds
Ingolstädter Str. 58, M 45
6 p.m.-5 a.m. If you fancy a Big Mac in the night.

Schmalznudel
Prälat-Zistl-Str. 8, M 2
5 p.m.-2 a.m.This is where the seasoned night owls meet up with the market people of the Viktualienmarkt.

SHOPPING

SHOPPING AREAS

The main shopping centre in Munich is the **Pedestrian Precinct** at Marienplatz. There are shops next to the one another between the department stores. There are shoe shops, boutiques, jewellers and more, offerring anything you could wish for. If you don't find what you're looking for in Neuhauser- and Kaufingerstraße then you can try Sendlinger Straße in Tal or Rosental. The high spot of the inner city is the popular **Viktualienmarkt.**

For the gourmet, there is Germany's best delicatessen **Dallmayr** in Dienerstr. 15. Game specialities may be purchased in **Zerwirkgewölbe**, Ledererstr.3. Munich could not be without the fashion store **Beck** at Rathauseck, known for its ever changing decor, created by well-known artists.

For the elegant and exclusive, such as furs, antiques and porcelain, the following streets are where to look: Theatinerstraße, Residenzstraße, Brienner Straße and in the **Kunstblock** (Art Block) at Ottostraße 3 near the Lenbachplatz. For art lovers, **Maximilian-straße** is a must, where there are 25 galleries to browse through, and to spend in. For lovers of Bavarian tradition, special gifts can be found in the boutique **Et Cetera** in Wurzerstraße 12, Lederhosen (leather shorts) at **Karl Wagner** in Tal 77. Bavarian aristocracy dresses are from **Loden Frey** in Maffei- straße. Exquisite little gifts, porcelain and fabrics are found in **Radspieler** in Hackenstr. 7.

For those of more modest means, clothes may be found in Hohenzollernstraße. Bargains can also be had in Leopoldstraße. If you are looking for particularly lovely bouquets of flowers, then **Tropica** is the place, in Nordendstraße. Open wines, to please the most discerning palate, may be found in **Nordendquelle** in the same street. In Schelling-, Türken- and Amalienstraße behind the university.

MARKETS

Viktualienmarkt, a popular market in the city as mentioned in the main guide.

Elisabethplatz (Westschwabing): Schwa-bing's smaller version of the Viktualienmarkt (daily except Sun).

Großmarkthalle: Thalkirchner Str. 81; größter europäischer Vegetable and fruit market (daily except Sun 5 a.m.-1 p.m.).

Christkindlmärkte(Christmas Fairs): Annually from beginning of December to Christmas Eve. Here Christmas tree decorations, cribs, candles and Christmas biscuits are on sale. By far the largest Christmas Fair is on Marienplatz, but there are smaller markets at Münchner Freiheit, Weißenburger Platz and on Rotkreuzplatz.

There are also weekly markets selling mainly for fruit, vegetables and flowers at various locations in the city:

Tuesday
Neuperlach, Plettstr. (8-12 p.m.); Haidhausen, Weißenburgerstr. (8-12 p.m.), Johanneskirchen/Oberföhring, Fritz-Meyer-Weg (1-6 p.m.); Berg am Laim, Baumkirchener Str. (1-6 p.m.).

Wednesday
Blumenau, Blumenauer Str. (8-12 p.m.); Sendling, Konrad-Celtis-Str./Jean-Paul-Richter-Str. (8-12 p.m.); Fürstenried-Ost, Berner Str. (1-6 p.m.); Neuaubing-Westkreuz, Mainaustr. (1-6 p.m.)

Thursday
Hasenbergl, Wellenkampstr. (8-12 p.m.); Moosach, Nanga-Parbat-Str. (8 a.m.-6 p.m.)

Friday
Johanneskirchen/Oberföhring, Fritz-Meyer-Weg (8 a.m.-12 p.m.); Berg am Laim, Baumkirchener Str. (8-12 p.m.); Neuperlach, Hanns-Seidel-Platz (1-6 p.m.); Giesing, Perlacher Str. (1-6 p.m.)

Saturday
Fürstenried-West, Graubündener Str. (8 a.m.-1 p.m); Neuaubing-West, Mainaustr. (8 a.m.-1 p.m.); Großhadern, Guardinistr.(8 a.m.-1 p.m.)

FLEA MARKETS

Flea markets are held at irregular intervals. Exact details may be obtained by telephone on Tel. 233-1 .

Venues are: Münchner Freiheit, Olympiapark, Dachauer Str. 128, Aschauer Str. 26, Neubiberger/Ecke Berghamstraße.

SECOND-HAND SHOPS

These shops abound with all kinds of clothes, such as petticoats and leather jackets, especially in Glok-kenbachviertel and in Schwabing.

Glockenbachviertel: There is **Alexa's**, Utzschneiderstr. 10, and **Humana**, Westermühlstr. 8. Also there are the **La Rumo**, Hans-Sachs-Str. 13, **Schicki-Micki**, Pestalozzistr. 3, Der 7. **Himmel**, Hans-Sachs-Str. 17, **Second-Hand Kinderladen**, Kapuzinerstr. 41 and **Kinder-Second-Hand-Shop**, Goldbergstr. 71.

Schwabing: There is **Flip**, Fallmerayerstr. 16, **Freie Selbsthilfe**, Theresienstr. 66; **Randis**, Zentnerstr. 5, the **Second Hand Boutique**, Siegesstr. 20, **Squirrel**, Schellingstr. 54, **Tonxedo**, Georgenstr. 80; **Zsa Zsa**, Görresstr. 13 and Nordendstr. 39, **Cri-Cri** (for kids), Kai-serstr. 57 and **Mausis Kinderladen**, Zentnerstr. 15.

SPORTS

PARTICIPANT

There is a brochure published by the Sportamtes München, which may be purchased at Neuhauserstr. 26 at the Karlstor, which gives details of sports open to anyone. Further details of sporting events in the city may be obtained from: Tel. 2338715.

SWIMMING

Munich has several **outdoor pools** which are opened between May and July, 9 a.m.-9 p.m and between August and September, 9 a.m.-8 p.m. The following is a list of them:

Dantebad
Dantestr. 6, M 2
Tel. 152874,
Take Bus No.8 and 17 to Dantebad, Tram No. 20 to Baldurstraße.

Floriansmühle
Floriansmühlstr. 23, M 45
Tel. 325522, Bus No. 290, 292, 69 from U-Bahn Studentenstadt to Floriansmühle.

Georgenschwaige
Belgradstr. 195, M 40
Tel. 309913, U3/U8 to Scheidplatz.

Maria-Einsiedel
Zentralländstr. 28, M 70
Tel. 7231401, Bus No. 5 goes to Maria Einsiedel.

Michaelibad
Heinrich-Wielandstr. 16, M 83
Tel. 407691, U8, Bus Nos. 59, 92, 93, 94 and 137 will get you there.

Schyrenbad
Claude-Lorraine-Str. 24, M 90
Tel. 653715, Bus No. 5 to Claude-Lorrain-Str., Bus No. 5 to Humboldtstr. and the U8 to Kolumbusplatz.

Ungererbad

Traube-Str. 3, M 40
Tel. 369842, U6 or take bus No. 4 to Dietlindenstraße.

Sommerbad-West
Weinbergerstr. 11, M 60
Tram 19 to Gräfstraße.

Sommerbad
Allach, Eversbuschstr. 213, M 50
Tel. 8125427, Bus Nos. 7 or 70 serves Sommerbad Allach.

Prinzregentenbad
Prinzregentenstr. 80, M 80
Tel. 474808, Tram 18, Bus No. 51, 54, 55.

INDOOR POOLS

Müllersches Volksbad
Rosenheimerstr. 1, M 80
Tel. 2338946. With Roman-Irish steam baths.
Rosenheimer Platz. Tues/Thurs 8 a.m.-7.30 pm., Wed 6.45 a.m.-7.30 p.m., Fri 8 a.m.-8.45 p.m., Sat 8 a.m.-5.30 p.m. and Sun 7.30 a.m.-12.30 p.m.

Nordbad
Schleißheimerstr. 142, M 40
Tel. 180091, Trams 12 and 18 serves Nordbad U8 and Hohenzollernplatz. Wed 10 a.m.-5 p.m. Tues/Thurs 8 a.m.-5 p.m. Fri 8 a.m.-8.45 p.m. Sat 8 a.m.-8 p.m. and Sun 7.30-12 p.m.

Südbad
Valleystr. 37, M 70
Tel. 761569, Take Trams 16 and 26. Wed 10 a.m.-5 p.m., Tues/Thurs 8 a.m.-8.45 p.m., Wed/Fri 8 a.m.-7.30 p.m., Sat 8 a.m.-6 p.m. and Sun 7.30 a.m.-12.30 p.m.

Westbad
Weinbergstr. 11, M 60
Tel. 885441, Serve by Tram 19 to Gräfstr. Tues/Thurs 7 a.m.-8.45 p.m. Wed/Fri 7 a.m.-7.30 p.m., Sat 8 a.m.- 6 p.m. and Sun 7.30 a.m.-12.30 p.m.

Michaelibad
(see outdoor pools) Mon 10 a.m.-5 p.m. Tues/Thurs 7 a.m.-7 p.m. Wed/Fri 8 a.m.-7 p.m. Sat 8 a.m.-5 p.m. and Sun 7.30 a.m.-11.30 a.m.

Giesing/Harlaching
Klausenerstr. 22, M 90
Tel. 6925517. Take Trams 15 and 25 to Kurzstr. Wed 10 a.m.-6 p.m. Tues/Thurs 7 a.m.-8.45 p.m. Wed/Fri 8 a.m.-8 p.m. Sat 8 a.m.-6 p.m. and Sun 7.30 a.m.-6 p.m.

Forstenrieder Park

Stäblistr. 27b, M 71

Tram 16 and 26 go there. Mon 10 a.m.- 6 p.m. Tues/Thurs 7 a.m.-8.45 p.m. Wed/Fri 8 a.m.-8 p.m. Sat 8 a.m.-6 p.m. and Sun 7.30 a.m.-12.30 p.m.

Schwimmhalle Ridlerschule

Geroltstr. 44, M 2

Tel. 5025497, Take Tram 27 and Bus No. 32 that go to Messegelände (Trade Fair Site) West/Bayernhalle. Tues/Wed/Thurs 5.30 p.m.-9.30 p.m. Fri 4 p.m.-7.30 p.m. Sat 1.30-7.30 p.m. and Sun 7.30 a.m.-12.30 p.m..

Olympiaschwimmhalle

Olympiazentrum, M 40, Tel. 30613/390. U3/U6 to Olympiazentrum. Mon 10 a.m.-9.30 p.m. Tues/Thurs 7 a.m.-5 p.m. Wed/Fri/Sat/Sun 7 a.m.-9.30 p.m.

Cosimabad "Schwimmoper"

Cosimastr. 5, M 81, Tel. 911790, Bus No. 89, 189, 51, 151 to Cosimapark. Mon 4-9 p.m., Tues/Thurs 7 a.m.-9 p.m., Wed/Fri 8-21, Sat 8 a.m.-6 p.m., Sun 7.30 a.m.-6pm. This a swimming pool complex with a difference as it has simulated waves and slides to provide swimming and fun for young and old.

BODY BUILDING

There are several finess centres in Munich for one to relax, These are:

California-Gym

Drygalski-Alle 33, M 71, Tel. 7854785.

Sport and Fitness

Augustenstr. 54, M 2, Tel. 525292.

Athletic Fitness Center

LeStudio 3 F

Nymphenburgerstr. 136, M 19,

Tel. 1295748.

Busek Sport Center

Rosenheimerstr. 145a, M 81, Tel. 404046.

Club Vitatop

Berg-am-Laim-Str. 91, M 80, Tel. 433061.

There are also public sports facilities where there is free admission although no coaching instruction is availabe, The following is a selection of such facilities:

Agilolfinger Str. 6, Giesing, Tel. 656699.

Guerickestr. 6, Schwabing Nord, Tel. 3613780.

Feldbergstr. 65, Trudering, Tel. 421744.

Grohmannstr. 54, Hasenbergl-Nord, Tel. 3133033.

Eichmannstr. 11, Untermenzing, Tel.

8122778.

Open: April-October, Mon-Fri 9 a.m.-12 p.m and 4-8 p.m.

There is also a popular fitness park at Spiridon-Louis-Ring, M 40, Tel. 3061010. Mon, Wed, Thurs 2-11p.m., Tues and Fri 6-11 p.m. To get there take the U3/U6 to Olympiazentrum, and then the Olympiapark mini bus.

SQUASH

There are several squash centres with modern facilities for lovers of the sport:

Bavaria Squash

M 2, Bavariastr. 16, Tel. 774181.

Squash-Center Schwabing

Winzererstr. 47b, Tel. 3083516.

Park Club Nymphenburg

M 19, Stievestr. 15, Tel. 1782055.

Tennis- and Squash-Center GmbH

Munich South, M 70, Zielstattstr. 61, Tel. 786970.

Racket Sport-Centrum

M 19, Wilhelm-Hale-Str. 45, Tel. 1688686.

TENNIS

Tennis buffs can enjoy a game of tennis at the following centres:

Tennis Park St. Florian GmbH

M 45, Sondermeierstr. 77, Tel. 3233066.

TSC Tennis-Park and Squash-Center GmbH

M 50, Günzburger Str. 46, Tel. 1492875.

Tennis Allwetter Fideliopark GmbH

M 81, Freischützstr. 42, Tel. 937125.

WHT-Winterhallen-Tennis - GmbH at Wackerplatz

M 79, Demleitnerstr. 4, Tel. 761675.

Tennisplätze Herzogpark,

M 81, Flemingstr. 16, Tel. 980694.

USEFUL ADDRESSES

TOURIST INFORMATION

The **Fremdenverkehrsamt München** (Munich Tourist Information Office), represented in the main railway station and at the airport, has offices in Sendlinger Str. 1 and in the state courtyard of the Rathaus (Town Hall) from Mon-Fri 9 a.m.-5.p.m. here you will not only find help with accommodation, but also information in different languages, brochures and city tours. Dial the collective number 23911 for tourist information, in the German language.

For information on museums and galleries in German dial 2391-62, and for other languages - Tel. 2391-6 English, Tel. 2391-63 French, Tel. 2391-64 Italian, Tel. 2391-65 Spanish. For information on castles and other sightseeing - Tel. 2391-71 German, Tel. 2391-72 English, Tel. 2391-73 French, Tel. 2391-74 Italian, Tel. 2391-75 Spanish.

Other Information Bureaux

ADAC-Informationszentrale, Tel. 505061
Alpine Auskunftsstelle
(Deutscher Alpenverein)
(German Alpine Club)
Praterinsel 5
Tel. 294940
Deutscher Camping-Club e.V.
(German Camping Club)
Mandlstr. 20
Tel. 334021
Fremdenverkehrsverband München-Oberbayern e.V.
Sonnenstr. 10/III
Tel. 597347
Jugend-Informations-Zentrum
Paul-Heyse-Str. 22
Mo -Fr 11-19, So 11-17 Uhr
Tel. 531655

Landesfremdenverkehrsverband
Bayern e.V.
Prinzregentenstr. 18/IV
Tel. 229491-93
Presse- und Informationsamt
Rathaus, Marienplatz, Zimmer 241
Tel. 233/6447
Mon - Thurs 8 a.m.-3.45 p.m. and Fri 8 a.m.-2 p.m.
Stadtinformation Stachus-Ladengeschoß
Tel. 233/824 and 554459
Mon - Fri 8 am.-6 p.m.

EMBASSIES & CONSULATES

The following are the foreign missions found in Munich:
Argentina
Kaufingerstr. 7/IV, M 2
Tel. 263787
Austria
Ismaninger Str. 136, M 80
Tel. 9210900
Bangladesh
Wittelsbacher Platz 1, M 2
Tel. 2350040
Belgium
Franz-Joseph-Str. 15, M 40
Tel. 397096/97
Bolivia
Möhlstr. 17, M 80
Tel. 989704
Brazil
Widenmayerstr. 47, M 22
Tel. 227985
Burkina Faso (Obervolta)
Mozartstr. 18, M 2
Tel. 5309421
Canada
Maximiliansplatz 9, M 2
Tel. 558531
Chile
Mariannenstr. 5, M 22
Tel. 222011
Columbia
Ohmstr. 8, M 40
Tel. 347759
Costa Rica
Neuhauser Str. 16, M 2
Tel. 266646
Cyprus
Kardinal-Faulhaber-Str. 15, M 2

Tel. 227920
Denmark
Maximilianstr. 22/I, M 22
Tel. 220441/42
Dominican Republic
Pacellistr. 7/II, M 2
Tel. 299634
El Salvador
Landsberger Str. 289, M 21
Tel. 569962
Equador
Fraunhoferstr. 2, M 5
Tel. 265658
Finland
Löwengrube 12, M 2
Tel. 221493
France
Möhlstr. 5, M 80
Tel. 479800 and 475016/17
Gambia
Widenmayerstr. 18, M 22
Tel. 2283327
Greece
Prinzregentenstr. 78/II, M 80
Tel. 4701061-64
Great Britain
Amalienstr. 62, M 40
Tel. 394015/19
Guatemala
Grafinger Str. 2, M 80
Tel. 406214
Haiti
Sonnenstr. 6, M 2
Tel. 553067
Honduras
Blütenstr. 11, M 40
Tel. 2123211
Iceland
Mühldorfstr. 15, M 80
Tel. 4129/2214
India
Englschalkinger Str. 150, M 81
Tel. 9256206
Indonesia
Widenmayerstr. 24/III, M 22
Tel. 294606
Iran
Mauerkircherstr. 59, M 80
Tel. 984322
Ireland
Mauerkircherstr. 1a, M 80
Tel. 985723/25
Italy
Möhlstr. 2, M 80
Tel. 4180030

Ivory Coast
Fürstenrieder Str. 276, M 70
Tel. 7141063
Jamaica
Ismaninger Str. 98, M 80
Tel. 981855
Japan
Prinzregentenplatz 10, M 80
Tel. 471043
Jordan
Barer Str. 37/I, M 40
Tel. 282953
Liberia
Frankfurter Ring 220, M 40
Tel. 3232555
Luxembourg
Klenzestr. 101, M 5
Tel. 20242202
Madagascar
Akademiestr. 7, M 40
Tel. 3819020
Malaysia
Nymphenburger Str. 134/I, M 19
Tel. 1232178
Mali
Georgenstr. 104, M 40
Tel. 2717814
Malta
Adamstr. 4, M 19
Tel. 184522
Morocco
Prinzregentenstr. 89, M 80
Tel. 476031
Mauritius
Sendlinger Str. 64/IV, M 2
Tel. 2607240
Mexico
Vogelweidestr. 5/I, M 80
Tel. 981617
Monaco
Von-der-Tann-Str. 14, M 22
Tel. 282718
Nepal
Landsberger Str. 191, M 21
Tel. 5704406
Nicaragua
Osterwaldstr. 95, M 40
Tel. 3611230
Netherlands
Nymphenburger Str. 1, M 2
Tel. 594103
Norway
Promenadeplatz 7, M 2
Tel. 224170
Pakistan

Rückertstr. 1, M 2
Tel. 534880
Panama
Sendlinger Str. 44, M 2
Tel. 2604647
Papua New Guinea
Akademiestr. 7, M 40
Tel. 390074
Paraguay
Fritz-Reuter-Str. 25, M 60
Tel. 882757
Peru
Stollbergstr. 11, M 22
Tel. 296580
Philippines
Grafinger Str. 2, M 80
Tel. 400482
Portugal
Thomas-Wimmer-Ring 9/III, M 22
Tel. 299932
Sweden
Marienplatz 21, M 2
Tel. 264089/80
Switzerland
Leopoldstr. 33/II, M 40
Tel. 347063/64
Senegal
Rüdesheimer Str. 11, M 21
Tel. 5707020
Seychelles
Prinzregentenplatz 15, M 80
Tel. 476057
Sierra Leone
Frankfurter Ring 220, M 40
Tel. 3232555
Spain
Oberföhringer Str. 45, M 81
Tel. 985027/29
Sri Lanka
Schäfflerstr. 3/IV, M 2
Tel. 297893
South Africa
Sendlinger-Tor-Platz 5, M 2
Tel. 2605081
Surinam
Adolf-Kolping-Str. 16, M 2
Tel. 555033 and 594369
Thailand
Meglinger Str. 19, M 71
Tel. 781997
Togo
Mathildenstr. 1, M 2
Tel. 591860 and 594635
Turkey
Menzinger Str. 3, M 19

Tel. 176093/95
Tunisia
Adamstr. 4, M 19
Tel. 180012/13
Uganda
Theatinerstr. 44, M 2
Tel. 221297
Uruguay
Widenmayerstr. 32, M 22
Tel. 293669
Venezuela
Prinzregentenstr. 54, M 22
Tel. 221449
United States of America
Königinstr. 5, M 40
Tel. 23011
Yugoslavia
Böhmerwaldplatz 2, M 80
Tel. 988685/86
Zaire
Siegesstr. 22, M 40
Tel. 331495

AIRLINES

Aeroflot Soviet Airlines
Ludwigstr. 6
Tel. 288261
Aerolineas Argentinas
Karlsplatz 4
Tel. 557697
Air Canada
Oskar-von-Miller-Ring 36
Tel. 288451
Air France
Theatinerstr. 23
Tel. 2106-0
Air Malta
Oberanger 45
Tel. 269076
Alitalia
Neuhauser Str. 7
Tel. 23800-0
Alia
Türkenstr. 71
Tel. 23727-0
Austrian Airlines
Promenadeplatz 9
Tel. 226666
Canadian Pacific Airlines
Rosental 8
Tel. 2609004

Egyptair
Schwanthalerstr.9
Tel. 592618 and 592796
El Al Israel Airlines
Maximiliansplatz
Tel. 296888
Finnair
Oskar-von-Miller-Ring 36
Tel. 281023
Iberia
Schwanthalerstr. 16
Tel. 558491
Japan Air Lines
Pacellistr. 2
Tel. 225255
Jugoslovenski Aerotransport
Sonnenstr. 14
Tel. 54561
KLM Royal Dutch Airlines
Sendlinger Str. 37
Tel. 267081
Korean Airlines
Maximiliansplatz 16
Tel. 292921
Lufthansa
Lenbachplatz 1
Tel. 51138
Malev
Hungarian Airline
Salvatorstr. 2
Tel. 29343
Pan American World Airways
Lenbachplatz 3
Tel. 55161-20
Quantas Airways Ltd.
Australian Airline
Theatinerstr. 30
Tel. 292071
Sabena
Belgian Airline
Petersplatz 10
Tel. 2605054
Scandinavian Airlines System
Pacellistr. 8
Tel. 220636
Singapore Airlines Ltd.
Schillerstr. 5
Tel. 596654
South African Airways
Herzog-Wilhelm-Str. 35
Tel. 265071
Swissair
Schweizerische Luftverkehr AG
Marienplatz 21
Tel. 23630

Syrian Arab Airlines
Pacellistr. 2
Tel. 222067
Tap-Air-Portugal
Karlsplatz 3
Tel. 598086
Türk Hava Yollari A.O.
Turkish Airlines inc.
Bayerstr. 45
Tel. 539417
Tunis Air
Karlsplatz 3
Tel. 557085
TWA
Landwehrstr. 31
Tel. 97643
Varig
(Brazilian Airline)
Sophienstr. 2
Tel. 554901

ART/PHOTO CREDITS

ADAGP, Paris and Cosmopress, Geneva	160
Alte Pinakothek, Munich	184
Archive for the Arts & History, Berlin	60, 61, 270
Archive of Gebhardt, Heinz	64L, 64R, 67
Archive of Pfeiffer, Gerd	24/25, 26, 28/29, 31, 34/35, 36, 38, 39, 41, 42, 43, 44/45, 46, 48, 49, 51, 52, 53, 54, 56/57, 58, 62, 63, 65, 77L, 77R, 79, 80/81, 164
Bavaria Filmstudios	169
Burcher, Siegfried	87
Chwaszcza, Joachim	230/231
Furtner Fotostudio	266
Gebhardt, Heinz	91, 116L, 200/201, 207, 215R, 240L
Henninges, Heiner/Free Lance Press	157, 180/181, 194, 237, 259, 262, 264, 268
Holliday, Tony	92, 93, 190/191, 196, 198, 204
Lenbachaus, Munich	188
Lüring, Werner	18/19, 33L, 33R, 100, 118, 119, 130,137, 145, 152, 153, 154, 216, 217, 240R, 261
Neue Pinakothek, Munich	185
Pfeiffer, Gerd	Cover, 9, 20/21, 32, 70/71, 72, 73, 76, 78, 84, 83, 85, 86, 89, 90, 94, 96, 102/103, 104/105, 106/107, 113, 114L, 115L, 115R, 116R, 117, 120, 121, 122/123, 125, 126, 127, 128, 129, 132, 133, 134/135, 136, 138, 139, 140, 141, 142, 144, 146, 148/149, 155, 156, 158, 159, 161, 162, 165, 166, 167, 168, 170/171, 172, 173, 174, 175L, 175R, 176, 182, 183, 186/187, 192, 193L, 195, 197, 199, 202, 205L, 205R, 206, 210, 211, 215L, 220, 223, 224, 225L, 225R, 226, 227L, 227R, 228, 229, 233, 234, 235, 236, 238, 239, 244/245, 255, 257, 258, 265, 268L, 269, 272
Reuther, Jörg	242/243, 248, 250, 251, 252, 253, 254, 256
Reichelt, G.P.	75, 177
Schiemann, Heiko	209, 241
Schneider, Günter	14/15, 16/17, 22, 68/69, 74, 88, 108, 114R, 143, 178, 212/213, 218, 219
Srzentic, Robert	82, 163, 179, 208, 260
Tourist Association, Augsburg	263
Tourist Association, Oberbayern	271
Vestner, Heinz	3
Wassman, Bill/APA	131
Weltbild Möppert, Munich 2	189
Zange, Christoph	98/99

Backcover: (Lion Statue) Werner Lüring, (Conductor) Gerd Pfeiffer, (Singing Hatman) Gerd Pfeiffer, (Beer waitress) Gunter Schneider. Spine, top to bottom: Gerd Pfeiffer, Gerd Pfeiffer, Heiko Schiemann, Gerd Pfeiffer, Gerd Pfeiffer.

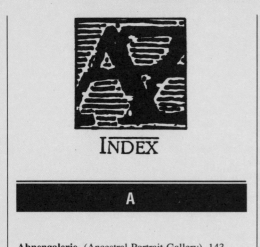

INDEX

A

B

C

D

E

F

N

O

P – Q

R

S

T